# The Lifeboat Is Full

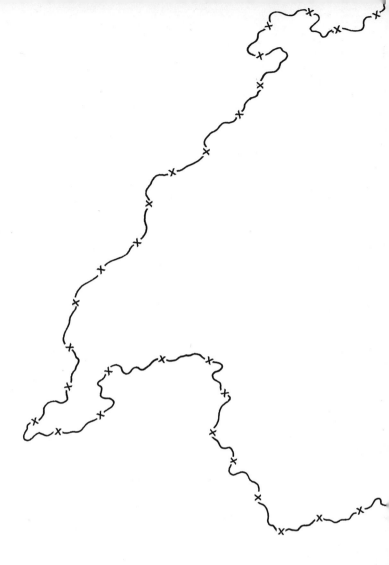

## by Alfred A. Häsler
Translated from the German by Charles Lam Markmann

*Funk & Wagnalls, New York*

# The Lifeboat Is Full

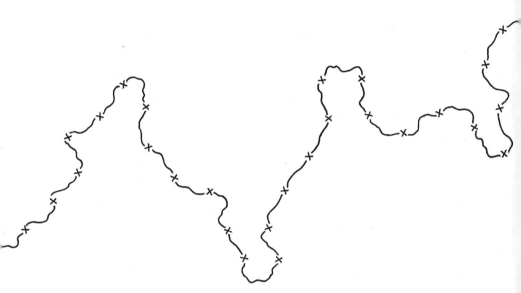

# Switzerland and the Refugees, 1933-1945

# Contents

# Contents

# About This Book

During the Second World War Switzerland gave asylum to almost three hundred thousand refugees for varying lengths of time. During the same years, she turned back uncounted thousands at her borders, and "removed" other thousands who were already in the country, or handed them over directly to the German persecutors. On every level of the population there were people—some of them very influential—who more or less openly subscribed to anti-Semitism, and there were also many others who combated racial hatred.

Official Switzerland was admittedly in the grip of a panic fantasy of inundation by foreigners. Humanitarian Switzerland saw the victims of the Third Reich as suffering brothers, members of the single human family. One side appealed to envy, fear, self-interest; the other, to good will. One side cried: "The refugees are guilty for our having so little to eat." The other retorted that at no time did the refugees amount to more than one-fortieth of the population—this being so, of every one-pound loaf of bread, exactly four-tenths of an ounce was eaten by the foreigners. The one side saw a threat to its complacent comfort, the other was unquiet in its conscience.

There was the Switzerland of the cautious, the fearful, the compromisers. And there was the Switzerland of the decent, of those prepared to resist compromise. The first group trafficked with the authorities of the Third Reich to keep the Jews away from Swiss borders, the others bargained under the sign of the Red Cross for their rescue. We Swiss cried out in horror at the National Socialists' concentration camps, yet we sent even innocent refugees into Swiss prisons like common criminals.

So refugee policy in Switzerland took more than one road during the time of the Third Reich.

It is the purpose of this book to make some contribution to the clarification of this period in our country's history—and to serve as a warning that its lessons not be forgotten.

# Acknowledgments

This work was undertaken on the initiative of the Zürich publishing house of Ex Libris Verlag. The following individuals and organizations were most helpful in making source materials available for my use:

Dr. H. B. Sagalowitz of Zürich, curator of the Juna archives dedicated to the persecutions of the Jews during the time of the Third Reich. He is the chief source of my quotations from Swiss newspapers and other publications that concerned themselves with Hitler's policy of persecution and Switzerland's policy toward refugees; in addition he supplied numerous reports from individuals, excerpts from transcripts of sessions of Jewish relief organizations, summaries of reports, and other helpful materials. Dr. Sagalowitz also assembled a great volume of material for the report prepared by Professor Dr. Carl Ludwig of Basel.

The Reverend Dr. Paul Vogt of Grüsch, Grisons, provided me with many letters, circulars, pamphlets, and reports from the archives of the Evangelical Pastors' Refugee Bureau and from his own collection of documents.

Dr. h.c. Gertrud Kurz of Bern; Dr. h.c. Regina Kägi-Fuchsmann of Zürich; Robert Risler, secretary of the Swiss Worker Relief Organization of Zürich; Dr. Arthur Emsheimer of the Swiss Central Office for Refugee Aid in Zürich; Dr. Emmy Oprecht of Zürich; Dr. Fritz Heberlein of Zürich; Prof. Dr. Hans Zbinden of Berne, president of the Swiss Writers' Union; Dr. Franz Beidler of Zürich, secretary of the Union; Dr. Edwin M. Landau of Zürich, author; and the Police Section of the Federal Justice and Police Department also made valuable material available to me.

In addition to those I have named, many other officials, lawyers, relief workers, and refugees who were actively or passively involved with the refugee policy, or affected by it, have been interviewed, as well as relief workers, officials, lawyers, and refugees. An outstandingly important basic source was the remarkable report on *Switzerland's Refugee Policy in the Years 1933–55* prepared by Professor Dr. Carl Ludwig of Basel.

It is appropriate to recall in this connection that it was the *Schweizerische Beobachter* of Basel that provided the impetus for this important Ludwig

Report through its revelations concerning Switzerland's refugee policy and, in particular, the part played by Dr. Heinrich Rothmund.

To all who made this work possible and who contributed to it I offer my heartfelt thanks.

ALFRED A. HÄSLER

# The Lifeboat Is Full

My question now is: Must we be inhuman in the present for the sake of an uncertain future danger, or in other words must we "stockpile inhumanity in advance"? Must we fling fellow-men out into misery and death when they flee to us for mercy, simply because there is a possibility that later things will go badly for us as well?

—*Dr. Albert Oeri in the National Council,*
*September 1942*


That Switzerland is the haven of the dispossessed is our proud tradition. This is not only our thanks to the world for centuries of peace but also and especially our acknowledgment of the great enrichment that has been brought to us by homeless fugitives since time immemorial.

—*Inscription on a mountain road to Swiss*
*National Exposition, 1939*

# The Anti-Semite in Us

The caretaker of the Jewish cemetery in Berne discovered among the gravestones one early morning a couple that had spent the night there. Husband and wife, both young, they were Belgians of Jewish origin who had been secretly slipped over the Swiss border and brought to Berne, after a dramatic escape from Belgium and through occupied France, in order to escape deportation to the east. In Berne they went immediately to the Belgian Embassy, which gave them money and directed them to the organization for refugee assistance. Afraid lest they find no effective help there, they then spent the night in the Jewish cemetery. It was also to be their last night of freedom. The cemetery caretaker informed the refugee-relief office, whose staff immediately took over the couple and, in the belief that this was the proper thing to do, notified the police without delay. The policemen, who were completely sympathetic to the young couple and conveyed them to the police station with every evidence of good will, had to hold them there until appropriate orders were received. The orders from the Police Section were explicit: The two refugees were to be deported at once to the occupied territory from which they had come. This launched a battle between Police Section officials and representatives of the refugee organization, who, assisted by outstanding personalities outside the Jewish community, waged a last-ditch fight to save the couple from eviction, inevitable separation and death. At the proper time there will be more to be said of the detailed circumstances of this two-day battle; we must confine ourselves here to the painful statement that all efforts were unsuccessful and the Federal Police Section uttered its fateful word of command. The Berne police were authorized and ordered immediately to proceed to remove the couple by way of Pruntrut. Since then the refugee organizations have had no further word of these two persons who were thrown back into the vast ocean of monstrous suffering. Are we to keep silent about these things? Does the Swiss people approve this practice?

That was the article that Hermann Böschenstein, head of the federal capital bureau of *Die National-Zeitung* of Basel, telephoned to his office on August 24, 1942.

In a bitter tone he added:

And still our ears are ringing with the beautiful words uttered over the radio by the President of our country on our national independence day this year: "There is no suffering of others that we would not feel too in our own souls. . . . Surrounded as we are by the roar of guns, we fulfill to the limits of our strength, in accordance with higher law and higher duty, the singular mission entrusted to us so that the fire of love and salvation shall not be quenched."

After the war, the Jewish community of Berne confirmed the report, which Hermann Böschenstein repeated, and it learned further, to its sorrow, that the young couple—the girl was about nineteen, the man three years older—had been captured shortly after the "removal" to France. The man was believed to have been shot at once and the woman deported. Nothing more has ever been heard of her.

A unique instance? A bureaucratic mistake? A regrettable example of an overzealous official in the Federal Police Section?

Or the logical consequence of a substantively anti-Jewish policy on refugees?

> In each of us, somehow, a smaller or larger anti-Semite is lodged. I feel him moving back and forth in my breast. But we do not want to give in to him; instead, if he turns too rowdy, we must tear him out of our hearts. . . . We want always to keep in mind that above races and nations a universal human sphere is enthroned with its unalterable law, in which alone we Swiss conceive of life as still worth living.

These were the concluding sentences of the address delivered to the people's representatives in the federal legislature in Berne by the Mayor of Biel, Dr. Guido Müller, a member of the National Council and a prominent figure in the Swiss Social Democratic Party. The date was December 7, 1938.

In the spring of that year Hitler had forced the annexation of Austria to the Greater German Reich. The Munich conference in the autumn, in which, with the consent of England and France, Czechoslovakia's existence as an independent state was sacrificed, had impressively enhanced the dictator's prestige.

During the night of November 9–10 of that same year the National Socialist rulers of Germany had once more made it unmistakably clear to the world that they were in earnest about the expulsion and extermination of the Jews: Synagogues were burned, Jews' houses and places of business were wrecked and looted, thousands of Jews were beaten, many Jews were murdered.

It was obviously not at all the time for ripping anti-Semitism out of one's heart. Quite the contrary. Hatred of the Jews was to be furthered with even better propaganda.

## Alien-Minded Elements

When the subject of Jews, or gypsies, came up in conversation in Switzerland, people would descant on "foreign-minded elements that were difficult to assimilate." Dr. Heinrich Rothmund, who built up and headed the Federal Alien Police after the First World War, and who subsequently became chief of the Police Section, had his own very definite views on the matter. Until 1920, two years' residence in Switzerland had been enough to enable a foreigner to apply for naturalization; in that year, a six-year requirement was inaugurated. "When jurisdiction over naturalization was subsequently transferred to the Police Section, in practice a minimum residence requirement of fifteen years was strictly adhered to for immigrants from eastern Europe, who can be assimilated only with the greatest difficulty." Thus spake Dr. Heinrich Rothmund in an address to the Independent Party of Zürich 1 on January 23, 1939. So, for example, in the city of Zürich special conditions were established for the naturalization of Jews from eastern Europe—in conformity with directions set forth by the City Council on November 3, 1920. These conditions were not removed until 1936. (On this matter, see also the special publication honoring the fiftieth anniversary of the Union of Swiss Jewish Communities, 1954, pages 207ff.)

In the same speech Dr. Rothmund declared further:

> The legally prescribed minimum residence of six years, however, was continually increased, so that we have now for some years been at the point at which absolutely no more applications will be accepted from foreigners who arrived here as adults, except occasionally in cases of very long residence. Toward Jewish applicants the utmost reluctance is practiced, even if they were born and brought up in Switzerland. If, however, they were brought up in a completely Swiss environment and are willing in addition to adapt, there is in our opinion no ground for refusing them. Another difference, too, is important in these cases: Intellectuals, whose activities may extend their influence over their immediate or more distant environments, must be subject to much stricter requirements as to assimilation than, for instance, an ordinary worker,

who as a rule is very quickly made to adapt by the influence of his environment.

Thus, from the beginning of his police career, Dr. Rothmund knew quite well what was and was not salutary for the Swiss nation. It was his firm intention to make the Police Section and the Alien Police a kind of state within the state. Over years of tenacious detail work he laid down his line of action in the cantons too, although at the start they did not share his opinion:

> By all means we have the right to say *no*, and certainly we are the most "infamous" of the federal offices because at all times we have made liberal use of it, regardless of all demands and complaints, even in spite of the constant attacks of certain newspapers. For a long time, too, some of the cantons refused to understand us. Only when we had curbed our original vehemence . . . did we find understanding.

Where some cantons engaged in resistance to the practices of the Alien Police, it sought "to slip in through the back door and appeal to the good sense of the men in control, in which, furthermore, it was increasingly successful." It was completely oriented to defense and filled with "concern for the prevention of the growth of foreign inundation, most particularly our own kind of alien elements." The "foreign inundation" of Switzerland, in Dr. Rothmund's view, was "the result of a wrongly conceived liberal outlook and at the same time of an irresponsible indifference." So he told the NHG in Zürich on April 3, 1937. He seemed thoroughly obsessed with his mission to make and keep Switzerland pure: "That is precisely what makes our task so challenging" (January 23, 1939). On the basis of this commitment to his self-imposed mission, he declared in the same speech "that the Alien Police cannot accept the responsibility for admitting more emigrants, even for transit purposes, unless their further travel is validly ascertainable by way of a visa for another country."

At this time—the closing months of 1938—he estimated that there were ten to twelve thousand emigrants in Switzerland. In official records of the Police Section the Jews were described without exception as "such persons," "such emigrants," "such elements," "foreign-blooded elements," "existences without passports that are shoved along from country to country."

A decree of the Federal Council on the treatment of "political fugitives" on April 7, 1933, first denied this status to Jews coming from the Third Reich unless they were in flight because of political activities. The German boycott of the Jews was not considered a valid political ground (see Dr. Carl Ludwig's report, Switzerland's Refugee Policy in the Years 1933–55, page 55).

In a proposal made to the Federal Council by the Justice and Police Department on March 26, 1938 (after the annexation of Austria), urging the revival of the requirement of a visa for the holder of an Austrian passport—which was first of all directed against the Austrian Jews—it was stated, among other things: "If we do not wish to create a justified foundation for an anti-Semitic movement unworthy of our country, we must protect ourselves with all our strength and, when necessary, without mercy, against the immigration of foreign Jews, most especially those from the east."

A justified foundation for a shameful anti-Semitic movement? In the same document it was explained why those in search of help must not be allowed in the first place even to approach the Swiss border: "Because otherwise the increasingly necessary ousters of travelers from distant countries must be viewed as brutal measures that would in addition expose us internationally to the reproach of the worst anti-Semitism." (See Ludwig, page 77.)

In actuality, during the spring, summer, and above all during the autumn of 1938 (after Kristallnacht—Germany's "Crystal Night"), the Swiss-Austrian border was the theater of scenes of exclusions of fleeing Jews that eyewitnesses denounced as brutal and outrageous and that created great agitation among border residents as well.

At that time Poland and Rumania refused to take back their Jews. Thereafter the Swiss Legation and consulates in "German Austria" were ordered to issue no further visas without the approval of the Alien Police.

The situation was described as dangerous because it was not to be taken for granted "that it would be possible to move the Israelites on into some other country after a short time." (See Ludwig, page 79.)

On June 24, 1938, the German minister in Switzerland wrote to his Foreign Ministry that the head of the Alien Police, Dr. H. Rothmund, had complained because German officials were openly encouraging the flight of Jews to Switzerland. "With the greatest earnestness," the minister said, Rothmund had emphasized to him "that, if it were not possible to discontinue this practice in Vienna, Switzerland, which could no more use these Jews than Germany could, would be compelled on her own initiative to adopt measures that, with the help of the Viennese police, would protect Switzerland from being overrun with Jews." (See Ludwig, page 82.)

The records of Ernst Woermann, head of the political section of the Foreign Ministry in Berlin, contain this entry under the date of August 10, 1938:

> The Swiss minister told me today that he wanted me to know, merely as a matter of advance information, that serious consideration is being given in Switzerland to means of blocking the flow of Jews out of Germany. The Swiss government is determined to prevent the Judaization of the country, he said, and it expects that we will understand its position. He added that it is possible that, in the course of the Swiss Federal Council's consideration of the measures to be adopted, a mode of cooperation with Germany may be evolved.

This document was not yet known to Dr. Guido Müller. But he did know the ways of the Alien Police. He knew the attitude of its chief, which was identical with that of many influential persons. And, as he himself had pointed out, he knew "the anti-Semite in us"—"I have nothing against the Jews, but I'd rather not get a whiff of them!" Undoubtedly one did not know any Jews personally, but one knew that they were usurers, that they owned department stores that put small merchants out of business, that they had crucified Christ, and that they had a firm grip on all the controlling positions in the economy, the banks, the few theaters, the newspapers, the publishing houses, the cinema, scholarship, and the arts. There were also the *Protocols of the Elders of Zion*, that alleged document that supposedly sought to lead the Jews to the realization of their desire for world domination.

If, indeed, one did know a Jew and the man was, by some chance, altogether likable, one did not really perceive him as "the Jew"—but nonetheless one was not altogether certain whether suddenly one day he might not try to usurp one's position.

One judged and convicted—on hearsay evidence based on centuries-old, ever more widely accepted prejudices devoid of proof—and without knowledge of the remarkable fate and the remarkable history of this people. Jews, gypsies, heathens, nomads—they were more or less all the same thing. Except that the Jews were more dangerous because they were so clever, so crafty, so devious.

In the 1930s many people were on guard against the "sinister race," while at the same time presenting themselves as being particularly respectable, dedicated to their homelands, and Christian. They draped their virtually traditional—and at the same time thoroughly fashionable —antipathy, and perhaps their bad consciences too, in a handsome garment.

Many who did not publicly admit the fact were in agreement with the National Socialists. The well-known physician and army officer, Dr. Eugen Bircher of Aarau, was the author of speeches and articles preaching the highest virtues, to which everyone could often subscribe, in order at the same time to give overt expression to his deep antagonism to "emigrant circles."

There was outspoken anti-Semitism and there was hidden anti-Semitism, "unworthy" and "worthy," the cold and cruel, the easy-going and "humane," the extremist and the "normal." But where was the dividing line?

## "The Jew-Lover"

E. B., an officer and a former *Gauleiter* in the National Front, wrote on June 3, 1936, in his organization's periodical, *Front:*

> . . . Out with those un-Swiss officers who belong to international organized secret societies with most un-Swiss connections and practices, or who belong to a race that has never felt Swiss! . . . We refuse to recognize it [the honorable designation of *Swiss soldier*] for the mercenaries of Jewish Marxism, who are concerned solely

with the defense of their International but never with the protection of our Fatherland.

There was another article in this publication at the same time:

FRONTIST VIEW TAKES OVER NATURALIZATION IN EASTERN SWITZERLAND!
Close observers have remarked with great satisfaction that for the past two years naturalization petitions in the *Ostmark* have been thoroughly examined as to the assimilability of the applicants. For the past two years the naturalization office in the city of St. Gallen has refused the applications of all Jews! Naturalization procedures have also been greatly tightened in the Thurgau.

In August 1937 a Zionist congress was held in Zürich. It gave the Swiss Nazis an excellent occasion for exceptionally venomous utterances against the Jews. The height to which this anti-Semitism rose is hardly imaginable today. That such incitements could go unpunished is still inexplicable.

Under the title, *The Jew-Lover*, a pamphlet was published by Benno W. Schaeppi, who was subsequently convicted of high treason. These are extracts from it:

For hundreds of years everything good has come out of Judah. Jewish military heroes have taken the field at the head of the stupid Swiss for the defense of democracy and humanity at Morgarten, Sempach, Näfels, and St. Jakob an der Birs, and only their celebrated talent is to be given credit for the fact that Fascism has never crushed the heart of Europe in its grip. . . . Indeed, the Swiss made themselves scarce for the refugees, so that the Chosen People could have free run of the streets and the sidewalks. But the Swiss are glad to do so, because they recognize the hegemony of Jewry in every respect. . . . So we bid a hearty welcome to our guests here in Zürisalem. If they should have bad luck again and fall into the hands of the Swiss Nazis, they can be confident of our sincere sympathy.

This was followed by *Ten Commandments for the Jew-Lover*, some of which read as follows:

When you see a man with a hooked nose, a bald head, flat feet, and similar characteristics, do not laugh, because he is a Jew and just as democratic as yourself.

If a Jew should lust after your wife or your daughter, give her to him, because as a good Christian you are filled with love for your neighbor.

Never forget that you are a servant but the Jew is a master, because he was "chosen." Conduct yourself humbly toward the Zionists and do not complain. If one of them slaps you on the right cheek, offer him the left as well.

If a compatriot comes to you and tells you that the Jews are swarming like flies, stinking up everything and spreading infection, close your ears (and, in case you smell something in Station Street, your nose too!). But turn your face away from him, for he who speaks thus of the Jews is a Fascist, and the truth is a bitter pill.

If Zürich stinks of Jewiness to high heaven, then think of the noble words of that great prophet in Bümpliz [this was an allusion to C. A. Loosli, a Swiss writer then living in Bümpliz, who as early as the 1920s and into the 1930s had waged a bitter battle against Swiss anti-Semitism when it tried to launch an anti-Jewish persecution on the basis of the forged *Protocols of the Elders of Zion*].

If by some accident you encounter an Aryan on Station Street during the Zionist congress, mark it down as a special event. It should not occur too often.

Dr. David Farbstein, a well-known lawyer of the time who was a Social Democratic *Nationalrat* (member of the National Council, one of the two national legislative chambers), was called by the anti-Semites the "Na—Zional Rat." The pamphlet did not overlook him: "He is not only a racial Jew—and what a one!—but also a religious Jew. . . . Yes, he is a sly Jew, our David. A stone of many colors*—the stone of the Elders of Zion. . . . And a stone to stumble over for every simple, solid Swiss. And a stone that will vanish from the country's public life when the time is right!"

Naturally, anti-Semites of the stripe of a Benno Schaeppi proclaimed themselves to be exceptionally loyal and racially pure patriots:

* The name *Farbstein*, literally, means *color stone*. —Translator.

The proud old Swiss Confederation, which was able to gain fame and honor throughout all Europe, was virtually totally Jew-free and entirely anti-Semitic in feeling. . . . And today? Too many sluts seem to have forgot what they owe to their race and their people. For the sake of filthy Mammon they fling themselves on the neck of some Jew and associate with the "dregs of the alien desert." . . . But God be thanked that slowly the healthy instinct is coming to life again in the Swiss people and they are again becoming anti-Semitic! Once more people have their eyes out for the Jews. We are coming out of that hypnotic trance in which we were told: "The Jew is 'the same as' we." Every schoolboy sees that the Jew is *not the same* as we and that he neither is nor ever can be a real Swiss. Fortunately there are ways enough of imparting a "lesson" in unmistakable fashion to those sluts who forget their race and still keep on running about with Jews. *We will get round to them one day.* Let the warning be clearly stated here!

Another article was headed WARNING TO RACE DEFILERS! In part it said:

[In ancient Zürich] a woman who forgot her race was put on top of a cart, a Jew's little hat was stuck on her, and she was driven through the whole city. . . . But the Jew who made advances to a woman of Zürich was very severely punished and then expelled from the country. Never again did he dare to return: The penalty was the loss of his eyes.

The disciples of humanity of our day will weep and howl at such "barbarity." But the ways and means that our forefathers adopted against sluts who forgot their race and against Jews were effective and wise.

*It is the highest duty of a true people's government to keep its people pure, independent, and healthy.* The race must not be befouled in its core. It must not sink to the level of a bastard people. Race defilement is a crime whose consequences are suffered by succeeding generations and for which there can never be reparation. Therefore the sternest measures are thoroughly appropriate.

Switzerland was apostrophized as a "liberal Jew-state" and a "Freemasons' democracy." "Jews have more rights than citizens," it was said,

and: "As a true colony of Palestine, we want to live up to our status.
. . . Switzerland for the Jews! Out with the Swiss!" Or: "Zionist
congress—and Zionist trial! We have become the classical land of Zion.
Verily times have changed, and we have changed with them." Head-
lines ran: "Who Are the Supporters of Marxism? The Jews!" or:
"Fellow-Citizens, Awake, and Rise Up Against Jewish Domination!" or:
"They Spread Like Weeds!"

The names and addresses of prominent Jews were published. So were
the travels and financial circumstances of Jewish citizens. The names of
the Jewish students at the University of Basel were published in a list
that was followed by a line in large type: "LONG LIVE JUDAH!" The
persecutory intent was obvious: The bearers of those names were supposed to be tormented and penalized.

## Fascist Hunters and Provocations by Jews

This was the "unworthy anti-Semitism." Upstanding citizens could and
would have nothing in common with such uncouth mouthings. It could
certainly be said that they found very little response in the people of
Switzerland. It was felt that the hysterical propaganda against the Jews
was fully as "alien-minded" as the Jews whom it denounced.

But, as we have said, beneath this "scum thinking," as Mommsen
labeled anti-Semitism, there were still various levels of a "civilized"
anti-Semitism. There was, for instance, the Swiss Press Service, which,
financed by prominent industrial and banking circles, distributed its
news reports to 250 large and small newspapers throughout the country
and, in a sense, subsidized their editorial budgets. The press service
spoke a different language from that of Schaeppi and his kind. It was
more cautious and more discriminating. But the spirit that had sired it
was nevertheless quite evident.

When, in 1938, the local government of St. Gallen banned National
Front publications, the press service trained its guns on "the merry-
hearted hunting down of Fascists that seems to have become the
fashion in some of the border cantons of eastern Switzerland. . . . Stern
warnings, however, must be issued against rash local measures of a
police nature toward foreign propaganda, and above all against one-
sided measures."

The press service further described the National Front as a "weak opposition" long after this movement had become a branch of German Nazism. During the crisis of September 1938, which was only temporarily resolved by the famous Munich conference, the press service distributed an article that said, among other things:

> In contrast to its fine words stood the contradiction of the intransigence of the Marxist-internationalist camp, which was able to count on valuable support from the emigrants and from Jewry, which is especially heavily burdened by the forced emigration. These people know and seek only *one goal*: the preparation of an international crusade against the Fascist powers, and particularly against the Third Reich. They distort the situation in such a manner that Fascism, which was once a defensive action against every national sentiment and force of subversive Bolshevism, is now portrayed by them as the devil at the gate who will destroy the world and who must therefore be annihilated by fire and sword.
>
> Wherever one's sympathies may lie, and whatever the sentiments in one's heart, reason must make it plain that the end result of the agitation carried on by this camp, inspired from Moscow through public and even more through clandestine channels, must in the very near future be a new World War that will finally hand Europe over to Bolshevism. It is the great merit of the British Prime Minister [Neville Chamberlain] that he has recognized this danger. Certainly it was not easy for him to remove his Foreign Secretary, Eden, who was firmly entrenched on the other side.

There was, of course, still another Briton who was also in the camp of Hitler's opponents at that time and who on that account was also denounced as a warmonger. His name was Winston Churchill.

Under the headline, "RICH JEW DEMANDS PRIVATE RELIEF ORGANIZATION," the Swiss Press Service fueled the small fire of anti-Semitism with the example of a man who had committed a minor offense. An established Swiss Christian manufacturer had placed an advertisement in the *Israelitische Wochenblatt* of Zürich, a Jewish weekly, in search of an immigrant able to make an investment of fifty thousand Swiss francs. The advertiser added that he would assist with the investor's application for a residence permit. The *Israelitische Wochenblatt* declared:

> The press service considered this to be the opportune time to enlist in the ranks of anti-Semitic propaganda through an article that dealt with this advertisement. Under the provocative headline, "Provocation by a Jew," the article was sent to Goebbels' paper, *Der Angriff*, which gave it prominent display. The press service forgot the standing obligation usually taken for granted by the Swiss press: namely, that of quoting accurately. As a result the advertisement was made to convey the false impression that it came from a trafficker in citizens' rights, whereas in fact it mentioned only a residence permit.

## Of Good and Bad Jews

Jacob Lorenz was then a well-known journalist and a man of thoroughgoing individuality in many areas. He was the editor and publisher of a weekly, *Das Aufgebot*, in which he wrote on December 16, 1936:

> We do not stand with anti-Semites and those who believe in race. We can no longer remain silent, however, when a minority that should have learned enough from history spreads itself farther and farther over our country. But it seems that the lure of money and influence obscures the thinking even of that people that usually claims to have been endowed with a very special wealth of astuteness.
>
> After an absence of several years, the writer of these lines recently returned to a Swiss border city. It was more than shocking to see how drastically the faces that one observed in the streets had altered. The visibly foreign and specifically Jewish admixture has been increased to a high degree and makes itself apparent in no agreeable fashion. In the same city, a once thoroughly respectable and large newspaper is now under Jewish management, and another in the same town must be described as outspokenly pro-Jewish. The number of Jews who write for the Swiss press under

assumed names or anonymously has risen markedly in recent years. The increased flow of Jewish students into the universities and their seizure of some places in certain academic professions are beyond description. Writers who were able through the inconceivable short-sightedness of our officials to become pseudo-Swiss but who are outspoken Jewish (not merely religious-Jewish) mouthpieces are making themselves conspicuous in immoral and revolting ways in dealings toward which we endeavor to maintain the greatest reserve in the Jews' own interest.

In increasing measure Jews are becoming more and more obtrusive in all activities. It is disgusting to read the advertisements in recent issues of one of the largest Zürich newspapers, which is blatantly filled up with Brann and Brann and more Brann. As if it were an occasion for special rejoicing for Switzerland that just in this particular time Mr. Julius Brann can celebrate the fortieth anniversary of his giant jumble shop in Station Street in Zürich and his avowed and unavowed branches all through the country. This is the same Mr. Brann for whom it was not enough to have a department store: He had to give us his super-department store, the Epa. . . . We are afraid, however, that those unscrupulous elements that limber up their guns whenever we even touch on such matters generally, like one Mr. Marx of the Jewish weekly, on whose naturalization certificate the signature is not yet quite dry, will not listen to our well-meant warnings but will yap about anti-Semitism and cry for official protection against provocations of a minority. . . . The Jewish communities would be well advised to believe us when we say that even in Switzerland the camel's back can break. . . . We should like to . . . counsel the Jews in Switzerland as a Jewish mother advises her children: "Precisely because you are Jews, you should not push yourselves too far up, otherwise you will be disliked, and arrogance brings on contempt and persecution."

The good Jew, the assimilated Jew, in the opinion of the Police Section and many civilians, was the frightened, quiet, inconspicuous Jew who made himself as unobtrusive as he could and, if possible, denied his Jewishness and his origins. Then he would be left in peace, accepted, tolerated. Granted that this restraint, this "mild" anti-Semitism was not so bad as that of Schaeppi and his cronies. But somewhere was a point at which the "hard" and the "soft" Jew-haters met, the fanatical xenophobes, the eighteen-karat patriots, and the Aryan men of honor. For the Jew, who in this heartless period of obsession with inundation by foreigners was sacrificed to Helvetian conformism and who was therefore turned back at the Swiss borders into the teeth of the National Socialist meat grinders, the end result was the same as for those others whose luck did not extend so far as flight to Switzerland. All of them arrived at the same end of the line: Auschwitz. The road from Brussels by way of the Jewish cemetery in Berne and back by way of Pruntrut into the hands of the vicious enemies of humanity was only slightly longer than the direct route. We Swiss did not want the persecuted to die like that, but we accepted it as part of the bargain.

It was the extreme but, at the same time, the inescapable consequence of any kind of anti-Semitism.

## History of the Jews in Switzerland

How little validity there was to the uproar over the Judaization of Switzerland, how minimal this "danger" was, was clearly demonstrated by Professor Carl Ludwig in his previously quoted report (page 60). A few figures dealing with the proportion of Jews in Switzerland's population will suffice:

|      |      | *Jews* |
|------|------|--------|
| 1900 | 3.7% | (12,264), including 4972 Swiss and 7292 foreign (19% of the foreign population). |
| 1910 | 4.9% | (18,462), including 6275 Swiss and 12,187 foreign (22%). |
| 1920 | 5.4% | (20,979), including 9428 Swiss and 11,551 foreign (29%). |
| 1930 | 4.4% | (17,973), including 9803 Swiss and 8170 foreign (23%). |
| 1941 | 4.6% | (19,429), including 10,279 Swiss and 9150 foreign (41%). |
| 1950 | 4%   | (19,048), including 10,735 Swiss and 8313 foreign (29%). |

Approximately 80 per cent of the Jews living in Switzerland were residents of the cantons of Zürich, Berne, Basel (city), St. Gallen, Vaud, and Geneva, and indeed for the most part they lived in the cities of those names. On the basis of these figures, Professor Ludwig rightly observed, it was impossible honestly to speak of a "danger of foreign inundation" of Switzerland by way of the Jews in 1933.

Yet anti-Semitism has its tradition in Switzerland as in other nations. For hundreds of years Protestants and Catholics have unremittingly preached and practiced hatred against Judaism and against individual Jews. Our history offers many instances of bloody and inhuman anti-Semitism. It was only a hundred years ago that the Jews whose families had lived among us for generations were admitted to full civil rights.

Previously, Jews were not allowed to settle in most cantons, or even to show their faces. They were driven out of the cities. In many places Christians were forbidden to give Jews shelter. About 1634 the mayor and council of Zürich issued orders to all officials and their subordinates "to drive the useless, godless swarm of Jews out of the city and its territory with hue and cry." No Jew would be allowed to enter Zürich again, and violators of this order who gave refuge to Jews would be severely punished. The Diet in Baden ordered its representatives to expedite the eviction of Jews from the earldom of Baden "as a godless, worthless rabble."

Pagans, gypsies, Anabaptists, and Jews faced a bitter fate in Helvetia in those days. The principle of the preservation of solidarity was conveniently adopted into law. In 1642 Luzerne asked that gypsies and Jews be expelled from the entire Confederation. In 1695 the magistracy of Zürich denounced Israelites in Switzerland as an "accursed swarm of Jews," or, more laconically, referred to them as the "pestilence."

The guilds would not accept Jews as members. Thus they were excluded from all artisan occupations. Agriculture was barred to them because foreigners were prohibited from owning land.

In 1776, for the first time, Oberendlingen and Lengnau were expressly designated as the only places where Jews might settle. Marriages between propertyless Jews were forbidden. Foreign Jewesses were allowed to marry resident Jews only if they brought dowries of at least five hundred gulden. Christians and Jews were forbidden to live under the same roof.

In 1787, in spite of the toleration in Oberendlingen and Lengnau, the mayor and council of Berne issued a strict prohibition against trade by Jews, and in general against their residence in all Bernese towns and rural territory.

It was only with the French Revolution that a change began to appear. Duke Johannes of Effingen and Hans Konrad Escher von der Linth joined other prominent Swiss in a public demand that the rights of human beings be extended also to Jews. In 1800, for the first time since 1379, Basel allowed residence to two Alsatian Jews.

But there were continual reversions. Berne and Zürich in particular repeatedly embarked on fresh initiatives against the Jews. It was not until 1866 that—under French pressure—the Jews received full political rights.

It was another long, bitter road that the Jews had behind them in Switzerland before they were recognized as children of the same God to whom their compatriots prayed. Augusta Weldler-Steinberg describes it best in her book, *History of the Jews in Switzerland*, published in 1966 by the Federation of Swiss Jewish Communities.

How inhuman and barbarous we Swiss could be toward "foreign-minded elements" was shown also by the methods that were adopted against the gypsies and other nomadic groups in many cantons. One ear, for example, was cut off every gypsy and he was then expelled from the country. If he returned, he was thus easily identifiable, and his punishment was still more severe. The Bernese author and folklorist, Sergius Golowin, gives an instructive account of the subject in his *Gypsy Stories*. How many gypsies sought safety among us during the Hitler time, were sent back, and were then shipped to the gas chambers is a question that is hardly raised among us. Nor could it be completely answered.

"It is the highest duty of a people's government to keep its people pure, independent, and healthy," Schaeppi, the Swiss National Socialist, proclaimed, and many a Swiss echoed him. *How* this purity was achieved and maintained is another story.

## A Heritage of Responsibility

Side by side with the tradition of inhumanity there was—and is—the tradition of hospitality, of solidarity with the persecuted and the tormented. There was and is the tradition of a Niklaus von der Flüe, a Heinrich Pestalozzi, a General Dufour, an Henri Dunant, an Alexandre Vinet, an Eugen Huber. There was and is the tradition of humane civilization, of the Red Cross.

In the years of the brown terror this heritage of responsibility was the support of those men and women who kept faith with their belief in humanity and democracy. They remembered the hospitality that the Swiss had extended to the Huguenots in 1572 after St. Bartholomew's Night and in 1685 after the revocation of the Edict of Nantes—in 1572 Geneva alone took in 2360 fugitives, of whom 1600 became permanent residents. And for a period in 1685 six to seven hundred refugees sought and found refuge in Switzerland every day; in the course of two years no fewer than twenty-eight thousand persons persecuted for their beliefs entered the country. Swiss men and women of good will remember that during the almost forty years after 1686 some one hundred forty thousand fugitives traveled through our country, many of them going on to Germany, Holland, and England. Twenty thousand religious refugees remained in Switzerland for twenty years. In Berne alone some six thousand were given haven with both state and private help.

> Switzerland had no occasion to regret the heavy sacrifices occasioned at that time. Scholarship, art, and the economy drew fresh strength and vital stimulation from these new settlers. In various cities they established new businesses and industries that are in large part still flourishing today . . . and many families contributed outstanding sons to their new homeland. [See Ludwig, page 14.]

One of these eminent sons was Heinrich Pestalozzi. Others bore such names as Zschokke, von Orelli. Georg Büchner taught and died in Switzerland.

After 1789 many French aristocrats fled to Switzerland and found a welcome. Later it was the political fugitives from the nations of the Holy Alliance to whom we Swiss gave asylum. In 1848 the German democrats were hospitably received. The population showed the liveliest sympathies for the fifteen thousand persecution victims. In 1864 some two thousand Polish freedom fighters sought protection in the Confederation. At that time too the Federal Council was urged to send the hunted along their road. But in a circular letter of June 8, 1864, to the cantonal governments, the Council expressed the hope that "that humane spirit that the cantons had always manifested before toward victims of political persecution will not prove to be any less vigorous among all officials again in these times." (See Ludwig, page 18.)

Gottfried Keller was the secretary of the Swiss-Polish Aid Committee.

The bonds of friendship that were forged then between the Polish and Swiss peoples are still strong today.

In 1878 it was German Social Democrats who sought and found asylum in Switzerland from Bismarck's persecutions. August Bebel is buried in Zürich, and Hermann Greulich was the real founder of the Swiss Social Democratic Party. He is above all to be thanked for the fact that the democratic sectors kept the upper hand over the extremists.

> One of the most precious rights of sovereignty is the right of asylum. Since the distant past we have opened the doors of our house in the most liberal fashion to political refugees, for the most part not out of sympathy for individuals or their teachings but out of human kindness. This has given rise to innumerable difficulties for us, and since 1815 this has been almost the only question that has consistently caused us disputes with our neighbors. But we have always stood firm on this sovereign right of ours, and we intend to continue to do so. [See Ludwig, page 20.]

This was the pledge made by Federal Councilor Numa Droz on March 20, 1888.

When this sovereign right, which derives from the humanitarian tradition, is as sailed and undermined from within or without, when totalitarian and anti-libertarian ideas are forced on us, then indeed it is proper to speak of "foreign inundation." When the bearers of hate, envy, and brute force seek to spread their message among us, then we must be on guard. Then we must sound the alarm, resist, and—if necessary—employ the power of the state. The German National Socialists and their Swiss imitators were a real danger to our country. After the annexation of Austria to the Third Reich, *The German News in Switzerland* asserted on June 25, 1938: "The Austrian campaign and occupation are therefore the model for all groups abroad, they are the obligation of all party members in our foreign organizations wherever they may be."

Whoever called then for defense against the inordinate pretensions of the National Socialists, whoever appealed for loyalty to the spiritual foundations of the Swiss national and political existence and to the unique historical development of Switzerland, whoever defended this individuality and exalted it in the people's consciousness stood on firm Swiss ground. He had no need of patriotic camouflage.

*Der Schweizer Spiegel* stated it in this way:

> But it is not only blood and soil, not only history, that shape a people, but will. The nations of today were certainly not always here. They grew. Often they were born not at all in the course of centuries but in much shorter periods. And, if the Swiss nation did not already exist, it would be born today. We have no wish to be Germans—not Germans by blood, or Germans by race, or Germans by culture, or Germans by language, neither redeemed nor unredeemed Germans.

Not conformity and political coordination but diversity should mold the character of the Swiss nation; not a single language but a variety of languages. It is not centralized control but the increased autonomy of cantons and communes that expresses the Swiss spirit. We Swiss are proud of our varying dialects, customs, habits. That is precisely what holds Switzerland together—that we have the right to be different from one another in the same nation, that every man can be and fulfill himself within the limits imposed by every society.

It is the unsentimental, the profoundly productive belief in a humane mission for Switzerland in this world that we must strengthen, because it keeps us clear-thinking and skeptical with respect to vainglorious panaceas of every stripe. Free men do not believe in paradise on earth; they believe in tolerance, in live-and-let-live. They know that perfection in man is unattainable, and that he who attempts to attain to the absolute by force leaves mountains of corpses behind without ever reaching his goal.

Tolerance nullifies the power of the lies of those who believe in force. The man who is strong within himself can be humane. Fear of being overrun by "foreigners" is a sign of weakness.

# The Unwanted

In 1938 Switzerland was the home of approximately ten to twelve thousand refugees. Admissibility was becoming even more restricted than it appeared to be. What were the other nations doing?

On the initiative of President Franklin D. Roosevelt of the United States, a conference representing thirty-two countries was inaugurated on July 6, 1938, in Evian, on Lake Geneva. Its purpose was the solution of the refugee problem. The countries participating were Australia, Argentina, Belgium, Bolivia, Brazil, Canada, Chile, Colombia, Costa Rica, Cuba, Denmark, the Dominican Republic, Ecuador, England, France, Guatemala, Haiti, Honduras, Ireland, Mexico, Nicaragua, Norway, New Zealand, Panama, Paraguay, The Netherlands, Peru, Sweden, Switzerland, the United States, Uruguay, and Venezuela. The conference was also attended by representatives of the High Commission for Refugees from Germany, the political department of the League of Nations, and a number of private relief organizations, mainly Jewish. The chairman of the conference was American Special Envoy Myron C. Taylor. Switzerland was represented by Dr. Heinrich Rothmund and his associate, Henri Werner. On July 11 Rothmund informed the conference that Switzerland always stood ready to offer help to the unfortunate: History was the proof. But her resources were not unlimited. The refugees from Germany and Austria whom she had admitted since March were a very heavy burden on the many public and private relief agencies and it could hardly be increased. In view of her geographical situation, her overpopulation by foreigners, and her years of unemployment, he added, Switzerland could be only a transit country for fugitives from Germany. Therefore she could not admit an influx of refugees into her territory without controls. Her borders were not sealed; all transit applications, and they were very numerous, were carefully investigated. In individual cases entry was granted within the limits of feasibility. But it was self-evident, he said, that these limits were dependent on the ability of the German refugees to obtain legal admission to other countries. (See Ludwig, pages 84–85.)

All in all, the readiness of other countries to accept fugitives from Germany was minimal. When their representatives at the conference were confronted with the statistics of the problem, states that had hitherto been quite generous in accepting victims of German persecution became suddenly silent. Australia and the nations of North and South America, with their vast expanses of territory, instead of opening their borders, reduced the number of refugees they were willing to accept.

The net result of the conference was the creation of an intergovernmental committee with its seat in London, the establishment of subcommittees, and unanimous adherence to a resolution that stated the urgent need of giving consideration to a comprehensive program of aid to refugees. The activities of the intergovernmental committee bore no fruit. At the end of 1938 its first director, Rublee, an American, resigned his post.

Der Völkischer Beobachter summed up the conference in its own way: "No one wants to have the mishpokha.* Most governmental

---

* A Yiddish word meaning family or tribe, which the Germans adopted pejoratively to mean Jews as a whole. —Translator.

representatives refuse to open the gates of their countries to a gang that brought about the ruin of Germany."

In his book, *The Mission*, Hans Habe quotes the Bolivian ambassador, who represented his country at the conference, as saying:

> We have the smallest Jewish population of any country in the world—three or four hundred. Last year (1937) we entered into an agreement with the German Reich that authorized the immigration of three thousand Germans—provided that they are Aryans. Aside from this, our laws restrict the entry of Russians, Poles, Arabs, and Jews, and they prohibit the entry of Chinese, Negroes, mongrels, the ailing, cripples, degenerates, criminals, and Communists. In 1936 we did permit the immigration of certain German Jews—Bolivia is closed to eastern Jews.

And again from the same book:

> There are already two hundred seventy thousand Jews living in Argentina; true, this is only 2 per cent of the population, but of the twenty-one thousand most recent immigrants no fewer than 10 per cent were Jews. . . . Since the inception of the National Socialist government in Germany, Brazil has granted asylum to a total of seven thousand Jews; recently, however, applicants for visas have had not only to present baptismal certificates but also to answer the question whether they are Aryans, Semites, or Mongolians.

Venezuela demanded a bond of a thousand bolivars for each immigrant; Peru required two thousand sols; Uruguay's fee was six hundred gold pesos (which it at least returned to the immigrant in installments of fifty pesos each); Chile admitted only those families whose heads were not more than forty years old; Ecuador could use only land workers, and in 1937 she had expelled all foreign Jews who were not engaged in agriculture.

On July 6, 1938, *The Times* of London asserted: "It must be granted that the presence of a large number of Jews within the state creates grave problems in certain countries, especially when they attain an importance there that is out of proportion to their number."

Of the one hundred fifty thousand Jewish refugees whom the Reich had allowed to depart, according to a report by the general director of

the Council of German Jewry, fifty-two thousand were living in Great
Britain, thirty thousand in France, twenty-five thousand in Poland,
twelve thousand in Belgium, ten thousand in Switzerland, and five
thousand in the Scandinavian countries. They amounted to barely
one-tenth of 1 per cent of the populations of these countries.

On the day after the annexation of Austria, democratic Czechoslovakia—Hitler's next victim—had hermetically sealed her frontiers with
Germany and Austria. German Jews who crossed illegally were punished
and then turned back to the Germans. Czechoslovakia's minister of the
interior was an anti-Semite.

He was not alone.

A great opportunity was thrown away in the Evian conference. Most
of the delegates to the conference were fully aware of their obligations
as human beings. They underestimated the dangers that haunted the
Jews, or they wanted not to see them; in any case they had no wish to
have "foreign-thinking elements" sully their pure Christian countries.
They indulged themselves in petty calculations of the burdens that they
would impose on themselves by taking refugees, and in tortured logic-
chopping on humanity and cruelty. Since no one wanted the Jews, it
was "more humane" to let their persecutors have them.

This too gave Der Völkischer Beobachter an occasion for comment:
instead of taking in the Jews,

> . . . everyone adopts precautions to protect himself against an
> influx of immigrants, for everyone clearly recognizes the damage
> that comes with Judaization. . . . There still remains one possibil-
> ity: the Soviet Union. But this Jewish-run country took no part
> whatever in the Evian conference. Why indeed did not Lazarus
> Kaganovitch send Litvinov-Finkelstein to the Lake of Geneva? . . .
> In Finland too this question is looked at no differently. Only
> recently, in fact, fifty-four Jews who wanted to move to Finland
> from the Reich were allowed to land in Helsinki only after the
> most extreme precautions had been taken.

Unfortunately Der Völkischer Beobachter was telling the truth.
This commentary appeared in Der Münchner Nachrichten:

> Obviously Germany was not represented in this noteworthy confer-
> ence. Nor are we concerned with the decisions that were reached

there, since the Jewish question has been thoroughly settled as far as we are concerned and is being resolved step by step. . . . If the Jews in Germany are so dear to their hearts, they can certainly have them. We are delighted to give them up, and we will not even ask any price for them.

The Jewish question: resolved step by step. . . .

*The Daily Herald* of London was right when it said: "Responsibility has been abdicated." And *The New York Times* said: "If thirty-two nations that call themselves democracies cannot unite on a plan for the rescue of a few hundred thousand refugees, then all hope vanishes that they will ever be able to reach agreement on anything at all."

Pettiness, narrowmindedness, and prejudice against the Jews were cited all over the world as reasons of state.

The consequences were catastrophic.

# Marked Men

On March 28, 1938, National Councilor Miheim, a Radical from Luzerne, told the Council: "On August 27 of this year it will be one hundred fifty years since the rights of man were proclaimed in the French
Constituent Assembly. Today we have to defend and renew the rights of
man in the cultural and other realms."

On March 23, 1939, National Councilor Theodor Gut, also a Radical,
told the Council:

> The Western world does not depend on the flag that flies over the
> Hradschin Palace in Prague—so many have waved there in the past
> thousand years—but it can establish itself only on the spirit of
> humanity. This we must and will defend. . . . The concept of

confederation is born not of race and nationality but of the aspiration toward freedom and law. This aspiration must instill itself in our people and make it strong. Not only in iron determination to resist every threat to our independence, but also in fealty to what must be recognized as the ideal of every civilized man and the ultimate goal of the European community of nations: the concept of mankind that has found its incarnation in the peaceful communal life of the various stocks in our Confederation: "Switzerland as a miniature Europe at peace with itself!"

In spite of these professions of faith by two high-minded Swiss, who certainly expressed the philosophy of the majority of Swiss people, the practices of the Alien Police persisted in utter silence, more or less unnoticed by the public. As early as the spring of 1938 the federal authorities began trying to persuade the German government to mark the passports of German Jews in such a way that they would be readily identifiable to Swiss consular and border officials. In a letter of April 13, 1938, to the Swiss Legation in Berlin, the Justice and Police Department expressed the desire that German passports not be issued to Austrian—which meant Jewish—emigrants in the same manner as to "German Austrians enjoying a normal relationship with the state"; otherwise "we should be compelled to introduce a visa requirement for every holder of a German passport whose residence is in Austria." Emigrants, it was suggested, should be given Austrian passports, or German passports valid for a shorter term than the normal. Visas would then be required only for the holders of such restricted passports. "We hope that the German government will be receptive to a solution that will enable us to limit the entrance of such emigrants by means of visa inspection, and we are prepared to propose to the Federal Council the measures that will limit this control as much as possible to such foreigners alone." (See Ludwig, page 95.)

Privy Councilor Roediger, the representative of the German Foreign Ministry—after the war he was assigned to the German consulate in Zürich for a time—made no secret of his revulsion at this Swiss initiative to prevent the entry of German and Austrian Jews into the Confederation. During a conversation with the Swiss minister to Germany, Dr. Paul Dinichert, he supposedly allowed himself to be persuaded that this protective measure was of the utmost urgent need to Switzerland and

that it would obviously serve German interests as well if a solution
could be found by means of which Swiss control over Austrian emigrants could be guaranteed with the maximum restrictions as to persons
against whom this control would be used. Roediger, to Dinichert reported,

> pointed out that Germany had a direct interest in the emigration of
> these people provided that on the other hand no one would be
> damaged by accepting them. On the other hand, it would hardly be
> possible to identify them in advance through their passports and
> thus make it more difficult for them to leave. There was also
> ground to fear that the Swiss precedent might establish a trend.
> From another point of view, Privy Councilor Roediger took into
> consideration, as the conversation proceeded, the fact that Ger-
> many would also be interested in preventing an agglomeration of
> such emigrants in immediate proximity to the Reich, though with-
> out blocking egress by way of Switzerland for those emigrants who
> had the opportunity to settle in some third country.

On May 16, 1938, Dinichert and Roediger conferred again, and this
time the German declared that the proposed solution was hardly relevant. He pointed out once more that no difficulties would be raised
against the departure of emigrants whose presence was not wanted in
Germany. It was, he added, the practice of the German administration
to issue passports to emigrants for a term that accorded with their
needs. Willingness to adopt some other method, however, was not yet
indicated. He said further that a special passport stamp for travel to
Switzerland would be an unsatisfactory measure and also would not
really serve Switzerland's purposes. If Switzerland insisted on visas for
German Austrians and also extended the requirement to all Germans in
general, Germany would adopt analogous measures toward Switzerland.
(See Ludwig, page 98.)

Dinichert's report to the Federal Council continued:

> The simplest solution, of course, would be to restrict the require-
> ment for a visa to non-Aryan German citizens. This is admittedly
> repugnant to our principles, but it could easily be justified in that it
> is also to the interest of Swiss Jews to be protected against any

further influx of foreign Jews. Inasmuch as other countries, such as Hungary and Rumania, are enacting more and more special restrictions on Jews, which are bound to lead to a new upsurge in the Jewish tendency toward migration, it might prove worthwhile to give closer consideration to such a regulation.

How keenly the Germans wished to be rid of their Jews could be seen from the fact that in the original territory of Germany they no longer marked passports as in the past: The second page was stamped *Valid only for exit*, in contrast to the earlier *Valid for travel inside and outside Germany*; and that in the case of Austrian Jews the right of reentry was specified in their passports—thus entitling them to visas—but only after they had signed a written declaration that they would not make use of this right, under very heavy penalties for any breach, and therefore would not return to Austria.

## The "J" Stamp Appears

On August 13, 1938 (August 13 seems to have been a fateful date in the history of Switzerland's refugee policy: on that date four years later the Swiss borders were hermetically sealed against refugees), during another discussion in the Foreign Ministry in Berlin, where Dr. Hans Frölicher had succeeded Dr. Dinichert as the Swiss minister, the suggestion of a special mark in Jews' passports was first voiced. The Foreign Section of the Federal Political Department in Berne had instructed its legation in Germany by telegram to lodge a protest against numerous illegal shipments of emigrants across the Swiss frontier by German border officials. Frölicher's report on his interview declared, among other things:

In my presentation I pointed out especially that some rule must absolutely be established that would enable Switzerland to supervise and screen arriving emigrants. Even the express assurance from the German administration that in every instance the Reich would take back the emigrants would not be regarded as adequate. I pointed this out because Privy Councilor Roediger proposed such a solution. There seems to be an unwillingness here to inaugurate a system of special identification of the passports of non-Aryan German citizens because this would put a tool in the hand of every country that would like to set up obstacles against their entry. In the course of the next week Dr. Franz Kappeler will have the opportunity to discuss this matter in more detail with the representatives of the Foreign Ministry.

A proposal submitted by Dr. Kappeler, the Legation counselor, to the effect that "German passports be issued to emigrants only when they have been assured of travel permits by foreign states," was graciously received by Privy Councilor Roediger. (See Ludwig, pages 100–101.)

In a report to the Foreign Section of the Political Department on August 20, Dr. Kappeler advised, on behalf of the Swiss Legation in Berlin, that the Foreign Ministry was seriously and obviously inclined to reach a compromise with Switzerland. On the date of the report, therefore, and at his request, German passport offices in Vienna, Cologne, Aachen, and Trier, as well as the German Consulate in Rome, which, according to Dr. Rothmund, had in the past issued German passports to Jews, were ordered by telegram not to grant passports valid for foreign travel to Jews in any case in which it could not be absolutely established that the passport would not be used for travel to Switzerland. In addition the German officials declared their willingness to issue orders to all passport offices that, whenever there was reason to suspect that a Jewish applicant intended to go to Switzerland, a passport be denied unless the Jew could prove that he had been approved for entry by Switzerland. Since Dr. Rothmund seemed at first glance to find this measure insufficient, Dr. Kappeler had already offered, in order to be able to dispense with the requirement of a visa, to investigate whether it would be possible to demand that after a certain date all German passports should bear the express statement that they were valid for Switzerland and that this endorsement be stamped into Jews' passports only on proof that they had Swiss entry permits. Dr. Kappeler was emphatic in his insistence that no means be left untried to prevent the introduction of visas into dealings with Germany. (See Ludwig, page 102.)

Professor Ludwig explains this attitude of the Swiss Legation in Berlin by its belief that in a time of imminent threat of war any further deterioration in relations between Switzerland and Germany was to be avoided. These relations had in fact become more and more strained as a result of the murder of Wilhelm Gustloff, the leader of the Swiss National Section of the German National Socialist Party, on February 4, 1938; the subsequent order of the Federal Council prohibiting the continuation of the German party's national and regional activities in Switzerland (February 18); and, on the one hand, acerb criticism of the National Socialist system by the Swiss press, countered on the other hand by the harassments practiced on Swiss citizens in Germany and by German officials' connivance in illegal border violations. (See Ludwig, pages 102–103.)

## The Bludgeon of the Visa

On August 22 Dr. Rothmund submitted the following proposal to Dr. Franz Kappeler, counselor of the Legation:

Agreement through exchange of notes.
In order to preclude the necessity for Switzerland, in the light of her absolutely urgent need of total control of the entrance of German emigrants, to introduce the universal requirement of visas on all passports, the following has been agreed on:
Aryan individuals whose return to Germany is prohibited, as well as all non-Aryans, will receive German travel passports only after a duly qualified German passport official has stamped the first page with the following restriction: "Valid for travel into Switzerland; visa of Swiss Consulate required." This restriction will be entered in already issued passports as soon as they come into the hands of the passport office for whatever reason. [Ludwig, page 103.]

In a report of August 27 to Federal Councilor Dr. Johannes Baumann, the director of the Political Department, the head of the Police Section once again emphasized the need for an emigrant control without loopholes; the report added that a new wave of emigration from Germany was to be expected as a result of the introduction of further severe measures against the Jews (exclusion of several thousand Jewish physicians from their profession; compulsory identification of all Jewish-owned businesses, and discrimination against their customers; special license plates for automobiles still owned by Jews; obligatory adoption of Jewish given names). The report sought to dissipate the Federal Council's well-founded apprehensions that the revival of visa requirements for holders of German passports might have unwelcome repercussions on foreign trade and travel. On August 30 the Council decided, as a precautionary measure, to abrogate the accord of January 9, 1926, with Germany for the elimination of visa requirements; its intention was either to revive the visa for all Germans or to induce Germany to make allowances for Switzerland's demand for complete control of all incoming Jewish emigrants from Germany.

On the same day the Swiss Legation in Berlin was handed a note from the German government, dated August 29. It confirmed the previous oral assurances and proposal with a view to issuing a confidential order to all passport offices that, whenever it was known or suspected that a Jew intended to use his passport for travel to Switzerland, it was to be issued only if the applicant presented proof that his presence in Switzerland had been approved. The German government, the note added, was all the more convinced that such a regulation would achieve the end desired by the Swiss because, as it was opportune to reiterate in this connection, an exodus of Austrian emigrants to Switzerland was in general undesirable from the German point of view, and its prevention, accordingly, would serve Swiss as well as German interests in the same way. At the same time the German government expressed the hope that thus it would be possible to avoid the abrogation of the visa agreement.

Dr. Kappeler telephoned the text of the note to the head of the Police Section and sent a written copy to the Foreign Section immediately. At the same time he urged that the whole problem be reexamined very carefully in the light of the German note. Dr. Kappeler pointed out further that

> the relinquishment of the visa should present no very great difficulty or consequences for border control, because the new tighter measures will have to be applied only to holders of passports issued since August of this year; in addition, as of January 1, 1939, German Jews' passports will be immediately identifiable because of the compulsory use of Jewish given names. To make matters more certain, it would be perfectly possible to request and demand of the

German government a further assurance that the Jewish given names actually be used in the passports. Under these conditions it is legitimate to wonder whether it would be justifiable during the transition period to take so far-reaching a measure as the introduction of a universal visa requirement. [Ludwig, pages 108–109.]

But the German proposal was anything but adequate for Dr. Heinrich Rothmund. He intended to

make every effort, likewise, to put an end to the current absurd situation, since every would-be emigrant can get a passport if he designates some country other than Switzerland as his designation. If he does not travel directly to Switzerland, then he will come to us in transit by way of some other country. The consequence of acceptance of the German proposal would be the issuance of thousands of German passports, and probably to emigrants who are already in other countries—Italy, for instance. If any doubt could have remained whether Germany wanted to dam the unregulated flow of Jews out of Austria and certainly, in the wake of the latest measures adopted against them in Germany proper, out of all German territory, and convert it into something systematized, without regard for the intake capacity of the receiving countries, the results of our negotiations have completely settled such doubts. In order to be able to push the Jews off on other countries as inconspicuously as possible, the Germans want to give them passports that are in no way distinguished from those issued to non-Jews. The statement also contained in the note of August 29, to the effect that Germany does not desire the exodus of Austrian Jews to Switzerland and therefore there is no question of German agencies' furthering such a Jewish influx into Switzerland, is mere talk. If that had really been what Germany wanted, she was in a position to accomplish it by accepting our latest proposal. But Germany persists in a ruthless deportation policy.

On this ground the head of the Police Section called on the director of the Political Department "with the utmost urgency" to prevail on the Federal Council to approve the abrogation of the visa accord with Germany. (See Ludwig, pages 109–110.)

In her answer to the German note of August 29, Switzerland declared on August 31 that she had "taken cognizance, with satisfaction, of Germany's opposition to the emigration of the Austrian Jews to Switzerland" and also that she was "grateful for the orders that the German government had issued in order to prevent to the fullest extent possible, pending the conclusion of a definitive agreement on Swiss emigrant control, the entrance of such emigrants with German passports into Switzerland." Then, however, Rothmund's views on the abrogation of the 1926 visa accord were set forth and notice of such abrogation was submitted. At the same time the hope was expressed that, before the expiration of the notice period, some other solution might be found that would make it possible to avoid the revival of the visa. For this reason Switzerland would refrain at this time from any public announcement of the intent to abrogate. (See Ludwig, pages 110–111.)

In a memorandum of September 1, 1938, to the Foreign Section of the Federal Political Department, Dr. Rothmund pointed out in this connection that the introduction of visas for German passports would result in considerably more work for the Swiss consulates in Germany and the Legation in Berlin, and that therefore it was advisable to start at once to examine the question of an increase in personnel.

> We must also be prepared, since that is certainly our intention, to issue the same instructions for granting visas to non-emigrants as for holders of Austrian passports; that means that these people, who will certainly constitute the majority, can get their visas without delay. I should think that we must demand proof of Aryan status from them. This, of course, can lead to quite a flood of correspondence. [Ludwig, page 111.]

## Technically Possible

From Dr. Rothmund's notes on a discussion with the German minister in Berne, Dr. Otto Koecher, it appears that Koecher asked the head of the Police Section whether it might not be possible to waive the visa if the holder of the passport was explicitly identified as a Jew.

> *Technically* [the emphasis is Rothmund's], I told him, this was certainly possible, but then we should have to introduce the visa

again for Jews. Whether the Political Department and the Federal Council could approve such a measure was of course open to question. All that I could tell him on the subject was that the solution was technically possible. After Mr. Koecher had read a sentence from his instructions aloud to me, pointing out that under the proposal submitted by us to Berlin the German Jews would be treated worse than the Jews of other countries and that Germany did not want such discrimination, it was clear, however, that we could not follow the course proposed by Mr. Koecher. . . . Nevertheless Mr. Koecher will make the proposal known to Berlin, with the added comment that its execution seems technically possible here but it is open to question whether it might not be impossible on some other ground. [Ludwig, page 112.]

Rothmund's memorandum further asserted that there was a definite impression that Germany was now attempting by every possible means to put Switzerland in the wrong with respect to the reintroduction of the visa, even though Berlin was quite well aware that its declaration of its opposition to Jews' travel to Switzerland could have no force unless, in addition to forbidding German border officials to direct such foreigners into Swiss territory, it armed the Swiss with the tools for a technically foolproof emigrant check. But, Rothmund added, Berlin knew perfectly well that this was not possible unless Germany identified emigrants as such in their travel permits. Since Germany refused on insincere grounds to do this, she wanted to reverse the positions and put Switzerland in the wrong. "Nevertheless we still want to make an attempt with Koecher's proposal," Rothmund wrote, "and therefore I will suggest that Mr. Kappeler try once more to further it from this side."

## The Germans Give Way

A telegram sent to Berlin by Otto Koecher described Heinrich Rothmund's memorandum.

In a letter of September 7, 1938, from the Swiss Legation to the Foreign Section of the Federal Political Department, it was reported that, after a conversation with Privy Councilor Roediger—in order to

reach a compromise with Switzerland to the fullest possible extent—the
Germans were prepared in principle

> . . . to employ some symbol to identify passports issued to Jews,
> and this symbol would appear in passports issued not only in
> Germany but also in Austria and, ultimately, in other countries. At
> the same time it was the understanding of the German government
> that the Swiss would reinstate the visa requirement for the holders
> of passports thus marked. Naturally this meant the Germans could
> not waive a certain reciprocity. In this connection I was obliged to
> convince the representative of the Foreign Ministry that special
> identification of the passports of Swiss Jews was impossible on both
> practical and constitutional grounds. Thereupon the Germans sug-
> gested that at least they be able to require visas for Swiss Jews
> without obliging Swiss officials to cooperate in the application of
> this rule. [Ludwig, page 114.]

Two proposals were offered as to the method of identifying German
Jews' passports: The first suggested that the holder's given name be
underlined in red instead of black ink ("this, however, entails the
danger that in any event the passport holder may later go over the
underline with black ink"). The second method was the imprintation
on the upper left quarter of the first page of the passport with a circle
about three-quarters of an inch in diameter containing the letter "J" or
possibly some other symbol that Switzerland might designate.

"It is my impression," Dr. Kappeler wrote, "that these identifications
will completely meet our requirements." He added this vigorous endorsement of the German suggestions.

> It is my opinion that the German government's suggestions repre-
> sent a very substantial compromise and that the solution proposed
> by Berlin is acceptable to us. It achieves the desired 100 per cent
> control over the entry of non-Aryan emigrants and makes it possi-
> ble to settle every case quickly at the border, where the presence of
> the stamp on the first page and, in appropriate cases, of the visa
> must be verified. Moreover, the partial reciprocity that the German
> government has requested for understandable reasons seems feasi-

ble to us. The number of Swiss Jews who have any occasion to visit
Germany in the existing circumstances must be very small.

The letter ended with a request that the German proposals be studied
and that Kappeler be notified as soon as possible whether he could
signify their acceptance, so that the agreement could be reduced to
writing and the new rules made effective as quickly as possible. (See
Ludwig, pages 114–115.)

## Dr. Rothmund's Hesitancy

The next day Rothmund telephoned to Kappeler, saying that discrimination against Swiss Jews was out of the question. Dr. Kappeler emphasized in a further letter to the Foreign Section on September 9 that he

> . . . was of the opinion that it would in no case be justified, in
> view of the small number of Swiss Jews who still travel to Germany
> under the existing conditions, to relinquish the exemption of all the
> rest of our citizens from the German visa regulations at the price of
> the consequences that would undoubtedly ensue from the general
> reinstatement of the need for Swiss visas for all travelers from
> Germany. Certainly further discrimination against Swiss Jews on
> the part of the German government would be undesirable. There-
> fore the Legation has consistently recommended that this question
> be thoroughly clarified. It has already been suggested in Berne that
> the idea be abandoned, and that the Legation be instructed to treat
> each Swiss Jew's case individually. Consequently we have already
> put up with a whole series of discriminatory measures without
> insisting on the principle of the equality of all Swiss citizens, and
> these, furthermore, as for instance in the domain of professional
> activity and the registration of Jewish-held property, have entailed
> much more onerously restrictive encroachments than the obligation
> of procuring a German visa before departure. What is to be
> avoided if at all possible is express consent to special treatment of
> our Jews. This, however, would have to be achieved through the
> phraseology employed in the proposed exchange of notes. It should

not be too difficult to justify to the public the introduction of German visas for Swiss Jews on the ground that our requirement of visas for German Jews is essential for reasons of urgent national interest and has resulted in the German counter-measure. [Ludwig, pages 116–117.]

Rothmund did not agree. "An arrangement with another nation under which Swiss Jews would be dealt with differently from Swiss non-Jews seems unacceptable to me," he wrote in an exhaustive report to the Federal Justice and Police Department. In his view Switzerland must in no circumstances allow Swiss Jews to be treated differently from their non-Jewish compatriots whenever Switzerland had a voice in the matter and could prevent such action. "It is more than enough that we must submit to the special treatment of Swiss Jews who live in Germany. In my opinion, therefore, the German proposal must be rejected at once insofar as it calls for reciprocity." As to the question whether the German proposal should be accepted if the claim for reciprocity was waived, Rothmund asserted that for a variety of reasons the suggested measures offered no guaranty of foolproof check on all German Jews before their entry into Switzerland. Furthermore he expressed doubt whether the Germans would live up to their agreement. At the very least there would a long period during which countless Jews would be given passports that did not bear the symbol.

"In earlier stages of the negotiations with Germany, in fact," the report continued, "we offered suggestions that, with the exception of reciprocity, amounted to the same thing as the present German proposal." Experience, however, Rothmund said, had shown that no further confidence could be placed in the German government agencies involved. As a result, the Swiss simply must not count on any supervision of the entry of German Jews. The National Socialist Party's fight against its opponents must and would continually intensify. As soon as the problem of German Jews' emigration could be resolved in the proper manner, Rothmund predicted, the campaign against the church would be revived, and the repressions of German nationals might take other forms than in the past.

Once more we should find ourselves defenseless against other categories of emigrants if we accepted the German suggestion: In other words, we should again be left hanging without any control over the entry of refugees. In that case, refugees whose passports were marked "political" would probably far exceed the Jews. What the consequences of this would be for our domestic politics I need not elaborate.

Still further reasons, however, influenced the head of the Police Section to revise his earlier views and to demand now that the requirement of a visa be reinstituted for all Germans and not merely for Jews.

The introduction of visas for Jews, however, even if we are dealing only with emigrants, would be extremely difficult for interested parties abroad to understand. The German press would give every encouragement to criticisms from the other side to the effect that such measures proved the virulent anti-Semitism of the democracies, and it would give them prominent display as evidence of our adherence to the racial axis. . . . All in all it would appear that, with her actions thus far and in particular through her latest proposal, Germany is making a great effort to draw us into anti-Semitism, or at least to make it appear to other countries that such is the case. . . . Since the establishment of the Alien Police we have maintained an unequivocal position. The Jews figure with all the other foreigners as a factor in the excessive influx of foreigners. Now we have assumed our share of the general obligation toward emigrants, and we intend to fulfill it humanely but with the utmost discipline through the Alien Police. The Swiss Jews are cooperating with us, and they clearly see their own stake in the matter. If now we come up with special measures that discriminate against them, we are simply alienating them from a healthy point of view. If they begin to protest internationally, instead of exerting their influence in their international circles on behalf of the measures that we have adopted, as they are doing today, we take the risk of setting the whole civilized world against us. . . .

All these considerations, in Rothmund's view, must lead to the rejection of the latest German proposal and to insistence on the revival of the visa requirement.

If we go back to the visa, Germany is completely free to give the emigrants whatever papers she pleases, and there is no need for her to identify them as emigrants. We would be able to identify them among those who would be unable to produce certificates of Aryanhood, party membership cards, German Labor Front identifications, proof of membership in industrial or professional federations or national associations, etc. Whoever can show such documents will get his visa at once. We would have a clean, orderly procedure at the border. The German plan would make us dependent on the good will of the German officials; at the same time, furthermore, it would result in far from adequate practical means of distinguishing between Jews and non-Jews at the border, and hence in innumerable unregulated entries by emigrants. . . . Besides, it would be a partial solution, simply a temporary makeshift, and undoubtedly it would result only in further friction in the future. [Ludwig, pages 118–119.]

## Conversation with Globke

The Germans' reaction to the stand taken by Dr. Rothmund was bitter. They were afraid that, if the requirement for visas was revived between the Reich and Switzerland, other countries might follow this example. This had to be prevented in all circumstances. Unimpeded entry into western European countries was too valuable to the Germans to be casually placed in jeopardy. On September 16, 1938, Koecher—who had just come back to Switzerland from Nürnberg—invited Dr. Rothmund to a new negotiation and explained to him that he ought to recognize that Germany was prepared to renounce any demand for reciprocity with respect to the Swiss Jews if her latest proposal were to be accepted. Rothmund, for his part, informed the German minister that he had submitted his documented proposal for the reinstatement of the visa to the Justice Department because he saw no other possibility of carrying forward a total supervision over the entry of emigrants.

At the request of the German Legation another meeting was held on the next day. It was attended, not only by the minister, Dr. Koecher, but also by the Legation counselor, Dr. Hans Globke, who was in Berne at the time to attend an international convention of vital-statistics officials.

(Globke had been a collaborator in the formulation of the Nürnberg racial laws. After the war he became a high official in Konrad Adenauer's government.) According to a memorandum by Dr. Rothmund, Dr. Globke offered a new proposal in this meeting:

> Reciprocity with respect to Swiss Jews will be completely eliminated. The identification symbol suggested by Privy Councilor Roediger and Dr. Kappeler will be included in all passports issued to non-Aryans in Germany. Within two weeks all passports already issued to non-Aryans in Germany will be marked with the same symbol. All passports issued to Aryan Germans living in Italy are stamped: "Valid also for Switzerland." Whoever has a passport not so marked is a non-Aryan. It would appear to be impossible to extend this to Aryan German individuals residing in other countries such as France, Belgium, and The Netherlands.

Dr. Rothmund himself then raised the question of the methods to be used toward other categories of emigrants that might possibly be created later—if, for instance, the campaign against the churches should be intensified. Koecher replied that this could affect only very small groups. Dr. Rothmund then observed that, in view of Germany's past performance and her efforts to get rid of her Jews, strict adherence to Dr. Globke's proposal was hardly to be expected; Dr. Globke retorted that he could guarantee the utterly flawless execution of his plan.

In conclusion Dr. Rothmund stated that, in spite of the recommendations that he had already submitted, he was prepared to suggest some other solution, provided that it would really result in the elimination of all loopholes in emigrant control. In this connection his memorandum said:

> It is still not clear to me whether the new project can effect a really foolproof control. In any case, the stamp, "Valid also for Switzerland," should be inserted in the passports of all Aryan Germans not only in Italy but also in all other countries, but this seems to me to be hardly practicable. [Ludwig, page 120.]

In a personal letter to Dr. Rothmund on September 17, Dr. Frölicher, the Swiss minister in Berlin, vigorously added his endorsement to the plan offered by Privy Councilor Roediger: for the time being the visa should be required only for German Jews, once assurances were had that passports would be made identifiable. Once Germany had agreed to these requests and declared herself ready to mark Jews' passports specially, it would not be feasible to require visas regardless in all German passports.

In a subsequent letter to Rothmund on September 19 Dr. Frölicher again expressed his disappointment that the head of the Police Section rejected the German proposals. He strove to convince Dr. Rothmund that the measures previously adopted by the Germans, coupled with the introduction of the "J" stamp, would reduce the unsupervised entry of German Jews to a minimum.

Dr. Rothmund, however, was not persuaded. In a report dated September 21 he also rejected Globke's plan.

## Journey to Berlin

After further consultations among Dr. Rothmund, the Swiss Legation in Berlin, the German Foreign Ministry, and the Foreign Section of the Swiss Political Department, the head of the Police Section went to Berlin, where he and Dr. Kappeler, the Legation counselor, conducted negotiations with the appropriate German officials from September 27 to 29, 1938. Once again Dr. Rothmund informed his interlocutors that total supervision of non-Aryan Germans before they entered Switzerland was imperative; he descanted on the campaign that the Federal Alien Police had been waging for almost twenty years against foreign inundation as a result of the immigration of more foreigners, especially aliens whom it was difficult or impossible to assimilate, a category in which the Jews above all belonged; he discussed too the situation into which Switzerland had fallen as the result of the unregulated immigration of penniless persons from Austria, whose number now totaled approximately twenty-three hundred. The restrictions could not be limited to those Jews who sought to enter Switzerland directly from German territory; they must be extended also to those Jews who were already in other countries, particularly Italy, as well as to Jews who in the future might go from Germany to some other country and then try to enter Switzerland from that country. (See Ludwig, page 125.)

In essence the negotiations concluded with this accord:

1. The German government will make every effort to the end that all outstanding passports held by German Jews . . . that are validated for travel abroad or for residence abroad be stamped as rapidly as possible with a symbol that identifies their bearers as Jews.

2. The Swiss government will authorize entry into Switzerland for German Jews whose passports contain the symbol required in Paragraph 1 above or, under the German regulations, should contain it, provided that the appropriate authorities have also endorsed the passport with an "assurance of permission to reside in Switzerland or to travel through Switzerland."

3. The designated German services charged with passport inspection and border patrol at the German-Swiss frontier will be instructed to prevent the departure of German Jews for Switzerland unless their passports are endorsed with the "assurance of permission to reside in Switzerland or to travel through Switzerland."

The German government reserves to itself the right, in agreement with the Swiss government, to require also that Jews of Swiss nationality obtain an "assurance of permission to reside in German territory or to travel through German territory" in the event that at any time the need therefor should be deemed by the Germans to have arisen.

The Swiss government revokes its notice of its intention to abrogate the German-Swiss accord of September 9, 1926 for the reciprocal elimination of visas.

In the event that the above regulations do not lead to a satisfactory solution, both governments will again enter into negotiations, particularly with a view toward agreement on the effective date for the introduction of general visa requirements if these should be necessary. [Ludwig, pages 128–129.]

Dr. Rothmund's detailed report on these negotiations concludes:

In his previous reports to you on the control of immigration of refugees from Germany, the first undersigned [Dr. Rothmund] has often expressed his views on measures applicable only to Jews. The present report deals only with the technical side of such control. The Federal Council will have to determine whether the said observations will permit its approval of the steps proposed in Berlin. [Ludwig, page 128.]

## The Federal Council Speaks

On October 3, 1938, the Justice and Police Department requested that the Federal Council take cognizance of the report of the delegates to the Berlin conference and subscribe its signature to the agreement reached. It was the department's view that, in the light of the solution decided on in Berlin, an effort should be made to see whether the measures to which the German government had committed itself would not permit the immediate seizure of all non-Aryan Germans presenting German passports at Swiss border posts. (See Ludwig, pages 129–130.) On the same day the Federal Council signified its unanimous approval of everything set forth in the request from the Justice and Police Department.

The accord was confirmed by an exchange of notes on November 10 of that year. The announcement of this far-reaching decision was made on October 4, 1938, by way of the following "communiqué":

In order to permit the Alien Police to regulate the entrance of German and Austrian emigrants into Switzerland and their travel through Switzerland before they have crossed the border, the Federal Council has adopted the following decree in its session today:

German citizens with German passports who are non-Aryans under German law will henceforth be permitted to cross the border at any point of entry on the Swiss frontier only if their passports have been endorsed with the entry of an assurance issued by a Swiss consulate for permission to reside in Switzerland or to travel through Switzerland. The requirement of visas for holders of Austrian passports remains in force as in the past.

In view of the large number of emigrants who are already living in Switzerland, they are reminded once more that Switzerland can be only a transit country for them and that during their temporary sojourns in Switzerland they are forbidden to engage in any form of economic activity. Nor does the acquisition of property or participation in Swiss businesses, etc., create any claim to permanent residence. The new decree of the Federal Council will be strictly enforced; it applies to border crossings not only from Germany but also from Italy and France.

This was a much diluted version of what had in fact been accomplished. In a circular letter to Swiss legations and consulates, also dated October 4, 1938, the Federal Council was more explicit than in this press release. In the circular letter it informed its diplomatic agents of the Swiss-German negotiations intended "to put into the hands of the Alien Police as complete a control as possible over all German and Austrian Jewish emigrants." It added that "the German government intends to mark all passports issued henceforth to German and Austrian Jews with a special symbol": specifically, "a circle on the first page, in which the letter 'J' will be imprinted." The German government, the circular letter said, was instructing its passport offices at home and abroad to follow this procedure, and passports already issued would be so marked when they were presented to issuing offices for renewal or for any other reason. The letter added:

> Since it will be extremely difficult to carry out border controls until the time when all German passports have been stamped with this special mark, we have a special interest in having the symbol entered as soon as possible in passports of such persons already outstanding. When German Jews whose passports do not bear the symbol apply at Swiss consulates, they are to be informed, before they are allowed to fill out any application forms, that their passports must be presented to the German passport office or consulate to be stamped with the symbol. [Ludwig, pages 131–132.]

The diplomatic representatives were provided with detailed instructions for their future procedures in the light of the new situation. They were admonished to follow these instructions to the letter. They were told that unfortunately a circular letter of March 29, 1938 (dealing with the renewal of the requirement for consular visas for holders of Austrian passports), had not been followed by certain consulates, so that, in addition to the three to four thousand Austrian Jews who had entered the country before April 1 on Austrian passports without visas, as well as the more than two thousand genuine refugees who had entered Switzerland penniless, several thousand more with visas on their Austrian passports had also gained entry. Experience had demonstrated that German Jews were striving to force their way into Switzerland by any and every means.

> We are encountering the utmost difficulties in sending those already here along on the rest of their journeys because all other countries have also introduced very strict controls over emigrants. The new regulations were devised in order to avoid sending emigrants back to Germany. We are resolved, however, to penalize all further persons entering illegally by returning them to Germany. The consulates can be of the greatest assistance to us in seeing to it that such measures can be confined to exceptional cases. [Ludwig, pages 131–133.]

## Between Legalism and Humanity

In actuality, not all border guards and not all consular and legation personnel were obsessed with the cruelty and ruthlessness demanded by the Federal Council when it came to sending back victims of persecution who were seeking entrance into Switzerland. When the pariahs appeared at the Austrian-Swiss border, singly or in groups, many of them thoroughly exhausted, hungry, freezing, broken by the hardships of their wanderings through a hostile country, it would happen that one or another border guard, with tears in his eyes, would allow entry to those whom under his instructions from Berne he was required to turn back.

The Swiss Legation in Rome and, above all, the Swiss consulates in Italy were besieged during the summer of 1938 by many thousands of Austrian Jewish emigrants pleading for visas for entrance into Switzerland. "What terrible scenes were sometimes enacted," Ludwig's report said, "can be grasped from the various reports by consular officials who were assigned to passport matters." One such report, in Italian, described how work had to be carried on "in the face of an invading crowd, clamoring its pressing desire to leave the country, ready to lie by

word of mouth and in writing in order to get visas, launching into
arguments and debates in reply to our requests for information." Another official described, also in Italian, "an impatient crowd that even
found ways of committing acts of vandalism against the furnishings of
the waiting room." Within a few weeks the consulates had issued some
three thousand entrance visas for Switzerland, so that several cantons
lodged complaints with the Police Section. On August 6 the Police
Section instructed the consulates in Italy to issue no more visas, even for
transit. (See Ludwig, page 84.)

The problem was aggravated by the fact that at the same time the
German and Austrian National Socialists were endeavoring to shovel as
many Jews as possible over the borders—after having first stripped them
of everything that they owned—and this led the Federal Council to
order the borders closed on August 19, 1938. The necessary precautionary measures were reinforced by the Central Customs Office and the
Military Department, which strengthened the border patrol forces.
"The closing of the borders will henceforth be rigorously enforced," a
new proposal to the Federal Council from the Federal Justice and
Police Department declared on August 25.

> For two reasons this is absolutely imperative in spite of the great
> hardships connected with the application of such measures. First of
> all, emigrants who are still in other countries must be made to
> understand that there is no purpose to be served by their entering
> Switzerland without permission. . . . It is to be anticipated that the
> battle with the refugees and most especially with the German
> border forces for the enforcement of our measures will go on for a
> considerable time. [Ludwig, page 91.]

How this battle went can be seen from Professor Ludwig's quotation
from a customs official who was stationed at Riehen from October 1938
until March 1939:

> During this time—and in fact since August, 1938—a mass of Israel-
> ites tried to get into Switzerland by every possible avenue. The
> border guards were under orders to prevent entrance into Switzer-
> land: in other words, to block any attempt to cross anywhere along
> the whole border. Two instructions were issued in this connection:

Refugees who were captured on Swiss soil in the vicinity of the border must be taken back to the frontier. In every case known to me, the refugee was actually moved over the frontier without the notice of the German officials. Often the Swiss border guards kept the refugees hidden until the German border patrols were out of sight.

Those refugees who tried to defend themselves—often in sheer desperation—against being sent back to Germany were taken to the Swiss customs post and then back into Germany by road; they were handed over to the German customs men on the other side of the border. It goes without saying that desperate refugees resisted being sent back by sitting down wherever they were, holding fast to whatever they could grasp, and so on, and they had to be put across the frontier by our border guards with physical force. Refugees who committed offenses against Switzerland were handed over to the police. I remember the case of one refugee who had pulled the emergency-brake cord aboard a train. He was taken to the police in Basel, who later sent him back to Germany by road. In other cases refugees were loaded into Swiss police vans and driven to the German customs posts. There was no departure check on them by the Swiss customs, so we did not know how these kinds of refugees had got into Switzerland and then into the hands of the police in Basel. I myself know of no case in which any exception was made and entrance into Switzerland was permitted. There were many rumors of such things, however. [Ludwig, page 156.]

## The Bad Conscience

With the introduction of the "J" stamp the German and Austrian Jews were branded in the sight of foreigners too as outlaws, banished and practically without rights. That Switzerland was an anything but minor accomplice in this is part of the especially black chapter of an official refugee policy that in any case is not rich in clean pages. We Swiss can and must admit that those responsible for it—and they included the Federal Council, which approved the German-Swiss accord in spite of Dr. Rothmund's criticisms; Dr. Heinrich Rothmund himself, for whom, in his fanatical obsession with defense, no regulation against foreign

Jews could be sufficiently severe, and Dr. Frölicher, the Swiss minister in Berlin, as well as his Legation counselor, Dr. Kappeler, who, in their dread lest they irritate their German partners, all too completely lost sight of the human aspects of the Jewish tragedy in the Third Reich—were not quite at peace with themselves.

Neither in the "communiqué" to the press that we have quoted nor in the Federal Council's reply to two legislative questions on the refugee problem—one raised by Dr. Guido Müller of Biel and the other by Trumpy of Glarus—and not in the annual report of the Federal Justice and Police Department for 1938 was even a word said of the fateful negotiations in Berlin.

A year after this transaction the Second World War broke out. The Swiss people had joined together at their unforgettable National Exposition in an impressive demonstration of their unity and unanimity in a democratic, independent nation. On the way to the fair every Swiss and every foreigner could read these words:

"That Switzerland is the haven of the dispossessed is our proud tradition. This is not only our thanks to the world for centuries of peace but also and especially our acknowledgment of the great enrichment that has been brought to us by homeless fugitives since time immemorial."

# Seen by the Blind

Was it possible that a branch of the Swiss government, and particularly the Police Section of a country that was Germany's neighbor, that spoke and read her language, that maintained innumerable personal, economic, cultural, and scientific ties with her, that possessed a legation and consulates in Germany—was it possible that this Police Section could not see what was really being done in the Third Reich? Of course it was possible that the officials had not read the National Socialists' guidebook, *Mein Kampf*—or had not taken it seriously. But all the same, things had been happening in Germany since January 30, 1933.

Very soon after the National Socialists seized power, grievous injuries were done to the Jews. "Let Judah croak!" the brown hooligans

54

screamed outside Jewish-owned businesses and Jewish-occupied residences.

In a number of places Jewish public officials and lawyers were forbidden to enter the courthouses. Hospitals in Berlin dismissed many Jewish physicians. Dismissals in the theater followed. Jews were publicly beaten. Jewish books were publicly burned. Jews were seized on the flimsiest pretexts in nocturnal raids.

On April 1, 1933, a one-day boycott of all Jewish-owned businesses was staged throughout Germany.

In Munich, Heinrich Himmler announced the opening of a Bavarian concentration camp to which five thousand Communist and other Marxist leaders were to be committed. Arrest orders were issued and carried out upon mere accusation by the police. On April 26 there were ten thousand persons in custody in Prussia alone and some sixteen thousand in the whole country.

The "elimination of the foreign-blooded" followed as the result of a law dated April 7, 1933. The "law of July 14, 1933, concerning the revocation of citizenship and withdrawal of German nationality" drew "the dividing line against those who have forced their way into formal membership in the national race without genuine right or who in criminal fashion have dragged the nation to which they belong in the muck in the sight of the world."

Non-Aryan lawyers, physicians, professors were forced out of their positions. Jews were no longer allowed to perform military service. Vocational groups excluded them. Other Jews were flung into concentration camps and "shot while trying to escape." No one knows how many they were.

The Nürnberg racial laws, on which the "specialist," Dr. Globke, collaborated, stripped the Jews of all political rights, prohibited marriage between Jews and non-Jews and extramarital relations between Jews and German citizens or persons of related bloodlines, banned the employment of non-Jewish women under the age of forty-five in Jewish households, and, among other prohibitions, forbade Jews to raise the German flag. (See Ludwig, pages 29–34.)

The National Socialist leaders increased their ever more unmistakably menacing activities. In July 1934, before an audience of one hundred thousand members of the Hitler Youth, Joseph Grohé, Prussian councilor of state and *Gauleiter* for Cologne and Aachen, shouted: "If peoples wish to live in harmony, the Jew must die" (*Westdeutcher Beobachter*, Cologne, July 24, 1934).

In 1934, through the Graphia Publishing Institute in Karlsbad, German author Gerhard Seeger issued his shocking report, *Oranienburg*, and in the same year another book called *Concentration Camps—An Appeal to the Conscience of the World*. At the same time the storm troopers were singing:

> When the storm trooper joins the fight,
> Sure, his courage is like wine,
> And when Jew-blood spurts from the knife
> Sure, things are really going fine!
> Soldiers, comrades, hang the Jews!
> Nail the bastards to the wall!

*The People to Arms*, another song, exhorted: "Germany, awake! And death to Judah!"

In 1935 the Swiss Mirror Publishing Company in Zürich brought out Wolfgang Langhoff's bloodcurdling book, *The Swamp Soldier*, a report on the German concentration camps. It went into many printings and was translated into many languages. In October 1950 the weekly *Schweizer Spiegel* related:

> Langhoff's book, *The Swamp Soldier*, the first documentary report on the German concentration camps, was typed on a machine in our offices. Since we did not know the author well enough to be able to accept his stories as reliable without investigation, we started a search for other fugitives from the same concentration camp. We finally found one of them in Paris. We brought him to Switzerland and had him verify every statement made by the author. Only after we had found a third refugee who confirmed Langhoff's findings did we publish the book. It became a worldwide success. We feel that with this book we did our part in enlightening the Swiss public and the world on the true face of National Socialism.

A year later the Europa Publishing Company of Zürich brought out *Dachau*, a book by Walter Hornung (Julius Zerfass).

In that same year Julius Streicher informed the National Socialist Party congress in Nürnberg that the only solution to the Jewish question was the extermination of the Jews. It was a mistake, he said, to think that this question could be resolved without bloodshed.

In November 1938 the National Socialists in Berlin staged an exhibition entitled *The Jew*. Reto Caratsch, the Berlin correspondent of the *Neue Zürcher Zeitung*, told his editors that this exhibit was nothing but "a solid call for his [the Jew's] extermination."

These and many other facts, written and oral reports from incontrovertible witnesses—namely, the victims themselves—were well known.

## The Federal Council's Eyewitness

Dr. Heinrich Rothmund prepared a report of his own for the Federal Council after his visit to the concentration camp in Oranienburg. While the treatment of the inmates was certainly not particularly indulgent, still the report gave no basis for inferences of mass murders of Jews in Germany or in countries under German influence, Federal Councilor von Steiger told Professor Carl Ludwig in a letter dated September 9, 1945. Rothmund's report said, among other things:

> The camp has accommodations for eighteen thousand persons and is at present occupied by fourteen thousand. Most of these are taken out every day to work at manufacturing, stone-breaking, etc. The working day begins at daybreak and ends at nightfall. The barracks are so laid out that they can be kept under surveillance from a watch tower. The routine is thoroughly military. The inmates are deliberately thrown together in a planned heterogeneity: incorrigible criminals, Jews, political offenders, anti-militarist Bible students, foreigners subject to labor service who have evaded it—all jumbled together. If I understood correctly, every new arrival is always immediately given a completely military "hosing." If he shows the required quick reactions to orders and the merciless discipline, he is assigned to a labor detail, if possible on the basis of his occupation. After three months' residence in the camp he undergoes his first investigation on the basis of his military-discipline records with the Gestapo and the camp leadership. If the

purpose of his detention seems to have been accomplished, he is released, frequently only provisionally, subject to good behavior and to residence in a specified place. The severest punishment prescribed is beating; this punishment is regarded as dishonorable, and it may not be inflicted by any SS man but only by other camp inmates in the presence of three witnesses. I was shown the barracks infirmary, which is equipped with everything necessary, including even an operating room. There are X-ray examinations for all sufferers from lung diseases, and reclining chairs for rest cures; extra food rations are provided for these patients. In general the rations seem to be abnormally reduced to the minimum required in order to keep the body capable of work. I was also informed that punishment by suspension of rations was no longer practiced, because the offender was unfit for work the next day. I cannot really believe that grown men can be reeducated into good citizenship through this denial of freedom and with these purely military training methods. As a rule one would have to be satisfied with superficially acceptable behavior.

Carl von Ossietzky, the German who had won the Nobel Peace Prize in 1935, held out for three years under this admittedly not exactly indulgent but nevertheless theoretically endurable treatment in a German concentration camp, but after his release he died of his education in citizenship.

Thereafter Rothmund's report was to serve the Justice and Police Department as the basis for the official view on the treatment of Jews in concentration camps. (See Ludwig, page 243.)

## A Disconcerting Warning

Other, less reassuring reports on conditions in Germany were as a rule either ignored by Swiss officials or greeted with disapproval. Dr. Emil Oprecht, a Zürich publisher, was one of those persons who excited Berne's disapproval only too often. First it was *The Front* that denounced him as a cultural Bolshevik when he began holding evenings of readings by exiled German authors in Zürich. "And who, now, go to hear these reading? In large measure the audience consists of Zürich

Jews and their royal court, the so-called 'better' society altogether—in other words, circles predominantly close to *Die Neue Zürcher Zeitung*. Cultural Bolsheviks! To the spiritual defense of our country!" (*Die Front*, August 29, 1933.)

Almost four years later Dr. Oprecht received a letter from Berne dated July 16, 1937:

In the recent past your publishing house has issued a number of books that deal with political conditions in Germany and especially with the personalities at the highest levels of the German government. These books, which are written by foreigners, most of whom are emigrants, seek to convince the reader of the harmful consequences of the present system in Germany. It is their purpose to undermine the authority of the official German institutions in the public mind. Consequently these books fall into the category of polemical and politically controversial literature.

The Swiss government has repeatedly taken the occasion to point out to the Swiss population, and especially to those persons who exert some influence over the formation of public opinion, that they must be guided in their judgments of non-Swiss matters by the fundamental principle of our country, which is neutrality, and at the same time, in their objective considerations of events abroad, they must not lose sight of the necessity of friendly relations with our neighbor states. Attention has also been called to the dangers that are inherent in the growth of an un-Swiss, unneutral, political emigrant literature.

Instead of being guided by these recommendations, you have for some time placed your publishing facilities at the disposition of these same foreigners, whose aim is to attack the political system in Germany.

We therefore find ourselves obliged to call to your attention the fact that, in the present serious period, the national officials responsible for the security of the country can no longer allow neutral Swiss soil, protected by international law, to be misused for propaganda attacks on foreign states with which our country seeks to live in peace and friendship.

If you should continue to publish or distribute such polemical books, the Federal Council will be compelled, in the furtherance of its obligations in foreign policy, to adopt whatever measures are appropriate.

In his pamphlet, *When Freedom Was at Stake,* published by Herbert Lang, Ernst Schürch, the editor in chief of *Der Bund* in Berne, said, among other things:

> What did we not get, especially in 1936, the year of the Olympic Games, listening to everything we heard from athletes, sailors, yodelers, and other fine fellow-citizens who had to make pleasure trips through the Reich and nowhere wanted to see even the most minuscule concentration camp! Some of them thought that reporters sucked such things out of their fingers, and almost all of them insisted that they would have been impolitely "meddling."

Indeed—as we have seen—it was not only athletes, sailors, and yodelers who thought and said such things . . .

## The Signal of *Kristallnacht*

In October 1938 a mass transport of Polish Jews, denaturalized and not denaturalized, was dumped by the Germans on the Polish border. All such unfortunates who did not have properly stamped Polish passports were turned back by force of arms. Seven thousand men, women, and children barely maintained their wretched lives in a no-man's-land on the German-Polish border—in Zbonszyn, under the worst possible conditions, in an old barracks and in stables. Accounts of their ordeal were published in the newspapers.

In desperation, a seventeen-year-old Polish Jew whose family had been deported to Zbonszyn fatally shot Ernst vom Rath, a secretary of the German Embassy in Paris. This act of desperation was followed by the infamous *Kristallnacht*—"Crystal Night" in Germany. From November 8 to 10, 1938, the pogrom raged: many hundreds of synagogues and more than seven thousand Jewish-owned businesses and residences were destroyed or heavily damaged by fires. The police rounded up between twenty and thirty thousand Jews, three thousand of them in Berlin alone. They included physicians, scholars, publishers, and poets.

Many wound up in concentration camps. Large numbers of Jews were killed. Many others killed themselves.

This occurred during the period when Germany and Switzerland were exchanging notes officially confirming their agreement on the "J" stamp.

The pogrom was "the prelude to the third period of the National Socialists' Jewish policy. It was elaborated with the death transports to the east and thus led to the 'final solution,' the period of annihilation, of extermination through mass murder." (From Professor Ludwig's report.)

The Jews of Germany were compelled to make restitution in the form of a fine of a billion marks for the act of the seventeen-year-old Polish Jew in Paris. A hundred thousand Jewish lives were destroyed. Jews were no longer allowed to enter specified streets, squares, public parks, and public buildings (for example, theaters, cinemas, concert halls, museums, stadiums, public and private baths).

In its issue of November 15, Himmler's newspaper, *Das Schwarze Korps*, demanded that the Jews be held within Germany as hostages for any attack on a German, under the slogan: "A thousand eyes for one eye, a thousand teeth for one tooth." A leading article in the same publication on November 23–24 said:

At the least, in these hundred thousand impoverished Jews we now have the breeding place for Bolshevism and we can observe the collection basin of the political-criminal subhumanity that is naturally formed on the margin of our own national entity through the process of selection. . . . Thus we are in the stage of development at which we face the harsh necessity of exterminating the Jewish underworld as thoroughly as we have pledged ourselves to root crime out of our ordered state: with fire and sword. The outcome would be the absolute and final end of Jewry in Germany, its utter annihilation.

Of this Reto Caratsch said in the *Neue Zürcher Zeitung*: "It would be completely wrong to interpret this threat as a mere shot in the air or a maneuver without serious intent. In the past year every proposal by *Das Schwarze Korps* for the handling of the Jewish question, however fantastic it might have seemed at the time of its publication, has been put into practice to the letter."

On December 1, *Das Schwarze Korps* declared once more: "On that day when a Jewish or Jewish-paid hand is raised to kill one of the leading figures in Germany, there will be no more Jews in Germany! We hope that we have expressed ourselves with sufficient clarity."

## Prophet Hitler

In his address to the Reichstag on January 30, 1939, Adolf Hitler declared:

> I have often been a prophet in my life, and most of the time I was laughed at. . . . Today I wish to be a prophet again: If international Jewish finance inside and outside Europe should succeed in hurling the peoples into another world war, the result will be not the Bolshevization of the world and the triumph of Jewry but the annihilation of the Jewish race in Europe.

On the day the war began, September 1, 1939, he reiterated his threat.

On November 16, 1941, Hitler's Propaganda minister, Josef Goebbels, referred in his newspaper, *Das Reich,* to this speech by the *Führer* and added: "We are witnessing the fulfillment of this prophecy."

On December 31, 1941, Hitler said in an address in his headquarters: "The Jew, however, will not exterminate the peoples of Europe; instead he will be the victim of his own assault." (*Völkischer Beobachter,* January 1, 1942.)

One month later, on January 31, 1942, the *Führer* reminded the world: "On September 1, 1939, I told the German Reichstag—and I do not allow myself rash prophecies—that this war would not follow the course that the Jews imagined: that is, that the European Aryan peoples would be exterminated; but rather that the result of this war would be the annihilation of Jewry." (*Neue Zürcher Zeitung,* January 31, 1942.)

On June 14, 1942, Goebbels said again in *Das Reich:* "The Jews are playing their criminal game in this war, and they will have to pay for it with the extermination of their race in Europe and perhaps elsewhere as well."

Can it be said that the leaders of National Socialist Germany left us in the dark as to their intentions and methods? Can it be said, as Federal Councilor von Steiger told Parliament on November 12, 1947, that, "if what was going on there in the Reich had been known, the range of the possible would have been broadened"?

Anyone could know that, under an ordinance of September 1, 1941, no Jew over the age of six was permitted to appear in public without his Jewish star. Anyone could know that the Jews in the Reich were being gradually cut off from food supplies and that in the end they could no longer purchase any meat, meat products, beer, wheat products, full-cream milk, skimmed milk, and other such staples.

Under the decree of September 25, 1941, illegal activities by Jews were removed from the jurisdiction of the courts and made punishable by the police, which was bound by no law. When a Jew died, his estate passed to the Reich. The Jews' scale of living was systematically reduced with the publicly declared intention of exterminating them.

## Beginning of the Death Transports

The first mass shipment of Jews out of Vienna to the east "for the purpose of launching the work of colonization" took place as early as October 1939. At the same time several thousand Jews were shipped to the east from Bohemia. Further transports to Poland from Germany and the Czech "Protectorate" were especially heavy in September and October 1941. The deportees were allowed to take with them only their minimum requirements in outer clothing and underwear.

More mass transports to the east followed in the spring of 1942. On May 1 of that year there were still approximately one hundred thousand Jews living in Germany, about half of them in Berlin. Those who were not drafted into forced-labor battalions were condemned to idleness. The rest of the Jews had been eliminated by hunger, disease, suicide, and deportations. According to other sources, the number of deportees alone was one hundred twenty thousand. Since the beginning of the war the authorities had shipped some forty thousand Jews to the east from Austria. (See Ludwig, pages 41–45.)

The first deportations from the occupied countries also took place in the spring of 1942. No Jew knew whether he would be seized as a hostage, deported, or arrested on some flimsy pretext. Attempts to flee abroad were deemed to constitute efforts to enter into relations with the enemy, and as such they were severely punished. (See Ludwig, page 189.)

In March 1942 the first deportations from The Netherlands and Belgium were made public. As early as January, in a speech delivered from London through the British Broadcasting Corporation, Thomas Mann said:

> The information seems unbelievable but it comes from an excellent source. A large number of Dutch Jewish families in Amsterdam and other cities, I am advised, has been plunged into the deepest mourning by the horrible deaths inflicted on their sons. Four hundred young Dutch Jews were taken to Germany to be used as subjects in experiments with poison gas. The full effectiveness of this chivalrous and thoroughly German weapon of war—a true Siegfried weapon—was expended on the young sub-men. They are dead—they died for the New Order and the military *expertise* of the master race. After all, they were good enough for this: they were only Jews. [The fifty-fifth in Thomas Mann's series of broadcasts to Germans, published in Stockholm in 1945 by the Bermann-Fischer Verlag under the title of *Deutsche Hörer!—German Listeners!*]

Bulletin No. 4 of the Dutch Legation in Berne reported on May 8, 1942, quoting official sources, that a tremendous number of young Dutch Jews had been arrested during 1941. They were deported to Mauthausen, where they were put to work in salt and sulphur mines but not provided with the necessary respiratory apparatus for the protection of their lungs. Several hundred died in the worst agonies. Others were used as guinea pigs for experiments with poison gas. A sharp protest by the Dutch Government in Exile in London went unanswered. The International Red Cross Committee was forbidden to visit the Dutch Jews in Mauthausen. It was established, however, that the victims were killed by six different methods, including the gas chamber.

In another broadcast in June 1942, Thomas Mann dealt with this tragic story again. He stated that in his January talk he had been guilty of a deplorable understatement of the truth.

I spoke of shameful acts by the Nazis and reported that four hundred young Netherlanders of Jewish stock had been shipped to Germany, where they were put to death with poison gas. Now, by indirect means, I have learned from The Netherlands that my report was almost 50 per cent short of the actual number: there were almost eight hundred men seized at that time, sent to Mauthausen, and gassed there. The exact figure has since been made public by The Netherlands government.

As early as November 1941 Mann had broadcast reports of the "unspeakable" crimes "that have been and are being committed in Russia against Poles and Jews." Mann's broadcasts were listened to by tens of thousands of persons in Switzerland.

In *Der Toggenburger Tagblatt* of July 2, 1942, the editor, Dr. R. Habicht, asserted in his leading article:

In Tuesday's issue of this newspaper we printed the assertion by a member of the Polish Parliament that approximately one million Jews had been done to death in this war; the word used in another official account is "exterminated," and the victims were not limited to men, but included women and children. According to reliable information from the most prominent Catholic sources in an occupied country, sixty thousand Jews were removed from Lithuania between May 7 and 10.

This article was distributed on July 8 by the Jewish press service, Juna, to the Swiss press as a whole.

In its issue of July 17, 1942 *Das israelitische Wochenblatt* of Zürich described a *Black Book* published by the Polish Government in Exile in London, according to which more than seven hundred thousand Jews had been killed in Poland. Two hundred thousand more were butchered in the German-occupied area of Russia.

A message from Churchill to a rally attended by twenty thousand Jews in Madison Square Garden in New York declared: "It is now known that more than a million Jews have been murdered by the National Socialists. Apparently Hitler will not be satisfied until every city in Europe inhabited by Jews has been turned into a gigantic graveyard." *Die National-Zeitung* of Basel and other Swiss newspapers printed this message.

## Report from Gurs

As early as the end of July and the beginning of August 1942, Switzerland was receiving positive information on the police raids of mid-July in occupied and unoccupied France and the deportation of ten thousand Jews to the east. At the beginning of the war some fifty thousand fugitives from Germany, most of them Jews, were living in France. As soon as war broke out, all German and Austrian nationals between the ages of eighteen and fifty-five were interned. After the German armies invaded The Netherlands, Belgium, and northern France in May 1940 approximately twenty-five thousand Jews fled south. Several hundred opponents of the Nazi system had to be handed over to the conquerors. On the other hand, releases from the camps were numerous. In August, however, there were again new military operations, and a decree of September 27 ordered that all aliens not required by the French economy either submit to residence in stipulated areas or be interned. In November the camps of Gurs, Vernet, and Argèles alone contained 27,200 inmates. These included 6900 Jews from Baden and 11,500 from the Palatinate whom the Germans had seized in the autumn of 1940 after the fall of France and shipped south—a gift from *Gauleiter* Wagner to his *Führer*, as this deportation was described by Professor Dr. Else Liefmann in a pamphlet memoir, *Bright Lights Against A Dark Background*. Professor Liefmann had been deported with her sister and her brother, an outstanding German scientist. The deportees also included the famous poet Alfred Mombert.

Many shocking reports of the dreadful living conditions in these camps were received in Switzerland. One letter to a relief organization said:

> I should like to point out to you that our need (we supplement our rations with kitchen waste, peelings, bones, and cattle fodder) is so great that only collective sharing of packages can be the general practice. . . . This is the only way in which we can meet our needs and survive the difficult times that still lie ahead for us. So we do

not bother with special requests but confine ourselves to things that will feed our hunger . . . because our permanent companion, hunger, constricts our stomachs at night and allows not even a thought of sleep. We need clothes, of course, especially warm things of all kinds. But again and always and first of all: food! food!

Another letter said:

You simply have no way of imagining how terrible the sufferings of the internees are. There is no limit to the needs of the insane, who do not get the slightest help because of their internment and who have nothing to eat. Many of the sick, in their agitation, weep and yell with hunger and tear food from one another's mouths. Sometimes they eat their own excrement just to lessen the pain of hunger . . .

A Jewish woman who was able to flee to Switzerland with her child after her husband's death reported:

Hunger! Atrocious hunger dominates our thoughts and feelings; our identities are eroded by despair and suffering and homesickness. Gruel twice a day and a tiny ration of bread! How long can we endure this? Have our torturers had some expert calculate just how long thin gruel and bread can keep a person alive? . . . Hunger, hunger! it throbs and stabs in the bowels, it gnaws into our hearts, it makes people rabid and vicious. Old people, some of them almost a hundred years old, invalids, the blind, the crippled, deaf mutes, children, babies—they all have to travel the same road of agony. A man sentenced to prison for a crime knows how long he has to serve; but we do not know when the gates to freedom and human decency will ever open again for us. For four weeks my three-year-old child whimpered and wept with hunger, and I had nothing to give him. Who can measure what this makes a mother suffer? There the child was, more apathetic every day, pale, thin; then high fever and diarrhea. "Dysentery," the doctors said. There were no medicines available. Soon there seemed to be nothing but two huge, wide-open eyes in the little childish face. I was never irreligious, but in those six weeks when I saw death hovering over my child I gained strength from prayer. True, there was a stove in the barracks; but there was nothing to burn in it. I had no dry underwear for my child, who was covered with his own excrement every ten minutes. We ripped rafters and wood out of the ceiling of the barracks so that we could make things a little better for ourselves by burning them, knowing that, if we were caught, we would be severely punished. But need listens to no orders. My husband, all this time, was in the men's barracks, suffering from dysentery in a horrible improvised infirmary. I was helpless. On my knees I begged for permission to visit my husband and give him a little care. I found him in a state of utter neglect and malnutrition. On the average there were fifteen to twenty funerals a day: typhus, caused by hunger, and dysentery. No one cared any longer who was buried where. First there was desperation, then resignation and numbness. Five children were deprived of their mother by death; their father died in a German concentration camp. The latrines were the most revolting that anyone could imagine. They were breeding grounds for disease. A good many people who had lost all their strength or had had heart attacks were found in these latrines.

Then these camps too had their turn. One August morning the police rounded up more than a thousand Jews—old and young, healthy and infirm—in Gurs alone, loaded them onto trucks and drove them north. There were heartrending scenes. The deportees were savagely hurled into cattle cars. Many of them died on the journey.

## The Persecutors in France

Here are excerpts from some of the letters that were received in Switzerland.

A woman wrote on August 14, 1942, from the camp at Rivesaltes:

A terrible fate lies ahead of us: we are about to be shipped off, no one knows where. We fear the worst that can still happen to us. What is dreadful for us is that we must leave our little Albert behind here. You are so good and so kind, perhaps you can do something to stand by the child. We give ourselves into God's hands and hope that he will stand by us. But we have no more hope that we shall ever again see our beloved children and relatives. Please send our warmest greetings and very best wishes to our dear sister and the relatives. If we have the strength, we will write to you so that you can give our dear children and sister news of us. Perhaps too you can write to our grown children when you get this letter and tell the eldest that for the present he should not send us any more money, only he must not forget his little brother and he must do everything in his power to have his little brother with him and to take care of him. My heart is almost breaking, I can't write more. All the best to you, and again all our deepest thanks for all your love, may the good God reward you in full. Best wishes to your dear relatives and to you from my husband and myself. Your E. I. [From the files of the Reverend Dr. Paul Vogt.]

A man whose wife had died wrote to his sister in Switzerland:

Now I and others are being moved, without knowing where we are going. And my twelve-year-old boy is left alone. I don't know whether or when I can write again. . . . Take care of the boy if you can, and, if it is at all possible, get him to Switzerland with you, because otherwise, I am afraid, he will have to follow me one day but not be with me. You understand. And I'd like to spare him that. I am beside myself, dear sister, and so helpless, and I have only one concern—the child. You'll take care of him, I want to finish, all my deepest love and a kiss. Your brother . . .

My beloved old mother is in danger of death. I beg you urgently to do everything possible to save her. Believe me, there is no finer woman. She brought us children to God. But now I can't see God any more, what he does is beyond my understanding. I *must* save my mother, and I would gladly be deported in her place. What can they do with an old woman? But I am young. How can I arrange to be taken in her place? . . .

A father wrote to his son in Switzerland:

My dear son: Unfortunately it has happened to me too, and now I must set off into the unknown. It grieves me particularly that now I cannot say farewell to your dear mother. The joy of seeing her again after so long a separation is now stolen from me, and who knows whether I shall ever again see her in life. I beg you, my beloved only child, take care of our poor dear mother and . . . just keep your head high and don't lose courage, whatever happens we want to *endure* it all. Please, my dear boy, make sure that you keep your job and behave yourself so that they will always be pleased with you. I hope I have written everything I wanted to say, and you will certainly understand that I am very nervous as I write and don't know any more what I'm saying. A thousand kisses from your father who is always thinking of you.

A woman wrote to her husband in Switzerland:

My dear husband: Just a note with all my good wishes—I'm leaving for some place unknown to me. *Don't upset yourself, I am quite prepared;* let us hope that we shall see each other again! Our child has not been home for two weeks. *Again, keep your head up!* If it is at all possible I will write to you. Don't bother any more about my immigration, it's impossible now. I've let everything drop; my sacrifice was for nothing. All my love . . .

This excerpt is taken from a letter written in Lyon:

Terrible things have been going on here for some time. Thousands of emigrants are supposed to be turned over to Germany, and for some time it has been like an animal hunt here for these unfortunates. Men and women, Jews and Christians, healthy and ailing, up to the age of sixty are on the lists; mostly they are rounded up in the middle of the night with trucks especially equipped for the purpose, thrown into camps, and then very shortly afterward transported, from all appearances, to Poland or Russia. Most of those who have not been arrested no longer live in their old quarters. All day long these Ahasueruses roam through the most obscure crannies. Night brings these people, who to look at them already have nothing human left in them, into the fields, the woods, public parks, hidden refuges, cloisters, churches, caves, wherever they think they may be halfway safe from the hunters. Every one of them, unwashed and unkempt, with his constantly shifting sleepless eyes, his ragged clothing, is like a hunted bird in quest of food. Most of them have no savings and are in no position to buy anything to eat. All it would need, to feed these persecuted people as if they were animals, would be always to carry something edible with one. And one must always carry money so that one can give at least a little help to these unfortunates, whom one encounters everywhere, including where one would least expect to find them. Hundreds of children above the age of two, who were forcibly taken away from their parents, have been placed in various institutions. Spiritual need cries out to high heaven as loudly as physical need. Why, you compassionate Savior, do you let such horrible wickedness flourish? Don't you see the anguish and the bitter tears of guiltless children of the tenderest years? Why, Almighty God, have you abandoned them all?

A Lutheran woman who had emigrated to Switzerland reported: "There are now eight persons among my husband's closest relatives who have been deported without our knowledge where; two others have committed suicide."

Another woman who had fled to Switzerland wrote:

Again today we have gruesome news. How often and with what horror I think of all the many people we love: all my cousins and nieces are gone, and now my dearest nephew, a wonderful man who lost his whole leg at the hip in the First World War and yet was always so brave and devoted all his life, a really, really fine man —he and his lovely wife and two delightful children, six and ten years old: now they have all been taken from The Netherlands.

Or another letter: "My wife is now in such a permanent state of upheaval over all her sisters and brothers in France, who are facing deportation, that often I do not know how to calm her. In the beginning of this year one of her brothers was killed in a concentration camp." (From Vogt file.)

## A Pastor's Diary

What horrible events occurred in France during this summer can be
seen from the diary of a French Reformed pastor, excerpts from which
appeared first in September 1942, before its full publication in 1943 in
the brochure, *Jewish Need and Christian Faith.*

*Saturday.* I have been in the camp since eight o'clock this morning.
I gathered my friends together. Right at the start I had a very
strong impression, which in the course of this terrible day was
confirmed with respect to not only my own community but all the
internees. First of all there was the frantic dread at the specter of
deportation; then, however, there was the courage with which in
spite of everything everyone was looking his fate in the eye, and
finally there was the love that everyone unwearyingly showed for
everyone else. Everyone strove to lighten his brother's cross and to
work for the rescue of his companion.

*Monday.* A succession of anguishes. Unforgettable farewells to
children under eighteen, who are to go to America. Horrible separation! A big handsome boy, sixteen or eighteen years old, held his
father and mother close. He did not weep, but he bent his head
first to one, then to the other, rubbed his cheeks against theirs,
slowly and softly, with all the tenderness in the world. Not a word.
Father and Mother wept silently, full of dread. This went on and
on. No one spoke. Finally the truck came. Then all of them, from
the biggest to the smallest, burst into tears. No outcries, no movement. But faces that bore a look as if they wanted to see eternity in
the next instant. The policemen round me were pale as ashes. One
of them said to me the other day: "I've been in the colonies, in
China, I've seen massacres and war and starvation, but I've never
seen anything so awful as this." In a moment no one could speak,
or even touch. The truck vanished. Finally one mother collapsed
into a heap on the ground in nervous exhaustion. . . .

The transport was fully loaded. The Quakers went through the
cars distributing food. The train was scheduled to depart at eight
o'clock Tuesday morning. We cannot conclude this brief report

without mentioning that a man and a woman slashed their arteries and were taken to the hospital in critical condition.

*Wednesday.* This horror-ridden day was marked by ten attempts at suicide. From ten o'clock in the morning on, the internees stood in the courtyard under a fierce sun. During the afternoon a policeman crossed the courtyard with a jug of water for his colleagues. He passed close to a group of internees, one of whom timorously held out his cup in a begging gesture, without speaking. The policeman stopped and poured insults on him. Later the policemen who accompanied the first group to the train did not omit any brutalities. . . . Mrs. L, who had not been arrested, surrendered in order to be able to go with her son. But he had already disappeared. In spite of all our efforts, Mrs. L was also deported, the victim of her own maternal love. . . .

Now it is night. Though it is beyond belief, I have confirmed the fact: Today a man's destiny was decided in thirty seconds. Suffering, degradation, revulsion, indignation, heartbreak, immeasurable grief, ruin, lives trampled out, indelible shame. The testimony of Israel: God has made it great and flexible. This whole people has suffered with dignity, with integrity, humility, with greatness. The magnificent example of the women who voluntarily came to be deported with their husbands. Everywhere a spirit of brotherhood and helpfulness. The close and deep communion that I felt with the rabbi. I must point out that I have seen how these doomed brothers concern themselves as deeply for one another as for themselves. How they rejoice at the liberation of their friends and share their griefs to the full. I have not, however, seen one of them attempt to harm another. What was loathsome and revolting was not of their doing. . . .

Sunday afternoon I encountered a group that was just moving off to the transport. One of them pointed out the man beside him and said to me: "He must not be deported: he is a Protestant and an Aryan. Please save him!" The man was in fact unlucky enough to have been arrested the night before, and in his bewilderment and desperation he was in no condition to explain or defend himself. On the ramp that led to the train he sobbed like a poor abandoned child. . . . When I went back a few minutes later to take him away, his Jewish companion thanked me with rejoicing. . . . I do not think that all anti-Semites would have been capable of such an attitude in the same situation. . . .

From August 25 on we plumbed the depths of our disaster. That night raids were carried out on a large scale. Everyone who was trapped by this roundup in the cities, the villages, and the farms was taken to the camp. The reports that we heard from the victims would in themselves form a mountain of suffering. How many homes and hearths destroyed, how many shattered peaceful happy lives, how many human qualities trampled down, and all in a whirlwind of a few minutes! A couple had had to watch as their young daughter threw herself out a window and was smashed against the street in order to escape the fate prepared for her. Women were snatched out of bed and made to dress under the eyes of grinning policemen. A man from the Occupied Zone—without the slightest idea what was taking place—had come to see his wife and two children after a long separation. At the station in X his papers were demanded. He is thirty-six years old, a Pole who has lived thirty-five of those years in France. . . . At the start of the war he had volunteered for service, with reputable and well-known Frenchmen as his sponsors; but he is a Jew. . . . He could not understand what was happening to him when he was arrested . . . and taken to the camp. And . . . when he was moved to another camp, he still understood nothing except for one single fact—that he could not see his wife and his little children. When the train stopped, he said with a dazed look: "I'm going crazy!". . .   · · ·

What was especially painful was the appearance of the small children, because at the last moment instructions were issued that all children above the age of two must be deported with their parents so that there was no further possibility of entrusting them to a relief agency. Extremely little children, shivering with cold and weariness in the night, weeping with hunger, clung wretchedly to their parents and asked to be carried; but the adults' arms were loaded with parcels and luggage—poor little fellows of five and six tried manfully to take some of the luggage from their parents and carry it until sleep overcame them and they fell to the ground with their loads. Everyone shivered in the night dew in a wait that for some groups dragged out to many hours; young fathers and mothers

wept quietly to themselves in the knowledge of their own impo-
tence in the face of their children's sufferings. Finally the order
came to leave the courtyard and board the train, and the pitiful
children took their places in rows and columns according to their
numbers, moving totteringly on their shaky legs. "This have you
done also unto me!" . . .

I cannot pay high enough tribute to the splendid behavior of the
guards and policemen during this day and night. They were sympathetic and humane, full of respect for everyone, sharing the griefs
and rejoicing, like the internees, whenever someone was set free;
they gave practical help of every kind, and they provided me with
special transportation on behalf of this or that group whenever they
believed that it could be useful. They investigated before they
loaded each person aboard, lest some fateful error be made. A pulse
of love had stirred their hearts, and the prevailing spirit was that of
general good will. . . .

Our task is not ended. It was only a prelude. Miserable, destroyed, hunted human beings, old people and women, the smallest
children, the sick and the strong, men torn out of life look to us
and to the church. What is important for us is not the judgment of
the world but only the solemn, awful judgment of that One who
said and will everlastingly say of any breach of the commandment
of love: "This have you not done unto me!"

SEPTEMBER 20, 1942.

Under the title *We Cannot Keep Silence, Die Berner Tagwacht* of
August 3, 1942, published a report from Paris, dated July 21, from which
these excerpts are taken:

It began at four o'clock in the morning of July 16 and it is still
going forward. Even now people are still being picked off the
streets. For the most part the victims are women and children of
foreign origin, but naturally the men are not excluded. We have
lived through hours of dreadful suffering. There have been accounts
of numerous instances of women throwing themselves from windows with their children. Nevertheless the operation is being carried forward to its conclusion. . . .

There is still no firsthand news from those in custody. It is said that some of those who were first taken to Drancy have already been shipped to Germany or Poland. . . .

The *Vélodrome* [*d'hiver*] is packed tight. Men, women, and children are all shoved together; they can sleep only sitting up. For everyone there is an interminable wait in line at the toilet. These poor people have been enduring great hardships for six days while they wait for their destinies to be decided.

And this dispatch appeared in the August 6 issue of *Die St.-Gallen Volksstimme:*

London, August 6 (*Reuters*)—According to information received by General de Gaulle's headquarters, Premier Laval has announced his assent to the German government's request for the delivery to Germany of all Jews of foreign origin in the Occupied Zone plus some ten thousand Jews in the Unoccupied Zone of France. The initial reports received in London indicate that thirty-six hundred Jews now held in the concentration camps of Gurs, Rivesaltes, and Vernet have been earmarked for deportation. On August 6, 8, and 10 about a thousand more Jews are to be shipped from Pau, Perpignan, and Marseilles to unidentified destinations. Mass arrests are to be carried out on Sunday in Lyons.

## What Swiss Observers Saw in the East

Swiss medical missions visited Germany's eastern front in 1941 and 1942. The members of these medical missions knew of the crimes that were perpetrated in Poland and Russia. Franz Blättler, who was a member of the second mission, described what he had seen in a book published at the end of 1943 under the title, *Warsaw, 1942—A First-hand Report by a Driver for the Second Swiss Medical Mission to Poland in 1942*. He described how the Jewish population was starved, tortured, bloodily beaten down, and done to death in the most varied ways. He also visited the Warsaw ghetto, which he called "a huge graveyard." The people who lived there had learned "that for them

there were only blows, hunger, and early death." He was ashamed "to
be able to walk out of such conditions of horror as a free man."

As the foreword to the edition published by F. G. Micha & Co. of
Zürich states, the book was not allowed to be generally distributed in
Switzerland until 1945.

Dr. Rudolf Bucher, a well known Zürich physician who had instituted
the army's blood-bank system, was a member of the first mission in
1941. In agreement with and at the request of the then chief medical
officer of the army, Brigadier Colonel Dr. P. Vollenweider, he lectured
on his experiences and observations in the east to various units of the
medical corps attached to the fortifications and the border troops. In
the course of these lectures he naturally described the horror-filled
matters of which he had knowledge. In all he made more than 150 such
talks, not only to the military but also to civilian audiences, physicians,
the Zürich cantonal police, and other groups. As he assured me in
conversation, his reports were heard by more than a hundred thousand
persons. He corroborated the statements made in Professor Ludwig's
report. Let me quote Dr. Bucher:

In January 1942 the chief physician in the northern military hospital of Smolensk, Captain Wagner, informed me that matters were
growing worse and more criminal from year to year, because more
and more Jews were being murdered in the most bestial fashions—
in fact, not so much through mass shootings (such as the massacre
of seven thousand Jews by machine-gun fire in the Minsk ghetto)
as by asphyxiation in the gas chambers and the mass burnings of
bodies in the crematoria. At all events, he knew that the construction of extermination camps of this kind, if not yet completed in
various places, had already been tested in Auschwitz.

On the outskirts of the city of Smolensk I saw some ten Jewish
women digging their own large grave. I did not wait to see them
executed, but at a later date I did see their covered tomb. In
Warsaw, closely watched by SS men, I saw a deportation train of
third-class cars packed tight with Warsaw Jews, from the very old
to the smallest children. One of the SS men informed that these
"Jew-pigs" naturally had no idea that in four days they would be
destroyed.

At the end of January 1942, in the building formerly occupied by the GPU in Smolensk, I was myself present at least at the start of a ghastly execution of sixty-two hostages that began at seven o'clock in the morning. Very few of them were Jews, but there was a random mixture of very old men and women and a number of very small children. The SS carried out these executions by shooting the victims at the base of the skull.

On my homeward journey in February 1942 a young blonde woman in the train from Breslau to Berlin told me that, although she was half-Jewish, she had been left in peace because she had willingly become the mistress of a high SS officer. . . . After a few hours of intimate conversation, she told me the mechanics of the undressing and washing procedures in the extermination chambers in Auschwitz. She also described the methods of execution and cremation and mentioned the so-called blue-cross gas (diphanyl-ar- sin), which was brought in in the conventional iron cylinders. This was when I first learned of the cynical delousing routine.

Dr. Bucher told me that in March 1942 he had reported his observa- tions in full to the then Judge Advocate General of the Army, Brigadier Colonel Eugster. In May 1944 Dr. Bucher was summoned to appear before the Judge Advocate General and Federal Councilor Karl Kobelt. He was accused of having, through his lectures on the war in Russia, broken his obligatory pledge of silence, and he was threatened with Article XVI of the Articles of War, which called for the loss of his rank and his expulsion from the army.

According to Ludwig's report, Kobelt and Eugster insisted that they had merely reprimanded Dr. Bucher for the breach of his pledge on his honor to maintain silence. Kobelt added further that there was never any discussion of the substance of Dr. Bucher's lectures or of any penalty of loss of rank. If Dr. Bucher had made the statements quoted by him, he would certainly have remembered them and embodied them in a report to the Federal Council. Judge Advocate General Brigadier Colonel Eugster expressed himself in the same vein.

Nevertheless Dr. Bucher stood firm on his own version. It would indeed appear strange that he should have been criticized for his lectures without any comment on what he said in them. The oath of silence could certainly have had nothing to do with the purely military and medical aspects, since other members of the medical mission also discussed them. Since the "risks for a neutral state in the light of the well-known German sensitivity" were brought up in the conversation among Kobelt, Eugster, and Bucher, or so Eugster told Professor Ludwig, this must have referred to those points in Bucher's lectures that might have been uncomfortable for the Germans—specifically, his observations on the massacres in the east.

Obviously no record of the three-party discussion exists. On the contrary, on May 6, 1943, with a covering letter, Brigadier Colonel Eugster returned to Dr. Bucher a diary kept by Sergeant Major W., a member of the same mission to which Dr. Bucher belonged. This diary contained such entries as these:

*October 23, 1941.* A young SA man told us that again yesterday three thousand Jews and others had been knocked off for sabotage. The Jews must be exterminated . . .

*November 7, 1941.* Women and children knocked off for shooting at German soldiers. A large grave was dug and each person was thrown on the bodies of the ones shot earlier, until the grave was full.

*December 1, 1941.* Every day at dawn, executions of Partisans, executions of the Jewish population in the GPU jail.

On February 16, 1942, in the name of the Federal Council, the Press and Radio Office of the General Staff ordered a strict prohibition on "the publication of reports, articles, statements, etc., dealing with observations and experiences of the medical mission or of individual members of the same." In April this prohibition was extended to cover the second medical mission, which was then at the eastern front.

Professor Ludwig also told of a Swiss who was living in a private capacity in what was then the Polish Ukraine and who at the beginning of August 1942 was an involuntary eyewitness to the mass murders of Polish Jews in Kamen Kasirski, a town situated in Rokitno-Sümpfen (Volhynia). The victims, who also included gypsies, were shot in the back of the head by two-man Special Commandos of the SS. Similar executions took place at that time throughout Volhynia and Galicia, whereas the executions in the Government General of Poland itself had already begun several months earlier.

Both orally and in writing, this Swiss reported what he had seen to the then Swiss Consul General in Hamburg, with whom he maintained a regular correspondence. Whether, as the eyewitness took for granted, his reports were forwarded to Berne it is now impossible to establish. In the country itself the man would have been unable to obtain work in any public post after his return. As a result of what he had seen he had suffered a nervous breakdown.

The first reports of mass murders of deported western European Jews also reached Switzerland in the summer of 1942—being received, specifically, by the Geneva office of the World Jewish Congress. The details, however, were so dreadful that, as Dr. G. M. Riegner, the director of the office, told Professor Ludwig, at first the reports were discarded as unbelievable even by Jewish circles. (See Ludwig, page 234.)

## August 13, 1942

It would appear from a report that was submitted at the end of July to the Federal Justice and Police Department by Dr. R. Jezler, Dr. Rothmund's deputy, in the name of his chief, that even in the Police Section there must have been some knowledge of what was going on in the east and of the monstrous fate that was awaiting Jews deported from western Europe.

Among other things, Dr. Jezler discussed the significant deterioration of the situation of the Jews in France in July 1942 because of the mass arrests for the deportations to the east. The first fugitives from France who tried to claim asylum in Switzerland were sent back to France.

> In the recent past [this is verbatim what Dr. Jezler wrote] we have been unable, however, to bring ourselves to continue such action. The unanimous and authentic reports on the methods by which the deportations are being carried out and on the conditions in Jewish areas in the east are so ghastly that it is impossible not to understand the refugees' desperate attempts to escape such a fate and equally impossible to assume any further responsibility for sending them back.

Jezler's conclusions were these:

The evolution of the military and political situation in Europe justifies the expectation that in the very near future an ever increasing flow of refugees is to be reckoned with. Switzerland's food situation, the difficulty faced by the refugees in proceeding farther, the large number of refugees still to be anticipated, certain considerations of foreign policy, factors of internal security, and the problems of housing the refugees are all factors that make strong reservations on the admission of refugees seem advisable. [Ludwig, pages 199, 202.]

Dr. Rothmund sent this report by Jezler, accompanied by a covering letter, to the new head of the Justice and Police Department, Federal Councilor Eduard von Steiger. Events in France, he said, gave ground for apprehensions that French Jews in the Occupied Zone too would soon seek to escape the threat of deportation measures by flight into Switzerland.

What are we to do? We admit deserters, as well as escaped prisoners of war by and large, as long as the number of those who cannot proceed farther does not rise too high. Political fugitives (that is, those who are in danger because of their political activities) within the meaning of the Federal Council's 1933 definition are also given asylum. But this 1933 law has virtually become a farce today, because every refugee is already in danger of death simply by reason of having fled, even though very few of them are persons who have engaged in political activity within the original meaning of the legislation. Shall we send back only the Jews? This seems to be almost forced on us.

Thereupon Heinrich Rothmund raised the question whether it would not be permissible to institute a special small, mobile, motorized reinforcement of the border patrol for a brief period—one to two weeks and at unannounced times—at those border-crossing points chiefly favored by alien-smugglers. It would be the major task of this force to prevent every attempt to cross the border, without respect to persons. Crossings where these reinforcements were not assigned would be permitted as in the past. In a very short time the border-control services would probably be so well coordinated that it would be possible to issue instructions to

them to give further attention to individual cases and, in especially
onerous situations, to make exceptions. (See Ludwig, pages 203–204.)

On August 4, 1942, the Federal Council decided to tighten still
further the restrictions of Article IX of its legislation of October 17,
1939, under which the cantonal authorities were obligated immediately
to send back to the countries from which they had come all foreigners
who entered Switzerland illegally. In future, therefore, expulsions of
foreign civilian refugees would have to be made on a much larger scale,
"even if the foreigners who fall within this legislation may have reason
to anticipate the most serious consequences (danger to life and limb)."

On August 8 Dr. Rothmund and some colleagues toured the border
in the Jura as far as Les Verrières

> . . . and found everywhere, beyond contradiction, the same condi-
> tions: woods and deep ravines where it was utterly impossible to
> patrol the border, conglomerations of Jews of various nationalities
> in the French Jura, inadequate controls at the Belgian-French
> border and in Occupied France, travel preparations completed even
> in the refugees' prior places of residence, where everyone knew the
> names of the restaurants in Belfort, etc., in which professional
> alien-smugglers could be contacted.

Besides, the border officials had assured Dr. Rothmund that nothing
happened to the refugees who were turned back. . . .

Acting under the authority of the Federal Council's law of August 4,
1942, Dr. Heinrich Rothmund ordered the borders hermetically sealed
on August 13. At this time Federal Councilor von Steiger was away on
vacation.

In a confidential bulletin to all cantonal police departments and their
subdivisions one sentence was fateful: "Refugees in flight solely because
of racial reasons—Jews, for example—do not qualify as political refugees."

# The Ruthless Frontier

That August 13, 1942, was a black day in the history of Switzerland's right of asylum. What happened then was the culmination of a course that had been initiated much earlier.

## At the Time of the Fair

On September 14, 1939, two weeks after the outbreak of the Second World War—the Swiss National Exposition was at its apogee—the Reverend A. Hübscher reported in *Das Recht* that three days earlier, on orders from Dr. Rothmund and in spite of every effort and plea on their behalf, a number of refugees of the Jewish faith had been delivered by

the Zürich cantonal police to the Swiss border town of Schaffhausen
and forced to return to Germany. The Reverend Hübscher printed the
letter that he had written to Dr. Rothmund on September 13:

Early last week, by means of the press and the radio, you ordered
that all refugees residing illegally in Switzerland be registered with
the police, and you also put into effect an ordinance that determined the future fate of these people. Thereupon I went to the
Zürich Alien Police on September 6, 1939, and declared that since
the end of June of this year I had been harboring a Jewish refugee
under my protection and in temporary domicile in my parsonage
and that I had come to register him. When I expressed my apprehension lest he be subject to enforced expulsion at the German
border—the border of that country from which, under the cover of
night and fog, he had fled in order to escape the threat of confinement in a concentration camp—I was officially reassured. It was
explained to me that there was no ground to anticipate such action
and that the registration was merely a preliminary measure for the
purpose of taking a census of these illegal residents.

The next day the refugee himself went to register with the Alien
Police. He too was given to understand that he could remain with
me undisturbed.

At 6:15 A.M. on September 11 the refugee was arrested in my
parsonage by a detective attached to the Zürich cantonal police and
taken to police headquarters. An hour later the cantonal police
official on duty informed me, when I expressed my apprehensions,
that he would issue instructions to the Alien Police for the canton
and that he would handle the matter in duly legal fashion. When I
told him that assurances had been given to me on September 6 in
the office of the Zürich Police Commissioner that, in the event of
expulsion, I should immediately be given the opportunity to intercede again for the refugee with the Police Commissioner, the
duty officer took official cognizance of this and once more reassured
me.

At 3:30 P.M. of that same day the refugee telephoned me from
Schaffhausen to say that the police had taken him there and that
within a half-hour he would be transported to the German border.
All subsequent efforts addressed to the Police Commissioner, the

cantonal office of the Alien Police, and yourself (through a colleague of mine in Berne) came to nothing. The only official
communication that I received from the police was a notice that I
would be charged with violation of the registration order.

Today, after having confirmed that on that Monday not only my
refugee but also others, including a young Jewish couple with a
two-year-old child, had been taken to the German border, the
Zürich Police Commissioner informed me that for the present no
more refugees will be removed to the border. Gratitude for this is
owed to this official's efforts. This change in practice, in contrast to
what was done on Monday, proves only that on Monday too it
would have been possible to suspend the execution of the expulsion
order for twenty-four hours, as we had earnestly pleaded be done.
Since all sources in the Zürich police department have informed me
that it is you, Mr. Rothmund, who are responsible for this matter, I
find myself compelled in good conscience, as a Christian and a
Swiss citizen, to protest against this action, for which I cannot find
an adequate description. I do so on behalf of many Christians
whose devotion to our country is beyond challenge but who still
believe that Switzerland is true to herself only when she does not
abandon human decency even in the case of one man. I protest in
the name of our Reformed Church, which insists that the preamble
to our Constitution—"In the name of God, the Almighty"—is no
mere phrase. This church would be betraying its Lord and Master
if it played the dead dog in the face of this action by your Police
Section. On this we cannot keep silence.

## By Means of Deception

To his letter the Reverend Hübscher appended the following:

1. The order issued by press and radio, in contrast to the assurances given, was intended not for the purpose of making a census of
refugees in illegal residence but for that of carrying out the plans of
the Alien Police regardless of all assurances and promises.

2. It is clear that under pressure by Mr. Rothmund, who is
accessible to no one and whose orders the cantonal police depart-

ments can hardly challenge openly but must simply execute even at
the price of their own debasement, the cantonal police was compelled to resort to the most despicable deception of other persons
in official positions, such as pastors of the national church, merely
in order to carry out Mr. Rothmund's orders in the case that I have
described.

3. It is a matter of record that on Monday Mr. Rothmund stated
that no individual case could be reversed as a result of protests, but
that twenty-four hours later, under the influence of the most vigorous protests, which had already been laid before him on Monday,
all expulsions were temporarily suspended as of Tuesday afternoon.
This, however, does not remedy the injustice committed on September 11.

There remains only the hope that, in cooperation with the police
departments, the refugee-relief organizations will succeed in propos-
ing to Berne, and winning its approval for, a solution of this painful
problem that will be humane and creditable to Switzerland. There
have been enough victims.

## Dr. Rothmund's Advice

Dr. Heinrich Rothmund, the chief of the Police Section, wrote a
"Clarification of the Refugee Question" that appeared in *Das Volksrecht* on September 21 and in which he did not dispute the Reverend
Hübscher's account. He referred to the instructions issued by the Federal Council, under which emigrants who had not complied with the
immigration regulations before they crossed the border would be sent
back. In this article Rothmund expressly accepted the responsibility for
their exclusion. Then he continued:

I should like to pose a question to the Reverend Hübscher: does he
consider it proper, and can he answer to his own conscience for it,
that, when he had violated a law, he first went to the official sources
to inform himself as to the punishment entailed and then, when he
had got his answer, he committed or risked another violation? He
should find the answer in his own education as a citizen, totally
apart from his position as a pastor, which requires exemplary
behavior of him in the first place. By speaking of himself in his

article as a man in an official position he further emphasizes this obligation. And the emigrant in question? Does the Reverend Hübscher not think that it would have gone less badly for this man if he had been sent back immediately after his illegal entry instead of having been allowed to spend a few months here and build up the firm hope that he would not be sent back to his country of origin? You are answerable for that, Reverend. In any event it ill becomes you to utter further reproaches. . . .

Anyone who henceforth in any way infringes the regulations or disobeys the orders of properly qualified officials of the Alien Police, and particularly anyone who does not register or who works without a labor permit, will be shipped back without delay. . . .

I advise the Reverend Hübscher to enlist in one of the existing organizations for refugee assistance if he does not think it preferable to devote himself to the service of one of the relief agencies of which today the Swiss have such great need.

The Reverend Hübscher did not keep Dr. Rothmund waiting for an answer to his *Clarification*. The next day the pastor set forth in *Das Volksrecht* the practical reasons that had motivated him to withhold the registration after much deliberation. Then he added:

There was also, however, a question of principle involved, and it was this: The detective who questioned me included in my testimony his own statement that I had broken the law because of the obligations of my calling. This simple man of the people understood better than Dr. Rothmund that a clergyman has not only the duty of exemplary behavior, as Rothmund's reproach pointed out, but also another vocation. It will be . . . within Dr. Rothmund's knowledge that in antiquity criminals could find sanctuary in the temples. Even in those days, in "darkest" antiquity, there was a conflict of conscience between religion and punishment. Within Christianity, fortunately, this problem has not diminished but, rather, become more acute.

It arises most especially today in the refugee question and in the light of the principles that Dr. Rothmund has thus far represented. These, invoking the name of God, clash with our Christian conscience, and that I cannot help. That Switzerland should make distinctions between Aryans and non-Aryans in the issuance of visas before the recent inception of universal visa requirements is unbelievable from a Christian point of view to those of us who are not adherents of the Third Reich. Moreover, we find it inconceivable when subordinate branches of the Alien Police, . . . in two authenticated cases of which I have knowledge, belabor these refugees with insults to which they cannot reply and so abandon themselves to the drunkenness of power that one can feel nothing but shame for the Zürich cantonal police. I am ready at any time to offer for investigation the evidence now in my possession. [From the files of Juna, the news service of the Swiss Jewish community.]

## Regrettable—but Not Wrong

In the summer of 1940, when German troops were trampling down France, the eminent historical philosopher and teacher, Dr. Wilhelm Foerster, was visiting Geneva on a three-day visa that had been granted in order to enable him to confer with his publisher. On June 22—eight days after the fall of Paris and three days before the cease-fire between France and Germany—Foerster applied to the police department of the canton of Geneva for an extension of his visa until the airline connections between Locarno and Barcelona had been resumed. The Geneva officials forwarded the application to the Federal Alien Police. The application was rejected, however, on instructions from Dr. Heinrich Rothmund, head of the Police Section. So on July 10, 1940, Professor Foerster left Switzerland. Premier Salazar of Portugal had personally invited him to go to Portugal after Switzerland threw him out. The Police Section contributed a thousand francs to the Swiss Relief Committee for Protestant Refugees, to be applied to the cost of the Foerster family's journey to Switzerland. The reason given for the order issued by the head of the Police Section was this: "The Locarno-Barcelona airline will certainly not be back in service for a long time. Foerster's presence is a terrible burden on us. He should try to reach Spain by way of Savoy and southern France. Until then he must remain in Geneva in complete retirement and make every effort to expedite his departure from Switzerland." In addition Professor Foerster was reminded that he was a French national and therefore he risked no danger in France!

The "Foerster case" had occupied the government before. Professor Foerster had been compelled to leave Germany because of his pacifist activities and his opposition to the government, and on March 13, 1936, he had formally applied to the president of Switzerland from Paris for permission to cross the border into Switzerland in the event that the international situation should make it impossible for him to continue to live in France. The request was denied on procedural grounds. Later, however, Professor Foerster was granted an entrance visa for a lecture tour in Switzerland; in addition, he received a six-month residence permit in 1938. Shortly after the outbreak of the war, in September 1939, Professor Foerster applied to Federal Councilor Giuseppe Motta, then the head of the Federal Political Department, for a special visa. At the same time he promised, as he had done before in 1936, to abstain from all political propaganda. This application too was denied, but the Swiss Consulate in Lyons was authorized to give Professor Foerster an ordinary visa for a lecture tour.

When the matter was raised in 1944 in a newspaper article, Dr. Rothmund replied, according to an official statement of August 6:

> However regrettable it may be in retrospect that we could give this eminent German no permanent asylum, this was unquestionably the only solution possible at that time. Given the conditions of our relations with Germany, Professor Foerster in his unbridled fashion might have aggravated them to the point of rupture. And then what? Where then would the eighty thousand refugees and above all the twenty-five thousand Jews have gone? Professor Foerster, however, was able to flee to another country. Moreover, he was not beset by the application of a deadline like the ordinary refugee; the head of the Alien Police explained to him not only that his permanent presence in Switzerland was out of the question, but also why. So: admittedly regrettable—but not wrong.

"The reception in Portugal was a dramatic contrast to the expulsion from Switzerland, where I had spent sixteen years as a teacher and lecturer," Professor Foerster, a prominent humanist, wrote in his book, *World History Lived*, 1869–1953. (See Ludwig, pages 186–187, and Juna files.)

## Out of the Question!

Professor Ludwig described another case, which was brought to his attention by a lawyer in Basel.

In the autumn of 1941, Jeannette W, a German Jewess living in Freiburg im Breisgau, retained a lawyer in Basel to obtain an entrance visa to Switzerland or any other country for her and her adopted Christian child. After a great deal of effort it appeared that a Cuban visa could be obtained and passage could be booked for the end of December. The municipal Alien Police in Basel, to which the lawyer applied for a transit visa for Switzerland, demanded a bond of two thousand francs. This was posted. Then, however, the Federal Alien Police, pursuant to the standard regulations, ordered that the transit visa be withheld until a transit visa for France was presented. Repeated attempts by the lawyer to obtain such a visa from the French officials were unsuccessful. On the basis of information from Mrs. W's lawyer in Freiburg that the matter had become most urgent, plus a report from an intermediary that the woman's deportation was imminent, the Basel lawyer went in person to the Federal Alien Police and requested that, because of the circumstances, the presentation of the French transit visa be waived. The petition was denied. Early in February 1942 the lawyer finally received word from Vichy that he could count on the issuance of the French transit visa. A few days later, however, the Federal Alien Police announced that any further entries into Switzerland, even with all the required documents, were now out of the question because the possibility of the emigrants' departure had now become minimal and even the group voyages officially organized by Switzerland would have to be suspended for a long period.

Jeannette W and her child were deported to the east. They did not return. [Ludwig, pages 196–197.]

## Under a False Name

Professor Dr. Ludwik Hirszfeld, a world-famous hygienist and biologist, took part in an international medical congress in Zürich in 1951. The

University of Zürich conferred an honorary doctorate on him for his research work in the fields of blood groups and heredity. Before the First World War he had studied and later taught at the university's Institute of Hygiene.

Perhaps, during this 1951 Congress, Professor Hirszfeld's thoughts went back to what had happened ten years earlier. When the Germans conquered Poland and the extermination of the Jews began, Hirszfeld was in the gravest danger. A friend in Zürich, Professor Dr. Silberschmidt, invited Hirszfeld and his wife and daughter to Switzerland. A Yugoslav transit visa was obtained. Hirszfeld, however, did not want to abandon his relatives, friends, and colleagues in a time of need. Therefore he requested a Swiss residence permit for his daughter, a scholar in her twenties who had suffered an emotional and physical collapse as a result of her tragic experiences in Poland. The University of Zürich was willing to accept Miss Hirszfeld as a student. Professor Silberschmidt attacked the problem of her immigration visa. It was refused. A year later Miss Hirszfeld died, another victim of persecution. Her parents had cared for her until her death in spite of the danger to their own lives. The twenty-three-year-old girl had to be buried under a false name. (From the Juna file.)

## The Tragedy of Jochen Klepper

No one has forgotten the tragedy of Jochen Klepper, the Lutheran poet, and his family. Born on March 22, 1903, in Beuthen an der Oder, Lower Silesia, Klepper was one of the most important religious poets of his time. His novel, *The Father*, laid the foundation for his fame. His church hymns were included even in the Lutheran hymnals in German Switzerland. In 1929 he met Johanna Stein, a widow and a Jewess. Her husband, Dr. Felix Stein, had died four years before. In 1930 Klepper married her, and they lived with the two children of her first marriage, Brigitte and Renate. "Hanni" Klepper, who was older than Jochen, was a strong woman who loved life and who was a marvelous partner for the sensitive, physically frail poet. Out of religious conviction she became a convert to Lutheranism.

When the Nazis came to power, this marriage was imperiled. Jochen Klepper could have saved himself without any trouble if he had abandoned his wife and their daughters. But that never even entered his mind. He was a member of the German Social Democratic Party and belonged to its religious wing. Politically—astounding though this may be—he had strong leanings toward a monarchy based on the Bible. From the start he was completely opposed to National Socialism. After 1938 the danger to his wife, and especially to her two daughters, grew much greater. Brigitte emigrated to England in 1939. Renate was as incapable of leaving her parents as they were of leaving her.

Klepper had close ties with Lutheran circles in Switzerland, particularly the family of a Zürich church organist named Tappolet. In November 1939 the first steps were taken to obtain admission to Switzerland for Renate, whose danger was the greatest. The sisters of Curt Götz, the writer, used their good offices for her with an attaché of the Swiss Legation; Götz himself, like the Tappolets, offered her his house.

On December 10 Klepper wrote in his journal: "After all our tremendous despair last year at Renerle's possible departure, we are now quite calm and working with the utmost patience of spirit on her emigration to Switzerland." This diary (DTV-*Taschenbuch* edition, pages 235–237) affords frightening glimpses of the dreads and burdens that beset the constantly endangered family. The news from Switzerland was not good. "The permission to enter Switzerland is going frightfully. Now Dessoir is working on her [Renate's] behalf with a nephew of his who is a secretary to the Federal Council. But as a matter of principle the Council wants to protect Switzerland against any excess of foreigners," Klepper wrote on January 20, 1940.

Rudolf Alexander Schroeder introduced Klepper to the Swiss minister, Carl J. Burckhardt, in Berlin. Burckhardt had been deeply impressed by *The Father* and wanted to intercede with the Federal Council on behalf of Klepper's stepdaughter. The aging Ernst Zahn wrote a letter of recommendation to Frölicher, the Minister. Frölicher endorsed the application. On March 19, however, the Tappolets wrote: "Approval as good as impossible." On May 15 Klepper noted in his diary: "The Tappolets write like the most devoted parents. In what good hands our Renate would have been there. Tappolet has filed another petition and been told in reply that to go on trying is absolutely hopeless. It is out of the question to get anyone into Switzerland now; in fact, in spite of the increased tensions of the war, every effort is being made to deport foreigners who already have their residence permits. So even someone like Professor Burckhardt would be unable to accomplish anything further."

For the first time thoughts of suicide begin to appear in the diary. On November 25, 1940, Klepper wrote: "However much she still hopes, Renerle is growing consistently more determined to kill herself if emigration fails and deportation becomes unavoidable."

Efforts were still continuing in Switzerland and also in Sweden. On January 8, 1942, Klepper turned to the Reverend Adolf Freudenberg in Geneva. Freudenberg enlisted the help of the Reverend Paul Vogt. "Impossible! Out of the question!" an official of the Alien Police in Zürich barked at Vogt. "This way anyone could come to us and get himself a housemaid cheap!" Another official, in Berne, explained that the case was not sufficiently interesting to warrant any exception to "the normal procedure." And Klepper wrote in his diary: "It is so unspeakably difficult to try to save a beloved human being by human means." Gertrud Kurz intervened; she too, this time, was refused a hearing.

Once more Klepper himself was advised to flee to Switzerland, and he wrote in his diary on November 25, 1942: "We know that this too has long been a utopian dream. We have reached the point at which we live under a constant burden of fear and terror, and above all the question what makes a man's life worth living when he is muzzled."

The danger was mounting from day to day. On December 2, Klepper wrote: "The destruction of Jewry in Germany, from all the evidence, would seem to have entered on its final stage. What anguish for our hearts even at this Advent season." Four days later: "Just to know the children were safe—that fills Hanni now with such suffering." And, two more days later: "God knows I cannot bear to let Hanni and the child go into this terrible and ghastliest of all deportations. He knows that I cannot promise him what Luther had the power to vow: 'If they take my body, my riches, my honor, my wife and child, let them.' Body, riches, honor—certainly! God also knows, however, that I will accept anything from him by way of test and punishment if only I know that Hanni and the child are really safe."

The miracle, apparently, came to pass: On December 5 Sweden approved an entry permit for Renate. Now it depended only on Adolf Eichmann whether she could leave. On December 9 Klepper noted: "Eichmann said: 'I have not yet given my final approval. But I think things will work out.' "

The final answer was to be given on a Thursday, December 10, 1942. Would Eichmann, the assiduous servant of his master, still want to protect himself with his *Führer?*

The final answer must have been negative. The last entry in Klepper's diary, dated December 10, read:

"This afternoon the negotiations with the *Sicherheitsdienst* [Security Service].

"Now we die—but even that is up to God. Tonight we shall die together. Above us in our last hours is the picture of Christ in benediction; he is all round us. Under his gaze our lives will end."

And thus it was.


## Too Late

The report that follows came to me from Dr. Käte Schuftan, a psychiatrist practicing in Berne:

Since, as a Jewess, I could no longer practice medicine in Germany, I came to Switzerland in the autumn of 1937. I worked as a volunteer in a public clinic in Berne; at the same time I could still get tuition money out of Germany, and I took my doctoral examination after a semester of study at the University of Berne. Shortly afterward, in the spring of 1938, I was hired as an assistant in a private hospital in Berne, and in the autumn I married a dentist in Berne and thus became a Swiss citizen. In the spring of 1940 I attempted to get my fifty-six-year-old mother, who was a serious cardiac case, into Switzerland for a two-month convalescent stay. The request was refused by the Federal Alien Police in Berne in spite of physicians' affidavits that the visit was urgently necessary.

In the autumn of that year (if I am not mistaken), I made a new application for entry and residence permits for my mother. Again I submitted a certificate from her family physician stating that she was a seriously ill woman in urgent need of a long visit to her daughter. I could prove that because of my work I could have supported my mother, since I was earning two hundred francs a month plus housing and maintenance for two persons.

After six months of worry and constant visits to officials, this application too was rejected. The reason: too many foreigners.

Once I was sent to an official in the central government and questioned by him (unfortunately, I can no longer remember his name). During a more than frigid conversation this gentleman said to me: "What guaranty have we that, as soon as you have your mother here, you will not try to bring in your father as well?" I told him truthfully that my father thought that he was in no danger and hence did not want to emigrate. I had no success.

Meanwhile I learned that other people had been able to get their relatives out of Germany and into Switzerland because they had posted bonds for them. Certainly no one had told me anything of this resort, either at the Alien Police or in the Jewish community; otherwise I should have tried right at the start to get the money together for such a bond.

During 1941 I had occasion to see documents assembled by the World Jewish Congress, including photographs brought out of the German concentration camps in Poland. They were horrible. I could no longer sleep, and hardly work. My mother and sister were writing the most miserable and agitated letters. Finally I was able to persuade my father-in-law, a high official in the Postal Department, to put up a bond of five thousand francs, and at the end of 1941 I filed a new application with the Alien Police.

In February 1942 I received a favorable reply. On April 28 my mother was notified by the Swiss Legation in Berlin to send her "valid passport," stamped with a German exit visa, to Berlin for her Swiss visa—just as if completely normal conditions had prevailed. The Germans refused the exit visa.

On June 7, 1942, my parents were deported to Auschwitz and— as I learned after the end of the war—gassed on the day of their arrival.

My sister, who, like my parents, lived in Upper Silesia, had married a physician who, as an active Zionist, had been able to emigrate to England—after several weeks in Buchenwald—and go into training there for agricultural work in Israel. My sister was waiting in Germany for the so-called means affidavit for Palestine. In the mistaken belief that this would come through without any

trouble, she made no effort to get to England as a domestic servant
—this was at that time the only way in which Jewish women could
emigrate to England. Then the war began. My brother-in-law wrote
to me that it was still possible for her to get to England as a servant
if she applied from Switzerland. Therefore I applied in 1941 to the
Federal Alien Police for permission for my sister to enter Switzerland for a stay of several weeks so that from here she could take the
necessary steps for emigration to England as a domestic servant.
The request was refused at once.

Early in July 1942 my sister was deported to Auschwitz. She was
thirty-nine years old. We have never heard anything of her since.

## Sent Back Three Times

This is the story of Dr. Edwin Maria Landau, who now lives in Zürich,
as he told it to me:

Hitler had already taken power when Dr. Landau, an editor for the
Circle Publishing Co. of Berlin, brought out the only book in Germany
at that time attacking National Socialism. In 1938, with the backing of
Benno Schwabe, a Basel publisher with whom he had business dealings,
he attempted to emigrate legally to Switzerland. His application to the
Federal Alien Police was denied because Dr. Landau's residence in
Switzerland would be of no "economic interest." The war caught him in
Paris. He was sent to a number of camps in southern France, from
which he and several companions fled in order to avoid deportation. In
spite of many perils, he made his way to the Swiss border, where a
monastery was his last refuge. When he was asked to take a crippled
woman with him, he at once agreed. Both were seized by the border
patrol almost as soon as they had crossed; they were sent to the St.
Antoine Prison in Geneva. This was in mid-August, 1942. Dr. Landau
explained his situation to the young official who interrogated him: He
was being hunted as a Jew and as a political offender. Dr. Landau asked
the official to allow him to establish contact with a Dr. G at the YMCA
in Geneva, who knew Landau. The young official flatly refused and
ordered Dr. Landau turned over to the French police at the border. He
was handcuffed and taken away.

Later he made a second attempt at flight. Here is his account:

On the second attempt I was caught with others right at the border, and, when it was established that I had already been sent back once in the preceding summer—the second attempt was made in January or February 1943—I was again sent back. This time, however, it was at night, and with instructions as to the best routes in order to avoid the Italians who were guarding the border.

A third attempt also miscarried. Nevertheless this time the commander of the border post at Chêne-Bourg considered the matter important enough to warrant an investigation in Geneva. There, however, as soon as the first two failures were brought out, I was ordered sent back to the border without any further investigation. This time too there were the same precautions for our safety as the time before.

Finally I was able to hide with a farmer who had a border-crossing permit. He alerted my friends in Geneva, and they reported the whole matter to Berne. There it was decided that I was in danger because of my anti-National Socialist past and therefore had a claim to political asylum. This time it was granted, and I was met at a specified place by a Swiss officer and then put into camp. This was on March 9, 1943.

## Thrown Out and Deported

In the annual report of the Swiss Evangelical Relief Organization for Affiliated Churches in Germany for 1942 this letter was printed:

According to information that I have received, my mother and my fourteen-year-old brother arrived in Geneva toward the end of September and spent about a week in a camp. From there they were sent back again to France. . . . You can imagine in what a state of anxiety I have been since then. . . . My husband's parents and his brother, who had valid visas for Switzerland and France, were turned back by the Alien Police at the Swiss border post of St. Margrethe on August 28, 1939, and had to return to Germany. My father was sent to the concentration camp at Buchenwald and died there on November 14, 1939. My mother was deported to the east on November 13, 1941, and since then there has been no word of her. One of my husband's brothers is in a concentration camp . . .

The Reverend Dr. Paul Vogt's files contain a letter sent to him on August 19, 1944, by one H. L. K. The letter lists the members of his family: Hersch Leib K, born in Warsaw in 1889; wife, Chana K, born in Warsaw in 1888; daughter, Sara Sch.-K, born in Warsaw in 1909; son-in-law, Max Sch., born in Oswi, Poland, in 1901; another daughter, Ryfka K, born in Warsaw in 1928; a grandson, Jacob Sch., eight years old, born in Belgium; another grandson, Reisel Sch., four-and-a-half, also born in Belgium.

In September 1942 Mrs. K was deported from Belgium, where the family had lived for many years. The letter continued:

These three children [the elder daughter, Sara; her husband, Max Sch., and the fourteen-year-old daughter, Ryfka] and the two grandchildren were seized when they crossed the Swiss border on August 17, 1942; they were then turned over to the Germans, who placed them in Section No. 119, Barracks 9, in the reception camp at Pothiviers. In September my elder daughter and her husband were deported from there, and my younger daughter and my two grandsons were sent to the Rothschild orphanage in Paris. Please try to find the address in Paris. In January or February 1943 Ryfka was transferred to Drancy and then deported (and not yet fifteen years old).

One J. K. reported:

I was interned in France at the outbreak of the war and was supposed to be deported by the Germans in 1942. I managed to spend nine weeks living in hiding in the woods in France and to enter Switzerland on October 18, 1942, but I was immediately taken back to the border because I am still unmarried (I am twenty-four years old). Two days later I managed to get into Switzerland again and to reach Geneva. Because I was running a high fever as a result of all I had been through, I spent eight weeks in a hospital in Geneva and then a week in the quarantine camp at

Champel. On December 28, 1942, after nine and a half weeks in Switzerland, I and nine other persons, including two married couples and five younger persons, some of whom did not have a centime in their pockets, were taken back to the border. I at once hid myself there; the others went on, and, according to what I heard from the French peasants, they were caught by the Germans. Who knows whether they are still alive? [Ludwig, pages 249–250.]

Another incident comes from a report by the Federation of Swiss Jewish Refugee Agencies:

During the period of extremely harsh restrictions on the entry of refugees into Switzerland from France, the sister of a Jewish refugee living in Geneva succeeded in joining him there illegally. At first the brother wanted to keep his sister with him illegally without reporting her presence to the officials. He was, however, advised not to do this, because there would be no danger if the sister registered. Thereupon the woman went to the police and was immediately taken back to the border and arrested in France; since then nothing has been heard of her.

Armand Brunschvig of Geneva, who was also active in assistance to refugees, told of one Auguste Hirsch, who entered Switzerland on December 15, 1942, and was thrown back across the frontier four days later. From the Gurs concentration camp he wrote to a woman friend in Switzerland that in that country he had been beaten on the Sabbath until he signed a statement. He was then taken by taxi to the border, where he was literally kicked across and greeted with sneers on the other side. (From the Juna files.)

## Last-Minute Rescue

The following incident was reported by Dr. Erwin Haymann of Geneva: A Jewish refugee about eighteen years old, who had been put into a home in Versoix, near Geneva, wanted to help endangered Jewish children to escape from Belgium to Switzerland. There were six of them, including a girl not yet fourteen years old. The children were arrested at the railway station in Pruntrut, a few miles from the border. At the same time Nathan Schwalb, who was active on behalf of Zionist organizations in the rescues of European Jews, was also arrested. Jewish groups took every possible measure, even appealing to the Papal Nuncio in Berne, to prevent the return of the children to Belgium. Dr. Rothmund, however, insisted that they be sent back across the border. The ground that he gave for this step was that their flight into Switzerland had been arranged by an organization.

The children were driven to the frontier in an army truck. On the way the truck had an accident, which resulted in injuries to some of the children. Three of them were taken to the hospital in Pruntrut, and the three others, with their young rescuer from Versoix, were put in prison. The chief physician of the Pruntrut hospital, Dr. M. Juillard, recognized the children's peril and raised an outcry. As a result, at the last minute they were able to escape expulsion.

## The Inflexibles

On September 2, 1942, *Das Volksrecht* reported the case of six Jewish refugees—a sixty-year-old mother, her daughter, and her son-in-law, as well as a fifteen-year-old girl, her seventeen-year-old brother, and an unattached man—who had been able literally in the last minute to avoid deportation from Belgium. Under the most hazardous conditions, hunted, exhausted, and virtually without food for six days, they crossed the French-Vaudois border illegally on August 28, 1942, and entered Switzerland. Since the village policeman was not on the scene, the villagers took in the pitiful group and provided food and shelter. As soon as the fugitives felt stronger they wrote to friends and relatives to announce their miraculous salvation.

It worked out otherwise. When the policeman returned to his post, he held a hearing for the six refugees and ordered them expelled at once. The villagers' protests were useless; under an escort of national police commanded by a young subaltern, the fugitives were compelled to march on foot to the border, two hours away.

> The refugees wept, and everyone who was present wept with them. . . . The two children had to hold the old woman on her feet. So they trudged off, up the slope. The policemen stopped to buy cigars

for themselves and then followed peacefully behind them. When he was asked why at least a truck had not been called to transport them, one of the policemen retorted: "Because they're Jews! So they can walk—the old woman too."

On the way the woman collapsed. "Shoot me," she begged in French. "Shoot: I can't any more." At this point the villagers went to their butcher, who had a car. He was a decent human being and he drove the absolutely worn-out woman to the hospital; the rest of the group was taken to prison. The farewell between mother and daughter was heart-rending: they were convinced that they would never see each other again.

Weeping and protesting, the refugees were taken by train to the border on August 29 and forced to cross back near the place where they had entered Swiss soil.

## Like a Novel

In Reverend Dr. Paul Vogt's *Armor Has No Fear*, published in April 1943, a letter was quoted:

> With aching feet and an even more aching heart I have just come out of—Switzerland! Yes, you are not mistaken, I was in Switzerland, even if only for six hours. On Sunday, the twenty-second [of November 1942], I made it into Wallis with a fellow from ———. What I went through cannot be put into words. My mountaineering outfit consisted of a pair of rubber overshoes, open at the top; I had no stockings, only wrappings. We climbed up to a pass fifty-five hundred feet high, through snow twenty inches deep, and, after twelve hours of walking through snow and ice, we entered Switzerland in the western part of Wallis. For food each of us had a half loaf of bread, plus melted snow. Our feet and lips were constantly chapped. But it was impossible to stop and rest, because my shoes were always full of water and, if I stopped, there was the danger that the water would freeze. . . . With all this we had snow and wind and police and customs men and soldiers to contend with. So at twelve o'clock, more or less, after exactly twelve hours of traveling, we came into Switzerland through the fifty-five-

hundred-foot high pass. Everything went all right in the border area, and we started down into the valley. After we had walked for about a half hour a Swiss border guard caught us. He interrogated us and said we must go back. When we pleaded with him and pointed out how bad my shoes were and how swollen my feet were, he took pity on us and took us with him to Champéry. . . . After a two-hour descent we reached the Champéry customs post, where we could rest for a half hour, and then, in spite of all our entreaties and requests at least to spend the night there and rest, we were compelled to make the four-hour climb back up to the pass through all the snow, which was now three feet deep, even though it meant sixteen hours in the high mountains. Without mercy we were ordered back to where we had crossed the border at nine o'clock. If a good-hearted customs man had not made hot tea for us and given us a little *pâté* to eat, we never would have got through without catching pneumonia. At ten o'clock it was back to France, in a snowstorm. Unable to see the narrow path, we made the dangerous climb down through the snow. In two hours, after a brief stop in a hut, we were in the valley. The rags round my feet were so stiff that they could stand upright in the room. Then, in spite of cold and hunger, I fell asleep out of sheer exhaustion.

This experience was so powerful and overwhelming that I am still not completely able to grasp it and I would think I had been dreaming, if it were not for the huge blood blisters on my feet and the prospect of the punishment camp. This was how it was in Switzerland on November 23 at Champéry in Wallis. In spite of the very different stories in the newspapers and all the rest. Believe me, I would never in my life have thought this possible. Even to me it all seems like a novel. . . .

This letter was distributed to Swiss newspapers by the National Press Service on February 17, 1943. But its publication was prohibited.

## Not Oversensitive

The files of Armand Brunschvig of Geneva contain a Geneva border-guard officer's report of a conference in Berne to which Dr. Rothmund summoned the higher border officials in August 1942. In this meeting

he instructed them that immigrants entering Switzerland illegally
should be handled in such a way that they themselves would prefer to
be sent back and that the others still waiting on the other side of the
border would be discouraged from making any attempt to flee into
Switzerland. (From the Juna files.)

This assertion is in no way unworthy of credence. Such a "recommendation" was wholly in the spirit of the "scare" policy. It was confirmed
in Jezler's report of July 30, 1942, to the Federal Council, cited earlier,
which observed, among other things: "Under today's wartime conditions, in which our country too, in a certain sense, must fight for its life,
one should not be oversensitive. Therefore we have unhesitatingly ordered the return of refugees who face the threat of more or less grave
consequences in the countries from which they came."

"Immediate explusion," Jezler's report continued, was to be ordered
for "all Jews who violate the general instructions of the Alien Police."
The same document recommended, at another point: "In general,
clearly undesirable elements (Jews, political extremists, suspected spies)
are to be kept out." (Ludwig, page 192.)

On August 20, 1942, *Die National-Zeitung* of Basel declared, with
justice: "[The expulsions] have been accompanied by indescribably
horrible scenes; no one has the slightest doubt that the ousted refugees
face certain death. Refugees who have been in our territory for days and
were living well in the interior of the country have already been turned
over."

Nevertheless the Police Section inspired a press dispatch that was
published in numerous papers on August 20, 1942, and that attacked an
article in the Socialist paper, *La Sentinelle*. The dispatch said: "For the
most part, however, it is not a question of refugees in the legal meaning
of the word, and it is not true that they risk severe punishment if they
are sent back. That is not certain. And the matter is handled with far
less inhumanity than *La Sentinelle* would have its readers believe."

So even deportation, "in the legal meaning," was certainly not a
punishment. It merely meant death.

## The "Dirty Business"

The Federal Council and the Police Section were particularly indignant
over the so-called alien-smugglers—people who guided fugitives into

Switzerland, at times in return for most impressive money payments. Federal Councilor von Steiger called this a "dirty business," and an article inspired by the Police Section and published in various newspapers in August 1942 asserted:

> Most of the people who come to our frontiers are assembled by an organized convoy service whose agents see to it that they are very well paid. Its clients are brought to the border at night with instructions to cross when the border patrol has passed or the guards are distracted in other ways. All this is a most shameful trade. If order cannot be restored through the suppression of this traffic, a veritable flood of refugees will pour into Switzerland.

When smugglers were caught, the Swiss courts imposed extremely heavy prison sentences on them. It was true that some of these "haulers" were shameless exploiters who profited by the helplessness of the refugees. But the question must arise whether it was so much more virtuous and honorable to punish the refugees who were in danger of death by sending them back across the frontier. A question was justly put at the time to Dr. Rothmund: How would he behave in a similar situation? But in his view the refugees were guilty on two counts: first, because they crossed the border illegally, and, second, because they accepted the help of smugglers.

There were also those—and they were by far the majority—who helped refugees to enter not because of a desire for money but out of love for their fellow-men. There is ample proof of the means by which Catholic priests and Protestant pastors, members of the resistance movements, and even officials and members of the French police selflessly endangered themselves to help endangered Jews to reach the sanctuary of the Swiss border. Abbé Pierre and Marcel Marceau, for instance, were among these rescuers, but so was the simple locomotive driver of whom the Reverend Dr. Vogt wrote in *Armor Has No Fear* and whose courage will have to serve here as witness to that of many others:

> One of our friends has told us of his flight and rescue. "It was in Grenoble," he said. "Through some divine miracle I fell into conversation with a locomotive driver whose regular run took him through part of Switzerland. With a violently thumping heart I

began to tell him my story. But already he was stopping me: 'You're the eighteenth. No, you don't have to give me any money. We'll meet tonight before the train leaves.' He hid me in the tender, under the coal. We set out. At the last stop my rescuer let out the steam from his locomotive. Under the cover of the hissing steam I was taken out of the tender. I wanted to thank him for having saved my life. 'Don't thank me,' he insisted. 'What have I done? helped eighteen desperate men a little farther along their way under a load of coal. Perhaps saved eighteen men from martyrdom and death. No, no'—he shook his head—'thank him, our Redeemer, who has saved us all.' Three days later I learned that, just when he was letting off steam from his locomotive in order to sneak his human cargo out from under the coal without being seen, my rescuer had been spotted and arrested."

But in the eyes of everyone who in those days lived in danger of death it was not the men and women who violated sections and articles who were guilty, but rather the others who for the sake of written statute forgot the unwritten law: not to cast out men in danger of death.

## "Our Compliments to the Federal Council"

Chief Rabbi A. Deutsch of the French Department of the Bas-Rhin testified to what follows. He was present at the railway station of Limoges when 750 Jews, all of them aged and frail and ailing, were deported. "If this isn't bad luck!" one of them said to him. "We were in Switzerland already and they turned us over to the Germans." Another corroborated this: "Yes, I was in Switzerland a week, and we were taken back to the frontier and delivered to the Germans." Rabbi Deutsch added: "I feel it as some mitigation of the excessive pain of my tragic memories and my consciousness of my own helplessness at having to see and hear these ghastly things that I can lay this testimony before the Swiss government in the hope of bringing to justice those responsible, who were the knowing accomplices of murder."

Lieutenant Colonel J. M. Rubli of the Swiss Army Medical Corps, who worked for the International Committee of the Red Cross during the war, told the Swiss Jewish Community Union of one of his experiences:

> During the final months of the war I was assigned by the Red Cross and the Federal Council to select among the inmates of the Mauthausen concentration camp those who should be given hospitality in Switzerland. During the medical examinations I was approached by two university graduates, Frenchmen or Belgians, who wanted to inform me that Switzerland's help had come too late. They were the last survivors of a group that had reached the Swiss border in 1942 and pleaded for admittance but had been turned back. Their bitter request that I convey their compliments to the Federal Council and inform it of these facts made me thoroughly ashamed of myself as a Swiss and as an educated man, and I did not know how to answer them.

## A Swiss Eyewitness

Gottlieb Fuchs, a Swiss who now lives in St. Gallen, offered me his testimony:

> During the war, with the knowledge and approval of the Swiss government, I worked in France as an interpreter for the German occupation forces. Since at the same time I was working for Swiss intelligence and the French Resistance—in this way I was able to save the lives of many Resistance fighters—and the Germans discovered both facts, I was arrested by the Gestapo at the end of 1943 and sent to the Buchenwald concentration camp. Subsequently I was moved to other camps. In August or September of 1942 I saw how the Gestapo in Dijon tortured to death two Jews who had fled into Switzerland but been sent back into occupied France by the Swiss functionaries. At Christmas 1943, when I was already a prisoner of the Gestapo, I heard how the Germans spent the evening celerating Christmas and singing Christmas carols—and also drinking their fill—and then dragged two Jews out of the cell next to mine and beat them until there was no sign of life in them. I also learned that the two Jews had also been in Switzerland and

been sent back from there. When I arrived in Buchenwald in the beginning of 1944, Jewish prisoners told me that they too had been in Switzerland and been thrown back to the Germans. Inasmuch as they knew that what lay ahead for them was death in Auschwitz, their feelings about Switzerland were understandably very bitter. And I was ashamed that such things could happen in the country of Henri Dunant.

# Who Was Dr. Heinrich Rothmund?

Who was this Dr. Heinrich Rothmund, head of the Police Section of the Federal Justice and Police Department, who in sovereign fashion and often over the government's head decided the destinies of men and women seeking help? In those days he was frequently known as the eighth Federal Councilor.

He was unusually tall, broad-shouldered, athletic—an imposing man to look at. His gaze fell from far above on everyone. Often he vacillated between pigheaded harshness and sudden, almost unbelievable weakness and conciliation. He was hot-tempered and gentle, despotic and charming, witty and cynical, moody as a prima donna, and paternally jovial. He was conceited and he was woebegone. He liked to live on a grand scale, yet for decades he had to endure the financial consequences of a broken marriage.

He had friends and enemies in all camps and parties, even among the refugees. Many dreaded him, a few admired him. Refugees who had been saved manifested an extravagant gratitude to him, but thousands of others spoke his name with hatred and loathing.

Many of his speeches and actions testify to his antipathy to the Nazis' power system, but his practice of democracy was authoritarian. A strict, paternalistic authority and upright, obedient vassals: Such was more or less his ideal. True, he professed to champion the right of asylum, but his stubborn endeavors to keep the doomed Jews away from our frontiers and thus to preserve our country "clean and healthy" and protected against Judaization were coldly ruthless in a time of crisis and at the cost of innumerable lives.

He was criticized by some for his love of power and his tyranny, and he was hailed by others for his toughness.

He had created the apparatus of the Alien Police and made it work, broken down the resistance of the cantons and the people by tenacious detail work and patience, "in spite of all demands and complaints, and too in spite of constant attacks by certain newspapers" (as he said in a speech on January 23, 1939, in Zürich). And he had infused this apparatus with an ideology of which he was the eloquent and almost fanatical missionary. But a state apparatus infused with an ideology almost necessarily becomes inhuman.

He was convinced that he was backed by the Federal Council, the supporters of the Fatherland Federation, and other champions of the theory of inundation by foreigners. He intended to be their leader and he was in fact their servant. In reliance on their good faith he took all the responsibility on himself.

Genuine fellow-feeling seemed alien to him. He totally lacked the ability to put himself in the place of a persecuted man. He saw only himself and his mandate. So he spoke of refugees as if they were merchandise that could be disposed of at random. People who were delivered defenseless to the National Socialists' manhunt and who clutched in anguish at the sanctuary of the Swiss frontier were to him "emigration-happy." Relentlessly he insisted on sending back even children, on the ground that their flight into Switzerland was "organized."

He instructed his subordinates to be so inflexible in turning back the unfortunates that they and others would abandon all desire to flee into Switzerland.

He professed to know people; basically, however, they were foreign to him. A man who knew him told this story: During the First World War Rothmund was a first lieutenant in command of a unit. He was absolutely convinced that he knew his men to the core and held them in the hollow of his hand—and he tumbled out of his cloud one day when a report was sent in denouncing him to the company commander over the signature of every soldier and noncommissioned officer in his unit. His self-assurance was his weakness.

He overflowed with good counsel for the German National Socialists with whom his duties brought him into contact, and he was fully convinced that they took him seriously even when they did not follow his advice. In his report to the Federal Councilor at the head of the Justice and Police Department after his negotiations in Berlin in September 1938, he wrote that at lunch in the Oranienburg concentration camp an idle conversation had presented the opportunity of going into the Jewish question.

> I attempted to make it clear to the gentlemen that the people and government of Switzerland had long since become fully cognizant of the danger of Judaization and had consistently defended themselves against it so well that the losses to the Jewish population were balanced by their gains, while this was not the case in Germany. The peril can be met only if a people constantly protects itself from the very outset against Jewish exclusiveness and makes it impossible. Then the Jew is a useful member of the popular community and in due time he can adapt to it. I pointed out that I had found outstanding persons among the Jews who had fled to Switzerland from Germany. The Jewish race has been tempered by the ordeal of history, made strong and stubborn against all persecutions. Thus far it has resisted all attempts at extermination and always come out of all of them stronger than ever before.
>
> On the basis of these considerations, I said in conclusion, it seems to me that the present German method is wrong and dangerous for all of us, because in the last analysis it hangs the Jews on

our necks like a millstone. Although I found no one in accord with my views, nevertheless those who heard them were certainly left with something to think about. The one and only thing that I could do was to make it clear to the proper people who have police responsibilities in the Jewish question that, as far as is needful, we know how to protect ourselves against the Jews and also to do so in such a way that we will not need or allow either help from abroad, whose methods we also reject as wrong, or interference. . . . To me the main thing is that we be left in peace, and I should have to be very much mistaken if on this point I was not clearly understood. If not, then it seems to me to be self-evident that we have to preserve the right of asylum without any regard to unfitness or the danger of some foreign attempts at interference, and not follow the disgraceful example of France. Furthermore, I said this to Mr. von Weizsäcker with the utmost clarity.

Dr. Rothmund had expressed himself similarly on the Jewish question in a detailed letter of August 10, 1941, to the Adjutant General of the Army, Troop and Quartermaster Section, while at the same time criticizing a passage, "The Swiss Society," in the *National Education Lecture Plan* on the ground that it might have been intended as anti-Semitic propaganda. In this letter Dr. Rothmund pointed out that, before Switzerland adopted National Socialist thinking, she must first not only examine meticulously whether such thinking offered us something needed or useful but also and at the same time consider the basic question of whether the idea could take root in the soil of our particular kind of democracy, produced through centuries of development and differing from that of any other country. Anything else, he said, would be superfluous and dangerous and therefore must be rejected. As for the Jewish question in Switzerland, the situation was this: As long as the Jew was not assimilated, he would be regarded as an alien element by all sections of the people; for certain of the Jews the process of assimilation takes longer than for others, so that first of all a distinction would have to be made between eastern Jews and those who have lived for a long time in western European countries. The unassimilated Jew, clinging to his foreign peculiarities and his customs and usages—especially in his business dealings—had always remained outside the national community, constantly isolated and having no other choice than to live his way of life in some other country. For this reason most of the unassimilated Jews had already left Switzerland. Today, with international freedom of movement virtually eliminated, this natural tendency could no longer be followed. For this reason the state must attack the problem much more vigorously than before. This, Dr. Rothmund said, was the gound on which the Federal Council, in its decree of October 17, 1939, had adopted such unusually strict special requirements for emigrants, almost all of whom were members of the Jewish race. Swiss Jews had understood this and also made considerable effort to explain the Swiss view of the emigrant problem to foreign circles. In these circumstances there was certainly no reason for Switzerland to allow the entry of German anti-Semitism in any form. On the contrary, Switzerland had every reason to approach and resolve the Jewish problem as in the past. (See Ludwig, pages 237–238.)

Here Dr. Rothmund once more exposed with complete clarity the true ground for his and the Federal Council's deportation policy: fear that the country might be Judaized. He overlooked all too completely the fact that in these years, and above all from 1938 until the end of the war, there was an even higher duty than the protection of the country from an influx of foreigners: to save as many as possible of the men and women whose lives were at stake. That an unbridgeable chasm lay between Switzerland's humanitarian mission and his own ideology of defense was virtually beyond his recognition. He looked on himself as the paradigm of a good Swiss. To him the spiritual successors of Henri Dunant were troublemakers. For the most part he treated them with loud contempt.

He saw a justification of his actions in the "anti-Semite in us."

He acted as if he were strong. But was he? Were his power and his strength not founded on weak and all too malleable department heads who allowed him to have complete authority because they were delighted to have him take the responsibility for those operations of his Alien Police that threw little glory and honor on their country? Dr. Johannes Baumann was a colorless Federal Councilor. Dr. Eduard von Steiger carried water on both shoulders. He was a versatile lawyer. The relation between him and Rothmund was strained.

Dr. G. Delaquis, whose father, Professor Ernst Delaquis, was Rothmund's predecessor as head of the Police Section, wrote:

I have known Heinrich Rothmund since I was ten years old. We children had an idolatrous love for "Uncle" Rothmund, who came to our house regularly, because he was gay, he seemed to be completely unconventional, and he always said the right thing to us. Later I often heard that my father—with a certain affection—spoke of him as a "young dog." . . . As far as his attitude toward the Jews is concerned, a certain primitive anti-Semitism is thoroughly rooted in our nature. . . . The description of the Jews as a "foreign-minded element" was by no means limited to Rothmund. That he used the term publicly proves only how little he recognized that it was no longer a question of inundation by foreigners, or of regulations and statutes, but of the fulfillment of a humanitarian duty that ranged far beyond all doubts. . . . Dr. Rothmund was not strong and independent enough, either in himself or as head of the Police Section, to stand up for views that were exclusively his own. I believe that in all his public statements he followed the clearly defined views of his superior in the department. Many, uncountably many errors were made, and very many of them were signed "Rothmund." But—and I stand firm on this—they were not his errors in their origin. But, because they bore Rothmund's signature, Mr. von Steiger was able to wash his hands of them in his final report to the other Councilors and blame the mistakes on the man who merely—and in a state ruled by law it is hardly possible to do otherwise—carried out the orders that were dictated to him from a higher level. . . . In the end Dr. Rothmund was sacrificed on the altar of Mr. von Steiger's prestige. If he did things that in retrospect seem inhuman, he did not do them alone and of his own volition.

When the war was over and the public accusations against Dr. Heinrich Rothmund surged up in repeated waves against the background of the savage crimes in the concentration camps, especially after the revelations by the *Schweizerische Beobachter* in March 1954, his day of power was finally ended. When he no longer held public office, when he was no longer needed, he found himself left in the lurch by his supposed friends. The Moor had done his duty.

Now Dr. Rothmund looked for support among those who in the past had often been made to feel the weight of his power. He sought out the

Berne editor of a major newspaper, who had broken off all relations with him because of his refugee policy, and begged to be allowed to speak to him again. He could not endure his isolation.

He had virtually no friends. The only people he knew now were people who pitied him. A woman refugee-relief worker told me how the once powerful police chief had wept like a child in her house.

Heinrich Rothmund was an all too dedicated functionary. The wrong functionary in the wrong function and at the wrong time. This was certainly no coincidence. But it was a tragedy for which thousands of innocent persons had to pay with their lives.

# Resist!

At the beginning of the war there were still approximately seventy-one hundred refugees in Switzerland. Re-emigration, therefore, had been vigorously furthered, if we reflect that a year earlier the total number of persons who had sought refuge with us stood at more than twelve thousand. So the "flood" of refugees was contained within extremely narrow limits until July 1942, partly because on the one side the Third Reich, fully engaged in war, had become even more totalitarian in its control methods and partly because on the other side Switzerland had now for the first time virtually eliminated the issuance of entry permits. In July 1942 the number of refugees was eighty-three hundred. But even this, supposedly, had already exceeded the "limit of capacity"!

On August 30, 1942, the Youth Church in Zürich-Oerlikon held its

annual national assembly. In the afternoon Federal Councilor von
Steiger addressed approximately eight thousand young Swiss of both
sexes, and in his speech he talked of the "little lifeboat." Among other
things, he said:

> Under certain conditions one must be absolutely hard and unyield-
> ing, one must endure insults and complaints and calumnies and yet
> be able to resist and not "break." What good does it do if we have
> a clear conscience and know that what we are doing is not for
> ourselves but for others? When conflict arises between sentiment
> and reason, when the heart is willing but duty cries *stop*, then one
> begins to understand what it means to resist. No one is exempt
> from this. The more imporatnt the position that one takes, the
> graver are such decisions.
>
> When one has the responsibility of commanding a tightly
> crowded lifeboat with limited accommodations and equally limited
> provisions, while thousands of victims of a shipwreck are clamoring
> for rescue, one must seem cruel if one does not embark them all.
> And yet one is thoroughly human if at the same time one warns
> against false hopes and tries at least to save those already aboard.
> [Ludwig, pages 393–394.]

## Heartless—Hypocritical—Ungrateful

A large part of the population held a different view. On the morning of
the same day, the Reverend Walter Lüthi, who was then serving in
Basel, had already stated the answer to the Federal Councilor:

> My dear friends! Today there is something that stands between us
> and God's love, and that is our bad conscience. Deep in our inmost
> hearts the assailant has struck, and there he attacks unremittingly.
> You boys and girls of St. Gallen are certainly not alone; indeed,
> many of us feel as you did when you wrote to me recently: "Of
> course we will come to our convention in Zürich, but we will come
> with heavy hearts, with deep distress and shame over what has
> happened."
>
> What has happened, then?
>
> These recent weeks have not been the first time when we have

forbidden entry into our country to fleeing strangers who sought safety with us. The officials who have ordered this decision have their reasons for it, and certainly they have stated them ten times over. We know these reasons, and too we know the background for them in domestic and foreign policy. Thus, for example, we know that Federal Councilor von Steiger, who will speak to us this afternoon, did not issue this decree without the approval of the entire Federal Council, including Federal Councilor Etter with his Catholic background and Mr. Pilet-Golaz with his west Swiss background. But even when we give serious thought to the known and unknown reasons and backgrounds and appraise them with the utmost deliberation, this decree weighs on us as Christians, and indeed in three respects.

First of all, it is *heartless.*

Official statistics have made much of the fact that in the city of Basel alone three thousand dogs are still well fed. I assure you that I do not begrude them their food. But, as long as we in Switzerland are still prepared to share our bread and our soup and our meat rations with perhaps a hundred thousand dogs, while at the same time we are worried lest a few tens of thousands of refugees, or even a hundred thousand, prove more than we can support, our attitude is one of extreme heartlessness.

In the second place, our position is *hypocritical.*

Almost more than there is any necessity to do so, we emphasize Switzerland's mission in the service of humanity. Almost all of us who are here today saw our love of mankind on exhibition here in Zürich three years ago. Such boasting and parading of one's human kindness, side by side with inhuman behavior, is hypocriscy.

And, in the third place, we are *ungrateful.*

Recently I asked approximately a hundred Sunday-school children, boys and girls, what each of them had to be thankful for. Virtually all wrote in their answers that the major reason was the fact that our country had not yet been drawn into the war.

And now it is precisely we, who as if by a miracle are still untouched, who have barred our gates against the most miserable victims of this world catastrophe. According to the Holy Scriptures, the sin of ingratitude is especially repugnant and insolent to God and his angels. . . .

That is why we have a bad conscience. We have every reason now to fear that God can no longer be with us, that because of what has happened God may become our enemy. Against such an enemy who wants to utter the cry: "Resist!"? When the enemy is entrenched in our innermost conscience and sits above us on the throne of heaven and earth, who then still thinks of calling for resistance? . . .

My dear Federal Councilor, do not trouble yourself to ease our conscience. That way you do our country a great disservice.

It was two different worlds that opposed each other in the presence of this national assembly of the young. There was the representative of the government, the spokesman for the state and reasons of state. Opposite him stood the spokesman of human conscience and compassion, the champion of genuine Christian humanity.

Both were members of the same church, citizens of the same country. Both accepted their responsibilities. Both thought that they were serving the nation to which they belonged. Both were determined to protect Switzerland against all perils from without. There were a hundred questions on which they were at one. But in this single matter they were not agreed. Here they were divided by a deep chasm.

Federal Councilor von Steiger spoke of good conscience. The Reverend Walter Lüthi spoke of bad conscience. This schism was not new. It had manifested itself in all its gravity over the fate of the Jews in the Third Reich.

On one side stood the avowed and the secret Jew-haters, who wanted to keep Switzerland free of "foreign-thinking elements." On the other side stood those who spoke of the guilt of Christians, of the injustices that through the centuries they had perpetrated against God's people out of baseless arrogance, hard-heartedness, and fanaticism.

"Resist your emotions, resist the influx of Jews and Jew-lovers!" the one group demanded, while the other urged: "Resist force and the use of force!"

## Fearless Warnings

When the satellites of racial follies began their unholy work in Switzerland in 1933, they encountered the opposition of such men as Carl

Albert Loosli, the Bümpliz writer whom no one could frighten, and Johann Baptist Rusch, the Catholic journalist. Under the title, "*Protocols of the Elders of Zion—the Greatest Forgery of the Century*," the editor and publisher of the courageous weekly, *Republican Press*, unmasked the lies and the fraudulent techniques of the anti-Semitic witch-hunters.

All anti-Semitism [he wrote] is a diversionary tactic on the part of those who, on the pretext of rescuing the peoples from the Jewish peril, menace them with the danger of their own rule by force and thus provide the safe protection of a preliminary reign of terror for criminals and their crimes. An anti-Semitic tide is always a new oppression of the peoples, followed by the destruction of all the rights and freedoms so laboriously achieved. . . . Anti-Semitism is a well-tested method of seduction in the hands of wily despots intent on winning the confidence of a people, a steppingstone in their climb to power. . . . Hatred of other races and classes, of other ways and customs, can never raise a people higher or enable it to master the problems of its time. Hate deceives and weakens, it is the fire that consumes understanding and reduces reason to ashes. No national prosperity can be built on these ruins. Therefore, in consciously responsible love of country, the nation must be protected from the temptation of hatred against fellow-citizens and fellow-beings.

How prophetic were these words written in July 1933 by a man who said of himself: "I too was seduced for years by this arrogant fraud . . ." J. B. Rusch spoke out untiringly, in his newspaper and in his widely read essays that were then appearing in the Saturday-morning editions of *Die National-Zeitung* of Basel, on behalf of Swiss democracy and humanity and against the enticements of power and the crime of hate.

He was not alone. There were many indeed who in those insensate times kept clear heads, who saw through to the real nature of National Socialism and of the totalitarian state in general, who fearlessly and steadfastly attacked the ideologies of race or class superiority. They were to be found in every party that called itself democratic, and in addition they were to be found outside all parties—individualists and independents loyal only to themselves and their consciences. They included the admirable publisher of the Liberal *Zürichsee-Zeitung*, Theodor Gut; the Basel liberal, Dr. Albert Oeri, editor-in-chief of *Die Basler-Nachrichten*; the economists and editors of the weekly, *Freies Volk*, Fritz Schwarz in Berne and Werner Schmid in Zürich; such journalists as Dr. Fritz Heberlein in Zürich, Paul Schmid-Ammann, Dr. Paul Meierhans, editor-in-chief of *Das Volksrecht*; Hans Vogel of *Die Berner Tagwacht*, Hermann Böschenstein of Berne, the intransigent Hans Schwarz and the daring Dr. Eduard Behrens, who together published the courageous *Schweizer Zeitung am Sonntag* until it was suppressed by the Federal Council. And there were the members of the staff of the weekly, *Die Nation*, who pledged themselves to combat National Socialist theories and aims.

At this time Gottlieb Duttweiler founded the National Independent Union for the purpose of uniting all men of good will from inside and outside all parties, lending new strength to the democracy that had been built up through many battles, and closing ranks firmly against all dictatorship and race hatred.

There were thousands upon thousands of individuals, known and unknown, who in their own lives and in accord with inner obligations solemnly vowed to withstand the seductions that were coming from north and south alike. In a pamphlet entitled *Is Democracy Curable?*, for example, a Zürich physician, Dr. Paul Cattani, wrote:

Above all I am thinking of the fatherly counsels that I should not speak so loudly and write so outspokenly against the dictatorships. But in my opinion nothing could give us better protection than if every day we were to shout across the borders at the tops of our voices with perfect clarity: "We don't want to be 'redeemed' and 'brought home' by you!" . . .

"If only nothing happens, if only we don't have problems!" This apprehensive theme song, so contrary to the contemporary spirit of sportsmanship, is certainly understandable in large part. A small nation cannot run its foreign relations with a bludgeon.

But the Swiss citizen should not be given a bad mark if he makes it clear in a very loud voice that he wants to have nothing to do with National Socialist ideas, that he abominates the whole statist system of the dictatorships from the bottom of his heart, that, if the need arises, he will take up arms for the defense not only of home and hearth and his beautiful mountains but also of his despised, ridiculed democracy with all its weaknesses and faults but also with its eternal principles of freedom, democracy, and humanity.

Konrad Falke, a Zürich writer who collaborated with Thomas Mann in the publication of a magazine called *Mass und Wert*, wrote in the 1930s:

Courage is not summoned into being by the call to arms; it is an attitude of the spirit and that is why it is so odious to those wolves in sheep's clothing whose purposes would be much better served if under the influence of official narcosis we all reeled like a herd of lambs into their "historical necessity." That, in fact—even in spite of all that we know and want—is what is actually intended to ensue from the present policy of the Federal Council; for anyone who is still minded to accept the official mealy-mouthed reports of outrages that prevail today is for the most part contributing to the subversion of ethics and also to the enfeeblement of our defenses.

When the Reverend Max Gerber wrote in *Der Aufbau* at the end of November 1939: "If we do not resolve to put up a vigorous, united battle in defense of what is right, we shall be destroyed in our isolation, one small nation after another," this sentence was stricken out by the censorship on the ground that it might be given a false interpretation.

This was plain speaking, and it required courage, for the neighbor to the north was a sinister one. Every day he demonstrated how he dealt with political dissent. He allowed no doubts as to what critics might expect if the National Socialists seized power.

His henchmen in Switzerland were not idle. Writers, journalists and publishers, actors and cabaret satirists, lawyers and politicians who took an outspoken stand against the National Socialists were bombarded with anonymous threatening letters. They were menaced and insulted on the streets. There was action as well. This was a time when it was not altogether safe to be an avowed democrat and enter the lists on behalf of human decency.

Among those who stood up unintimidated for humanity and the practice of brotherly love were Professor Leonhard Ragaz and his wife Clara. In the monthly magazine that Professor Ragaz edited and published, *Neue Wege*, he took a bold position on all contemporary questions. His contribution to the disclosures of what was happening under the National Socialist system cannot be evaluated highly enough in retrospect. In his September 1940 issue, under the title, "An Emergency Alarm," he published a description of the dreadful conditions in the French camps of Gurs, Vernet, Rivesaltes. At the same time he called for help. His daughter Christine was equally active. As a consequence, *Neue Wege* was subjected for the next year to prior censorship, the result of which was the suspension of its publication.

## In the Name of God

In June 1941 Professor Dr. Karl Barth, the world-famous Basel theologian, delivered a lecture in which he said:

> "In the name of God, the Almighty!" Because this phrase appears in our Federal Constitution and has meaning, we ask:
> What is the meaning of the treatment that Switzerland inflicts today on foreigners residing in her territory? These foreigners appear to be divided into two classes: we have welcome guests and we have unwelcome guests. The welcome guests are those whose papers from their countries of origin are "in order," and in 90 per cent or more of all cases this means that they are more or less convinced adherents of the political system so radically opposed to ours that encircles us with its power, and that voluntarily or because of compulsion they are serving its propaganda and sometimes something more as well. The unwelcome guests are those who were forced to leave their homes because of their opposition to this system or as its victims, and who came to us as so-called "emigrants" (in any connotation of this term). The welcome guests enjoy the protection of our laws on the basis of existing residence agreements for foreigners: even for such spectacles as that demonstration at the Basel Exhibition Hall and probably also for such

preliminary arrangements as their compatriots carried out before their invasion of The Netherlands. The unwelcome are subject to regulations that keep them on short leash as if they were anti-social or even convicts; they must run back and forth between Pontius and Pilate in order to be allowed to breathe our air under every possible restriction; from time to time they receive notices calling on them to perform the magic trick of continuing their travels; life goes decently for them, most assuredly, only if they are lucky enough to have secreted a substantial amount of money on their persons before they entered our country.

Here there is something wrong. Certainly the residence agreements must be respected, our own economic difficulties must be taken into consideration, and the genuinely undesirable elements even among the emigrants must be kept within strict limits. But can we be untouched by the disappointment, indeed the bitterness of so many reputable guests in this second class who came to us in the most optimistic confidence in that "free offer" of free Switzerland and who, once in the country, find themselves more or less explicitly punished for the fact that they are opponents and victims of the system whose victory Switzerland must resist to the end with all her strength in defense of her neutrality? Is there not ground here for reproach for the manner in which we have solved this problem? Whose interests, in fact, are we serving by such discriminatory treatment of our guests? . . .

What we are doing today in this matter, regardless of the fullest comprehension of our current difficulties, can be called neither generous nor far-sighted. What are we going to choose to do in *this* matter: give in or resist? Is it not clear as daylight: every franc, every act, every intercession that has been offered in voluntary assistance to precisely these less welcome guests is real Swiss resistance? Why indeed are there official "higher levels" at which this apparently has not yet been discussed?

The publication of this lecture was prohibited by censorship. Not until 1945 could it achieve a broader circulation, when the Evangelical Publishing Company in Zollikon issued Karl Barth's book, *Eine Schweizer Stimme, 1938–1945* (A Swiss Voice, 1938–1945).

## The Letter of the Three Hundred

We know the petition of the two hundred, who at a time of danger tried to persuade the Federal Council to mount somewhat greater opposition to the Third Reich.

But there were also others who demanded more firmness of purpose. In September 1941 the Theological Study Group of the canton of Berne protested to Police Commissioner Seematter of Berne because he had forbidden the delivery of a speech by Professor Barth to the annual meeting of the former students of the Muristalden Seminary in Berne on September 27.

Even more determination was shown by the three hundred persons who on November 17, 1941, attended the fourth Zürich congress of the Swiss Evangelical Relief Agency for Affiliated Churches in Germany. In an open letter to the Federal Council and the nation, they wrote:

As members of the Evangelical Church in a grave and critical period, we are all fully aware of our responsibilities to our Swiss democracy and we all pray for our government and our army. In this anniversary year, firm in our resolve, we pledge our allegiance to our homeland, its Constitution, and the rights and duties that that Constitution creates. We do this gladly and joyfully, with the single reservation that we place God's rule above all else and that God's universal claim through Jesus Christ on our entire private and public lives shall be violated from no quarter.

We are filled with grave concern by the encroachments of the Federal Council and the Press and Radio Section of the General Staff on church writings and free speech. We refer in particular to the prior censorship of Professor Ragaz' *Neue Wege* that compelled this publication to suspend its operations rather than be disloyal to its innermost convictions. We refer to the prohibition of the publication of utterances by eminent churchmen, whereas the words of political leaders of every stripe may be freely disseminated. We refer, further, to the ban on Dr. A. Frey's pamphlet, *Der rechte Staat* (*The Just State*), and on Professor Karl Barth's *Our Church and Switzerland in Today's Conditions* and *In the Name of God the Almighty,* as well as the prohibition of speeches by Karl Barth at the labor camp of Vouvry and to the Union of Former Students of the Evangelical Teachers' Seminary of Muristalden, in Berne. We are also more especially concerned with these prohibitions because at the same time the propaganda materials of an anti-democratic state are available in bulk in Switzerland and German harvest festivals are allowed to be held in spectacular fashion with political speakers.

It is our belief that the forbidden speeches and writings of our compatriots embody genuine Swiss thinking and can contribute substantially to the maintenance of our independence, and therefore there should be no question of prohibition out of mere regard for what will be thought abroad; especially since experience has shown that such deference has never saved any neutral country from foreign attacks. Great sacrifices for the defense of our country seem to us to be justifiable only when as a result our country and our people are preserved strong in their old rights to freedom.

In a letter from the General Staff on October 22, 1940, to the then editor of the Swiss Evangelical Press Service, Dr. A. Frey of Zürich, the view was presented that the church had no voice in political affairs. The only reply possible from our point of view to such a proposition is a clear and unmistakable: "No, never." Without this "No" we should be traitors to the fathers of our Reformed Church, Huldrych Zwingli and Johannes Calvin, both of whom accepted the universality of God's claims with the utmost seriousness. For us it is totally impossible to keep silence for "tactical" reasons when God's word bids us speak. We intend to be faithful to our Reformed religion, which in God's name bids us call right right and wrong wrong. Adherence to the Reformed faith and neutrality of feeling are as mutually exclusive as fire and water. The Reformed Church stands as the watchtower of faith, in the trust bestowed on it by its master. "Truly the stones must cry out when the apostle's mouth is stilled." The statement of position by the General Staff, as it was formulated in the letter to Dr. Frey, is therefore the occasion of special concern to us because this statement of position comes dangerously close to that of National Socialism. Indeed, the ideological director of education in the Third Reich, himself a minister, has made it plain: "The churches have only one mission: namely, to instruct in the churchly belief in the next world those persons who are interested in it. The earth on which we live, this world, has absolutely nothing to do with the church."

We consider it our duty further to make known to you the increasing anxiety in Reformed circles in our country over the state's encroachments on freedom of information. The stress is growing greater, because we take our stand on the words of Peter: "One must obey God rather than men."

In order to leave no effort unmade on our side that in a difficult and critical period might lead to a reduction of tension, we appeal to the responsible officials not to take a narrow view of the wishes of the Reformed Church but rather to give its publications, its church union, and church teachers the opportunity to speak their private views, and to halt all further inroads on freedom of expression. May God guide our beloved Reformed Church through his holy spirit!

May God in his grace preserve our beloved homeland!

May God grant us all wisdom, courage, faith, and fearless hearts indomitable in their belief!

Neither Hitler nor his menials, neither the cautious nor the all too fearful could silence these unfrightened sentinels!

## The Revolt of the Initiate

On August 20, 1942, the Central Committee of the Federation of Swiss Jewish Communities met in a session at which Dr. Rothmund later also appeared. The committee chairman, Saly Mayer, had no good news to report. Eleven days earlier the first indications of a new wave of refugees had been made public. Two days after that, Dr. Josef Weil, a physician representing the OSE, a Jewish relief agency, in France, sent to Zürich a shattering report on the details of the deportations. Appalling information on the conditions of the Jews in the east had been received. On August 12, Mayer had attempted to reach Dr. Rothmund by telephone in order to acquaint him with all these facts. On the next day he had a conversation with Rothmund in Berne. Rothmund said on this occasion that a new flood of refugees was imminent, the equal of that of 1938. Since July 29, 1942, 293 persons had come to Switzerland, most of them from Belgium. A few days earlier Rothmund himself had investigated the whole situation at the frontier, and the border officials had assured him that nothing happened to the refugees who were sent back to their homes. Those who had entered Switzerland earlier had been interned by the Swiss authorities in the punishment camps of Bellechasse and Witzwil. In no case would any new arrivals be allowed to remain; if they were discovered, they would have to be sent back. The expected transports from Belgium must be turned back with strict measures. The Federal Alien Police was about to issue an explicit order that was founded on the Federal Council's decree of October 17, 1939. (In actuality, such instructions had already been given.)

As soon as Dr. Rothmund appeared at the Central Committee's meeting, he was given the floor. Thus far he had always made every effort—or so he said—to communicate with the Jewish organizations *before* the enactment of decrees. This time he had not thought it proper to do so because he did not want to burden the Jewish community. He then sketched the history of the refugee problem in Switzerland. He explained that in any decision as to admission or return the determining factor must be the interests of Switzerland, not those of individual persons or of foreign nations. From the Swiss standpoint the primary concern was the preservation of order and peace in the country; there were also the questions of employment opportunities and food supplies. As far as the Jews were concerned, he said, Switzerland was now an island in Europe. In order to remain so, she must continue to maintain order and ought not to "overstrain herself." The problem must be handled with caution in order to preclude any possible demagogic measures. Under the Federal Council's decree, all illegal immigrants except deserters and political refugees were to be sent back. Inasmuch as the influx had not been stopped from the other side, he said (here Rothmund contradicted himself, since in his covering letter with Jezler's report he had stated that flight alone incurred the risk of death), it seemed necessary to impose severe consequences in order to establish an example. Nothing had affected him so deeply as the decree of August 13. On the other hand, he knew from his long years of experience what efforts and sacrifices were required for the maintenance of those refugees thus far resident in Switzerland. (These sacrifices had been borne thus far virtually alone by Jewish and other refugee organizations.) It was impossible to help everyone, Rothmund insisted. He was well aware that hundreds of thousands of Jews were in jeopardy and that millions of other persons felt that they too were in peril. Switzerland, however, was in no position to take in all the refugees from neighboring countries. "It is better that we take care of those who are here and try to keep them with us."

During the discussion that followed, Rothmund was answered with detailed information on what was happening in France. Switzerland, he was told, must not close her eyes to what was being done in neighboring countries; she must ask herself what this wave of refugees would be sent back to. Reports of what fate befell the Jews deported to the east were so appalling that it was almost impossible to believe them, in spite of all the same kind of ruthlessness that had been experienced in recent years; but even the worst horrors could no longer be regarded as impossible. The government, it was urged, should no longer disregard the fact that the Jews who were now fleeing into Switzerland were doing so to save their lives. In the event that Switzerland should send back without exception everyone who had entered since August 13, it was further argued, there could no longer be the slightest doubt as to the fate of the deportees. In any case all evictions should be suspended until there was verified evidence of what happened to those deported.

According to the decree the refugee committees were obligated to report all new arrivals to the police even though they knew that as a result they faced expulsion and the danger of death. But, Rothmund was told, the refugee agencies could not accept the task of working as agents of the police. The men and women engaged in refugee work were, rather, Samaritans who wanted to help the least of those who had found safety in Switzerland as on a raft in a violent sea.

At least, it was argued, if there was no *right* to asylum in Switzerland, there was an old Swiss *tradition* of asylum. It was our duty "to rescue the last vestiges of humanity in this world." In their actual work, too, the police officials ought to keep this human aspect in the forefront of their thinking.

One member of the committee stated:

"According to reports, the old and ill are gassed and their bodies are used for chemical purposes. Even if the latter is not true, if in actuality the final destination of all the Jews is the Government General [of Poland] or forced labor, we know definitely, from all previous experience, that the fate that threatens them there, under the Germans' domination, is more horrible than death. . . . They die of disease or hunger."

Another member reported that he had been informed by a foreign consul that refugees who had been thrown out of Switzerland and caught in the occupied areas were in any event imprisoned, if not shot: "Without exception those who have left occupied territories without authorization from the officials are treated as deserters and punished accordingly." This speaker could not reconcile his conscience to the registration of illegal immigrants with the police and their condemnation to expulsion at the frontier. "We cannot become the accomplices of the persecutors and cooperate in hunting down the refugees for probable or apparently certain death."

Once more Rothmund insisted that the information that had been requested from German officials at the border had shown that nothing happened to the refugees when they were returned, except that they were compelled to work. He admitted the possibility that all might be faced with deportation later. Since the stream of refugees had grown constantly larger and on one day the total had amounted to eighty-two, it was no longer possible to temporize. The suspension of the decree of August 13 was therefore out of the question. He wanted merely to examine to what extent the approximately three hundred refugees who had arrived before August 13 might be able to remain in Switzerland. (From the Juna files, from the transcript of the committee meeting.)

## Decision on Mount Pélerin

But Dr. Rothmund had not reckoned with public opinion. Letters, telegrams, protests poured into Berne; the Social Democratic Party made an urgent appeal to the Federal Justice and Police Department on August 22

. . . to uphold the concept of humanity in the birthplace of the Red Cross in view of the current refugee emergency, to carry on with a generous heart the traditional Swiss right of asylum, to avoid the imposition of hardship on unhappy refugees, and under all conditions to abolish political expulsions, in accord with the basic legal principles of the Confederation.

The Federation of Churches and other organizations made similar appeals to the Federal Council.

But Dr. Eduard von Steiger was not in Berne. He was on vacation. In his absence, Dr. Heinrich Rothmund exercised his power of attorney and issued the order that the frontiers be closed to Jewish refugees.

Then something extraordinary occurred.

National Councilor Dr. Albert Oeri, editor-in-chief of *Die Basler-Nachrichtungen*, a liberal-conservative newspaper, and a man of great repute and great prudence, sent a telegram on August 22 to von Steiger in his vacation residence. In blunt words Oeri said that the new order had left him crushed, and that he foresaw the worst of domestic crises if it remained in force. Therefore he urgently requested that von Steiger immediately receive Dr. Gertrud Kurz, the director of the Christian Peace Center in Berne, and discuss this grave matter with her.

Federal Councilor von Steiger agreed. Dr. Kurz, "the mother of the refugees," was not unknown to him. He was fully aware of the devotion and the eagerness with which she labored on behalf of the refugees. He was equally acquainted with her utter integrity, her compassion for the persecuted, and her parallel understanding of the government's concerns.

The next day—Sunday, August 23—Dr. Kurz and Paul Dreyfus-de Günzburg went together to see von Steiger on Mount Pélerin. In a three-hour conversation in his hotel, Dr. Kurz dramatically depicted the desperation of the persecuted and the hunted and the fate of the deported. She spoke of the human and Christian duties of help; she pointed out that the order to close the frontiers was tantamount to a death sentence for those who would be sent back. In her own name and in the names of all the refugee agencies, in the name of the church and of all men of good will in Switzerland, she begged him to rescind the decree or at least to mitigate its terms.

"It was most painful for the Federal Councilor," Dr. Kurz recounted, "to think that in 'Goethe's Germany' there were people who could sink so low that they would herd Jews together and drive them into death."

As a witness to her facts, Dr. Kurz cited to the Federal Councilor one Dr. Silberschein, who had formerly been a deputy in the Polish Parliament and who now lived in Geneva. He had called to see her and in the greatest agitation he had informed her

> . . . that he had been summoned to the deathbed of a Swiss who had returned to Zürich from Poland and the dying man had told him of the savage horrors practiced on the Jews. These and many other reports seemed to impress Federal Councilor von Steiger; he told us frankly that as a result of these reports all the petitions that he had received from Christians known and unknown to him had now assumed more stature.

When he took leave of the ambassador of human kindness and her companion, she asked him whether she should look forward to a favorable decision, and he replied that he must now give the whole matter more and deeper consideration. Furthermore, the decision was not his alone to make; it lay also with the cantonal police commissioners.

On the same day, however, Federal Councilor von Steiger ordered that in special cases refugees not be sent back. Explicit instructions to that effect were distributed to the border personnel.

On Monday, August 24, the representatives of the Swiss Central Office for Refugee Aid met in Zürich under the chairmanship of their president, Privy Councilor Dr. Robert Briner; Dr. Rothmund also attended. If any doubt still persisted as to the views of these refugee workers, it was resolved at this meeting. It was like a revolt of conscience against bureaucratic inhumanity. In angry words the representatives of Henri Dunant's Switzerland protested against the abandonment of values that were as important to the survival of the nation as its military defense. The unanimous determination not to give any assistance to the expulsions and to withhold all cooperation from the authorities was made unmistakably clear. Some participants informed Dr. Rothmund that, if he continued in this direction with his refugee policy, they would turn to illegal action in order to defend human decency against official orders. Their "thus far and no farther!" could not be misunderstood or ignored.

The tempestuous session was almost at an end when Federal Councilor von Steiger telephoned to report that he was easing the regulations of August 13. In this round Dr. Heinrich Rothmund was the loser.

On August 25 he disseminated a circular letter to the cantonal police commissioners informing them that, since it was to be expected that the flow of refugees would be less, they were therefore expected to make some exceptions to the orders for the immediate return of all refugees. After all, the Police Section regarded it as its duty constantly to review the situation and not to bar any more refugees than considerations of state policy absolutely dictated.

The final orders were thus made contingent on whether and to what extent the cantons were prepared to admit some part of the interned and newly arriving refugees into their jurisdictions and place them with individuals or in institutions. (See Ludwig, page 210.)

## And They Were Not Silent

The echo in public opinion was no less unequivocal. Prominent persons of various temperaments and of various views raised their voices as spokesmen for the nation, presenting its position. In a letter to Dr. Heinrich Rothmund, Ernst von Schenck stated the dominant attitude in the ranks of the national resistance:

> To us all European refugees, wherever they flee from, are the victims of a system whose "blessings" have already been adequately demonstrated to us. . . . And, as for what concerns the Jews in particular, let us make no secret of the fact that every stone-hearted rejection of them represents an act of surrender to the Axis and every assistance that we can give them represents an act of resistance against it. Here an unprecedented distrust of our official foreign policy has been put on the alert. Even the simplest citizen knows today that anti-Semitic measures signal the beginning of the end. . . . We are of the belief that the extent of what we ought to and indeed must do for the victims of a policy of terror that we regard as criminal has not yet reached the so-called saturation point. Since, however, this should be the only point of view as to the limitations on our ability to help, we do not understand the

provisional restrictions at all. [Alice Meyer, *Accommodation or Resistance*, page 205.]

Professor Dr. Hans Zbinden gave expression to the views of other quarters when he wrote in the weekend edition (August 22–23, 1942) of *Die National-Zeitung:*

Until now Switzerland's obligation of asylum has not been brought into question. On the contrary, with greater emphasis today than ever before, it compels her to declare her humanitarian tradition, and the nation rightly views this obligation as compensation for certain privileges that have been bestowed on us. Human kindness, however, is not a thing to be bargained over. One of its characteristics is the fact that it is practiced not only when it assumes the diplomatically and bureaucratically safe aspects of the Red Cross and aid to children but also when it requires courage, character, and conviction. . . .

Today more than ever it is said that *Swiss* and *Christian* are synonymous. To send refugees back to the border and hand them over to their persecutors, however, is neither Swiss nor Christian because it is not human. It is the sign of a grave disorder of mind and conscience. . . .

What good is it to us to preserve and defend Switzerland if by imperceptible degrees we surrender the only thing that justifies the existence of our Confederation—our function as the protector of freedom and human kindness?

In *Die National-Zeitung* of August 28, the names of the Reverends Rudolf Schwarz, Walter Lüthi, and Samuel Dieterle of Basel were signed to this declaration:

Anyone who has had to deal with the Federal Alien Police thus far in connection with refugee matters has been appalled to observe that that organization is ruled by a spirit that places the protection of Switzerland against dangerous refugees so apprehensively and cruelly above all else that all human kindness toward the persecuted refugees is constantly forgotten.

It was an act of inhumanity to make so great a distinction between political and racial refugees. Inasmuch as the persecution —indeed, the extermination—of the Jews is part of the racial policy of our neighbor country, then even refugees who have come to us or who may yet come to us solely because of their Jewish origin are also victims of political persecution and must be admitted and treated as such, not turned away or tormented.

Dr. David Farbstein, a lawyer, wrote movingly in *Das Israelitische Wochenblatt:*

It is said that no right of asylum exists. I maintain rather that a duty of asylum is constant. It is the duty of those who are menaced by no danger to protect those others who are in peril. . . . I believe in a God of retribution. The God of retribution will punish those who seek through their inhuman behavior to harm the hunted Jewish refugees. He will punish as well those who stand silent and do nothing when their neighbors' blood is shed.

## Duty and Honor

In thoroughgoing fashion J. B. Rusch dealt with the arguments of the Federal Council and Dr. Rothmund in the morning edition of *Die National-Zeitung* of August 29, 1942. His analysis has lost nothing of its topicality, and therefore it is repeated here in its entirety.

Among the German-language newspapers of Switzerland *Die National-Zeitung* was the first to disclose the latest "traffic in lives" of the Police Section of the Federal Justice and Police Department. Its readers are also acquainted with the developments thus far in a matter that is hardly recommended for exhibition on the public highways. With satisfaction and approval we have all read the statements of the Evangelical pastors, some of them pulsing with anger, and we are grateful too to the Swiss Federation of Churches for having registered its protests.

Obviously it was not very pleasant to those responsible for the exclusion and surrender of all refugees on our borders to observe the extent to which public opinion had taken note of their "reasons of state" before it was altogether too late. It was even more uncomfortable to them to note the nature of the nation's reaction as soon as it learned of this enormity. That was the reason for the attempt, in an article hastily distributed to the press, not only to justify the inhuman actions in precipitate servility but also, indeed, to glorify them. I should like to state my position clearly and coherently on this effort, and, further, on the reasons for the growing resistance and also on the apologies filtering down to us from above; for the matter is one of urgent concern not only to the heart that feels but also to the mind that thinks.

The statement for the defense argued that these most improper precautions had to do with defense against "black border crossings" that had already mounted to "sensational proportions" and threatened to increase still further. "Disrespect for our borders" must be stopped. International law provided no right of asylum for any and all fugitives. Hence there was no right of illegal border crossings. The Hague Convention of 1907 stipulated merely that persons who crossed frontiers were to be disarmed, not that they must generally be allowed to enter. Thus, for example, it rested within the Federal Council's discretion whether to admit the Burbaki army in 1870 and the French Forty-fifth Army Corps in 1940. Moreover, the so-called right of asylum was after all not a right in the technical legal sense. There was also no legal definition of the concept of a "political refugee." We could not accept still more in addition to the fifty-two hundred emigrants already in the country. It must be clear to every "dispassionate Swiss" that the authorities did not wish to allow this figure to be increased under any conditions. Thought must be given, in such case, not only to the problems of caring for the refugees but also to the ensuing difficulties in the labor market. The bombastic attack on the "dupes of emotion" said in so many words: "Anyone who knows the situation will therefore *be compelled* to support without reservations *the firm position of the Alien Police* toward the late influx of refugees *without any diminution in his sympathy for these unfortunates.*" In passing it might be remarked that only a very small number of newspapers has endorsed this paean to the wise foresight of the Police Section of the Federal Justice and Police Department. And not one could have done so without having to expect immediate strong reactions from its readers. The typical bureaucratic obstinacy is weaker now, however, in its contention that the barred refugees also have no great punishment to fear in the countries from which they fled in desperation. But the authorities repeated that the influx was beyond the resources of our strength and also of our political capacity.

This is complete intellectual humbug! The argument of defense here is perhaps a not unsuccessful attempt to justify a thing that is stupid in itself—all brutality is stupid; because brutality is the forcible manifestation of lack of intelligence—on even more stupid grounds! Obviously we are dealing with "black border crossers." It takes a considerable amount of police intelligence to consider it improper for persons under the threat of being deported or held as hostages not to have followed the established procedures of obtaining Swiss visas, exit permits, and immigration authorizations in their homelands before they fled their persecutors! The attempt, after an agonizing flight undertaken out of urgent need and desperation, to cross "black"—that is, without papers—into the sanctuary of an asylum is not so black as the thinking of those who find it necessary to keep such desperate people away from the riches of their own safety! The "sensational proportions" of this influx of refugees have thus far risen to several hundred. Is that so terrible, and, if it were, would it be terrible enough to warrant the terrible act of debasing our country's honor and reputation in the world through police measures? *These fugitives have not shown disrespect for our borders.* In their belief in our humanity in a brutalized world, in their confidence that hatred had not yet consumed Switzerland's love for men who suffer, in their fear-ridden quest for our frontiers with this belief and this confidence, *they have shown respect for our borders* and honored them. Contempt for the meaning and the spirit of our country, unfortunately, has come from within! But, when a country invokes The Hague Convention of 1907, the *Accord on the International Laws of War*, against civilians, against women and the exhausted aged, it exalts itself to the height of policeman's prudence! The very stipulation that border violators are to be disarmed is cited unnecessarily in proof of the minimal extent to which consideration has been given to the fact that this is a provision of pure military law and has absolutely nothing to do with accords on the treatment of harmless, need-driven men and women. Just once I should like to see, in the Emigrant Museum of the Police Section of the Federal Justice and Police Department, the weapons that had to be taken away from these dangerous menaces to our borders. What in heaven's name have these few shattered victims of destiny, with their broken feet and their trembling hearts, to do with a Burbaki Army or a French army corps that was admitted to Switzerland in the midst of war? What is more shameful to our country: the way in which the Police Section of the Federal Justice and Police Department upholds our finest and most honorable traditions, or the way in which unbelievable actions are defended by bought hacks?

In a country with seven universities and thirty-seven academies such justifications are found for a baseless position!

Yes, this is again more technical legalism! But we want no "legal technicians" among us; we prefer men of authority who know what is right and who, when they do not know, do not in their intoxication with shadow power create a "right" of their own! The gentlemen seem not to know that rights arise not only out of claims but also out of offers, that not only the situation of the petitioner but also the integrity of the bestower is required to create a right!

We have never looked on the right of asylum as a mandatory duty on our part on the basis of topography, but always and only as our right to grant regardless whether it pleases foreign countries or whether on that account some other power threatens or whimpers. It is a question of *our* borders, it is a question of *our* country, and it is a question of *our* right! That is the foundation for our right of asylum, not The Hague Convention! And that equally ringing declaration that there exists no definition of the concept of a "political fugitive"! A political fugitive is anyone who, with or without reason, is persecuted by the political powers of his country without having been guilty of a common crime. A political refugee, therefore, is also one who, becaue of his beliefs, his racial origins, his rejection of a political point of view that prevails at the time in his country, would be in danger of persecution or, worse, destruction by those who hold power in his country. His even more guiltless wife and child are likewise political refugees.

That the fate of these tragic figures, for whom it is our duty and honor as human beings, Christians, and Swiss to provide help, left the "sympathies" of the Police Section of the Federal Justice and Police Department "undiminished" is certainly believable to us. But we demand of this Section an attitude that will also leave unimpaired the compassion of the Swiss people, the sovereign of the Confederation, for others' need and for sufferings that cry out to heaven! "Unreserved endorsement" of this horror, of this conscienceless indifference to the fate of human beings, will never be possible to envisage in our nation! We would be altogether too ashamed in the face of the past, the present, and the future, if we thought even of merely forgiving it, to say nothing of approving it. The intelligence of the justification shows the spirit of the program. If this program, which already has had such tragic consequences, has damaged the good name of our country without the knowledge of the people, that is sufficient atrocious ground for world condemnation of Switzerland! The world stands now definitively between two camps, one of the left and the other of the right. We want to maintain our honor in the face of both.

In *Libera Stampa*, a Social Democratic newspaper published in the Ticino, there appeared an open letter to Federal Councilor von Steiger from former National Councilor Francesco Borella, a prominent lawyer. The letter was also published in German-language newspapers. It dealt in particular with the young Jewish couple who had fled to Switzerland from Belgium and taken cover in the Jewish cemetery in Berne, and it continued: "This incident in particular is a grave accusation against the incumbent officials of the department headed by you and it will arouse the indignation of every fellow-citizen who remembers your recent speech in which you expressed understanding and promised help for those proscribed persons who seek to flee here in order to escape their persecutors and who are turned back to the countries from which they come. And every citizen must ask himself whether your functionaries read your speeches and are guided by your directives; perhaps in one or another of our compatriots the dreadful notion may occur that after all speeches are only speeches that are not followed by deeds."

In *Die Tat* of August 31, 1942, Félix Moeschlin, the writer, declared: "Just one word on the refugee question: There should be no official Switzerland that denies the best in the essence of the nation, what makes Switzerland what she is. Such officials do not serve their country; they harm it. . . . The maintenance of our right of asylum is part of the maintenance of our existence."

## It Must Not Be!

Under the title, "Switzerland Is Still Switzerland," Gottlieb Duttweiler wrote in *Die Tat* on August 29–30, 1942:

> In recent weeks all sections of the Swiss press have been concerned with the "extradition" of emigrants, most of them Jewish, who have fled to our country from Belgium, The Netherlands, and France.
>
> One has the impression that everyone everywhere had merely been waiting for the occasion of something directly affecting our country before it was legitimate to give voice to sentiments of genuine humanity. What unbelievable and inhuman events the Swiss press had to record without commentary! What horrors the reader had to ingest as if they were his daily bread! The most fiendish fantasies would lack the power to exceed the facts of the present World War. No one spoke.
>
> But now the time has come to prove our sentiments by our attitude.
>
> Quite simply, it must not be—that we ship refugees back across the frontier to certain death, refugees whom we could not keep out, who put their lives in peril in order to reach the country that stands beneath a flag bearing the cross. Are there thousands, then, hanging in this balance? No, their total number is three hundred—and that is going to be an "impossible" drain on our country?
>
> Once again the heart must triumph over the suffocating conspiracy of reasons of state. The heart is a force whose indomitability our freedom songs have well described. If the heart no longer dares to speak out, our battle is indubitably lost. It is more than time to

reinforce our sovereignty and our loyalty to our principles both
within and without. It is a question of making one thing plain:
Switzerland is still Switzerland. As tragically cruel as it is to forbid
entrance into our territory to those in fear of death, it is equally
impossible to throw back into the maelstrom of death refugees
whom fate itself has helped to set foot on Helvetian soil.

In the same issue, *Die Tat* quoted a news report and added a word of
its own:

> "In the first half of August, the conference was told, approximately
> twenty-six thousand Jews were deported from Paris alone. Hus-
> bands and wives were separated from each other by force and
> children were kept behind by reason of the destruction of their
> identification papers." Every father, every mother should take a
> moment's thought before agreeing that a few hundred people who
> wanted to save their families from this fate should be cast out of
> their Swiss asylum.

## The Sentinels of the Church

At the assembly of the Youth Church on August 30, 1942, to which
Federal Councilor von Steiger, as we have mentioned, addressed his
fateful words about the overcrowded little lifeboat, Superior Judge Dr.
Max Wolff, president of the Zürich Church Synod, presented the
greetings of the officials of the church. Most of the press ignored his
brief address. On September 11 *Die Tat* published it under the headline: "BRAVE WORDS FROM A CHRISTIAN AND COMPA-
TRIOT":

> We have recognized that the attack on Christian belief is also at
> bottom a direct assault on the innermost essence of our national
> freedom. This must be evident to anyone who reads the opening
> words of our Federal Constitution. . . .
> The best homage that the church can pay to the fatherland
> today is to show that it is really a church, that it truly fulfills its
> God-given mission to be a witness to the name of Christ. . . . This

ation2Resist!

entry duty of the church has always been diligently performed on the soil of Reformed Switzerland.

It is all the more to be deplored, then, that just in these times of the greatest spiritual menace to our country the warnings of the church have encountered no response from the controlling authorities of the state; rather, the freedom of church expression—that is, what must be cited from the Bible, orally and in writing, with relevance to current conditions of both domestic and foreign policy —is seriously threatened by the censorship of the press. We view such measures as a surrender to the spirit and method of a philosophy of the state that is absolutely incompatible with our Reformed belief. The church can and should not submit to the orders of the state in so far as they require it to betray its beliefs and its Christian conscience. It cannot often enough be repeated that it is the duty of the church in society to testify for the truth and to call right and wrong by their names: in a word, to give the nation its views, grounded on the Gospels, on all public questions, in all frankness and freedom but also with full responsibility. A Swiss nation that does not know and cannot openly say *why* it should not surrender to the powers that threaten it, why it must resist, will very quickly be deprived of its ability and its willingness to resist. The church must view it as its duty to arouse and actively sustain the innermost strength of our people, out of which alone an unbroken and invincible force of resistance can grow.

Therefore the church wages its battle for freedom of speech; therefore it raises its voice when the cross is defiled in its own country, when refugees in peril of death are hurled back into their agony. Therefore it absolutely refuses when in the name of neutrality it is called on to remain silent in the face of the worst injustice that the world has ever known, to look on, indifferently or fearfully, while peoples and races are exterminated, justice and freedom are abolished, God's word and human values are transgressed, when everything on which the ultimate foundations of Switzerland are based is defiled and destroyed.

Therefore the church defends itself against the reproach that denounces such unintimidated utterances as unjustified condemnations of foreign wrongs. Every pledge to the name of Jesus also embodies in itself a pledge against all injustice. If we forbear to

testify against injustice, we give it rein and we become equally
guilty with it. Christian belief means saying *yes* to Christ and *no* to
anti-Christian forces. . . .

Raise yourselves up, all you young people who have faith and
good will. Step forward. You—yes, you—are the foremost on whom
we rely. Our fatherland needs an independent elite that has nothing to do with schooling, social status, and political party but that
in its courage stands with the conscience of the entire Swiss nation.
In speech and print, in the press and on the radio, everywhere in
the country a new flame must be made to glow, in the cities and
the hamlets, in the hearts of the parties and the churches, in every
home. A people that thinks only of itself is doomed to destruction,
but a people that fights beside and for God is invincible. May God
assist us!

Judge Wolff was small, delicate, outwardly anything but a solemn
man. Now he stood as the spokesman for a faith and a courage that had
been forgotten by many in those days. The editors of *Die Tat* added
their own commentary to the report of his speech: "We welcome the
defense of freedom, human rights, and our highest traditions by men of
religion. Indeed, this is our hope, now that the responsible figures in
politics—undoubtedly against their inner beliefs—are silent."

The church council of the canton of Zürich took a different view. In a
public declaration it dissociated itself from the president of the Zürich
Synod. Dr. Wolff, the council asserted, had no mandate beyond that of
presenting the greetings of the Zürich church to the Youth Church in
Oerlikon. Anything further that he said was uttered on his own behalf
alone.

"Have we really gone so far that the mission of the official church of
the canton of Zürich is merely one of presenting 'official greetings'?" the
Reverend Walter Marti asked in the week-end edition of *Die Tat* on
September 19–20. "Why must the Zürich church council shoot its
representative in the back? Is that what matters to our national church:
that it operates in 'coordination with the state'? Does Zwingli's church
have the duty of disavowing a man who raises himself to the level of
Zwingli in his thinking and his sense of responsibility?

"It appears to us that, as a result of its statement of dissociation from
a declaration made by a man in the name of Christ, the Lord of the

church, the Zürich church council has imposed on itself the obligation
of providing a more detailed justification of its position."

Perhaps the Reverend Dr. Paul Vogt was also thinking of this when
he said in a sermon at that time:

> A church without love is a mechanical church. Perhaps it has a very
> fine organization. Everything functions remarkably. The budget is
> always balanced. The community can be proud of the beautifully
> restored church edifices. The roll of honor can bear the names of all
> the large contributors.
>
> But, although outwardly everything is as it should be, perhaps
> this church is utterly unperturbed by the grief and suffering of the
> times. It is silent when it ought to speak out against injustice and
> force. It is very prudent. For incautious remarks might endanger it,
> and that it wants to avoid at all costs. It wants to preserve what it
> has. So it says nothing. Its silence, however, is an unholy silence.
> The silence of a church that did not speak when synagogues were
> burned, but merely shrugged—well, it was only the Jews—is an
> unholy and unhealthy silence. The silence of a church that did not
> speak against the horror of the deportations, but merely shrugged
> —well, it's only the Jews—is an unholy and unhealthy silence. A
> church that is silent in the face of four million dead Jews keeps an
> unholy and an unhealthy silence.

Vogt and many of his colleagues were not among the silent. He
himself traveled about the country, roused people's hearts with his
innumerable lectures and sermons, and pointed out their duties as
human beings. He solaced and helped. He appealed to consciences. He
was never silent. Combat weakness and fear, believe in the strength of
the spirit! That was his guiding principle in word and act. He said of the
decree of August 13:

> It is contended that the limit of capacity had been reached by
> Switzerland in the matter of refugees. Massive crossings of the
> border supposedly posed a threat to internal security. The safety of
> the state was advanced more than any other factor as the basis for
> the decree. The voice of conscience and the law of God, however,
> pointed most unmistakably in those days to the indescribable suf-

ferings of the deportees and the inhuman and un-Christian fact of
sending back refugees some of whom had two or three emigrations
behind them and thought that in Switzerland they were safe. The
assurance of protection for the hunted and homeless and Switzerland's right of asylum . . . were endangered. [Annual Report,
1942.]

In a sermon on August 29, 1942, he said:

A Christianity so cold that it freezes Jewry to death is equally
doomed. It will be fearfully judged. For it knew its mission, it knew
its Lord's mission, and it has deceived and betrayed its Lord,
belittled and shamed and even crucified him; it is not one whit
better than Herod and Pilate, who crucified Jesus. . . .

The reputation of our humanitarian, Christian Switzerland has
often been shouted to the skies. Even by Swiss themselves, even by
Christians in Switzerland.

But God examines closely. God also sees the fifteen-year-old girl
who after a dreadful flight was sent back across the border four
times. And he sees those who pushed her back. God also sees that
mother in an internment camp who wrote: "One has the feeling
that a cloak of ice has been thrown over one's shoulders, that one is
totally covered in ice." And God sees those who place the cloak of
ice on her shoulders. [From *Ye Shall Love the Stranger*, page 21.]

## The Debt of Neutrality

In a study of Swiss neutrality in *Die Neue Schweizer Rundschau*, Edgar
Bonjour, a professor of history in Basel, wrote:

The finest heritage of neutrality is certainly the bestowal of asylum.
To offer political fugitives a sanctuary is a right belonging to every
state; Switzerland has simply handed it down from the past in
especially open-hearted fashion and thus has become the preferred
country of asylum. How firmly resolved she is to exemplify this
honorable tradition within the limits of the general standards of

international law has recently been demonstrated to us by a "ground-swell" of public expressions of opinion. The awareness of our obligation to precisely this part of our past is so deeply rooted in the nation, is so much a part of Swiss life, that it can perish only with the nation. How great is the potential of Switzerland's capacities in this area—in far greater degree than the current generation has any idea—is shown by many epochs of our history. One is astounded at the extent of the sacrifices that were made in a spirit of helpfulness barren of rhetoric, without regard to existing facilities or embarrassments to domestic or foreign policy, without a glance at the possible cultural enrichment brought by emigrants, but purely "for the sake of conscience, for the sake of God's mercy," because the fugitives too were "true members and guests of our Lord Jesus Christ." There were cantons that turned over as much as one-fifth of all public revenues for the maintenance of ideological refugees and that imposed a refugee tax, with penalties for its evasion, on their citizens, to say nothing at all of the vast private assistance given. Such a tradition creates an obligation. The surrender of the concept of asylum would mean a self-inflicted wound to the national pride, from which we could recover only with the utmost difficulty. For every betrayal of one's own ideals exacts a bitter vengeance. In fact, we should accept our mission of Christian love of our neighbor as a foregone conclusion beyond discussion. Our total neutrality obligates us to a total human kindness.

But it was not only prominent personalities who publicly expressed their advocacy of an unrestricted right of asylum. The newspapers were often completely overwhelmed with letters from students and soldiers, housewives and officials, secretaries and workers from every part of the country who voiced their revulsion at the exclusion of refugees and demanded human decency even on the frontier.

The authorities who conceived and administered the refugee policy consistently and increasingly called to witness their special responsibility to the nation, in whose obvious interest, they argued, they must be harsh. This special responsibility could not be disputed. On the other hand, however, we Swiss did not and do not live in an authoritarian state in which the high command or the government or anyone else alone bears the responsibility for the nation. In our direct democracy every citizen carries his share of responsibility. It is broadly based. The National Council, the Council of States, the cantonal administrations and legislatures, and the community councils all share in it.

If the well-meant justification of special responsibility in the refugee policy and the results that ensued from it were accepted as valid, this would mean that all other persons who did not agree with this policy, who criticized it and demanded more humanity, had acted without responsibility to the nation. The contrary was the truth. If these critics had not stood up, if the spokesmen for human conscience had not done what was within their powers—and often against the will of the authorities—Switzerland would indeed have suffered a moral wound from which it would have hardly been possible for her to recover. The fact that these citizens did not keep silent but spoke out because of their personal responsibilities as Swiss and Christians prevented the nation from being wholly and utterly reduced to heartlessness.

As the mentor and defender of the Confederation's conscience, the New Helvetian Society recognized what was at stake. On September 26, 1942, its central committee adopted a resolution, which was published in the newspapers:

> The refugee problem confronts the Swiss nation with a decisive test of its character. We must deal with it in fealty to our country's tradition of asylum in the spirit of humanity and Christian love of our fellow-men. In that way we shall also meet the requirements of a well-thought-out and far-sighted national policy. Every restriction or smallminded surrender of the concept of asylum is tantamount to the abandonment of a high spiritual value of the Confederation for which history will demand retribution. The principle of the right of asylum, acknowledged by Parliament and the Federal Council, must in the future be implemented by a generous application, particularly through a modernized revision of the concept of the political fugitive. Our supply situation, which fortunately is still favorable, has not yet reached its limit of capacity, which is the only factor that should influence Switzerland's course. This is all the more the case in that under the binding regulations of the

authorities newly arriving refugees are interned in labor camps for the duration of limited asylum period. The central committee of the New Helvetian Society supports all relief activities for the alleviation of the refugees' needs.

## The Press on Guard

The press, with few exceptions, was no less passionate and outspoken on behalf of a humane refugee policy. Hermann Goering, in Germany, taking cognizance of the opposition of our newspapers to National Socialism, had informed us that we had "excrement in the brain-pan." In Germany we were described as "Alpine Semites," and "Judeo-Marxist-plutocratic demoscratchers." Even in 1942 the press proved itself worthy of these honorific titles bestowed by the National Socialist rulers. All the leading newspapers from left to right demanded humane treatment of refugees. It would be impossible to reproduce all that was printed; let a few examples suffice:

Under the headline "WHO IS 'ARYAN'?", *Die Nation* said on January 22, 1942:

Inasmuch as the Zürich Alien Police has allocated one line of its Questionnaire B (Application for Issuance of Residence Permit) to an inquiry into the applicant's religious affiliation and added thereto the question, "Aryan?", one is compelled to inquire what law must be studied in order to be able to establish who is "Aryan." Is Switzerland now covered by the German, the French, the Italian, the Hungarian, or the Croatian statute of Jewishness?

In *Die National-Zeitung* of August 20 Dr. Fritz Heberlein proclaimed, with particular appropriateness at that time:

Anyone who keeps silent in the face of all suffering injures his country. The nation will have to pay if as a result of disregard for the right of asylum Switzerland's reputation suffers irreparable damage throughout the world.

From *Die Basler-Nachrichten* of August 22:

> Even in the great tragedy of our time Switzerland ought not to relinquish her right of asylum. The attitude of our Alien Police toward the poor refugees has aroused horror, and the reasons alleged for it seem devoid of validity. . . . In the course of her history Switzerland has learned, through a generous policy on asylum and settlement, to appreciate the benefits of such an attitude. This attitude, however, so fully expresses at the same time the inner essence of the Swiss people and state that its abandonment also indicates an inner weakening of our general capacity to resist.

Again on August 24 the same paper declared:

> It is simply not true that refugees who are sent back face no punishment. If they were not threatened by deportation, their number would never have risen so high. And it is difficult to envisage any more agonizing punishment. Granted that for the most part the Jews are not political fugitives: they are people, they are our fellow-beings, and they have a just claim on our help.

In an appeal to the President of the Confederation in the same issue, in which he was besought to prevent the revolting crime that "was now about to be perpetrated against the most unfortunate of the unfortunate refugees," the paper stated: "Every expulsion of such a refugee means death."

*Der Landbote* of Winterthur said on August 22:

> If our federal authorities take the position that deportation and race persecution or flight from the fate of imprisonment as a hostage do not fall within any concept of international law that gives rise to a claim for the right of asylum, one must certainly be amazed at such cynicism and such cold-hearted literal-mindedness. The mentality of the "new Europe" has already begun to operate here, or else no one dares to stand by the liberal interpretation of our tradition. They can say what they like in Berne: This is an exhibition of cringing to foreigners that is irreconcilable with Switzerland's right of sovereignty, with that spiritual defense of the

country to which the Federal Councilors summon us at every opportunity, and above all with Switzerland's mission of ministering to the needy that is always so eagerly preached in Berne. A large part of the nation will not go along with this, and the gulf between the Federal Council and the people will become wider.

Professor Valentin Gitermann of Zürich wrote in the Social Democratic press:

It is impossible to accept the statement of the Federal Police that no harm awaits refugees sent back across our borders or prevented from entering them. Perhaps these assurances are based on isolated inquiries; we possess sufficient evidence, however, to lend credence to quite different conclusions. Many persons who are sent back at the Swiss frontier *go to certain death*. It is beyond all doubt that the harshness of these exclusions violates that principle of humanity that Switzerland exalts as the ideal of her political position and that is bound up with the essence of her national dignity.

*Die Neue Zürcher Zeitung* said on August 25:

We should like to voice the hope that this Swiss sentiment will no longer be offended by reports of individual cases in the application of the right of asylum and settlement in which the "coldest of all cold horrors," the article-and-paragraph, has again won an unqualified victory over the contradictory concept of simple human kindness.

*Das Volksrecht* of Zürich declared on August 25:

The Swiss people will not permit the great historical heritage and mission of Switzerland in the domain of the right of asylum to be destroyed.

*La Sentinelle* of La Chaux-de-Fonds said:

We call on the Federal Council to wipe out this stain on our escutcheon, to give us back our pride of belonging to a democracy

that places the defense of the best of human values at the highest
level of its obligations.

*Die Evangelische Volkszeitung* of Basle asked on August 27:

Must not the treatment of the refugees be a curse on our country
beside which all the burdens imposed by these emigrants are mere
child's play?

*Der Tagesanzeiger* of Zürich said on August 25:

The will of the people to grant asylum has in recent days been
expressed in unmistakable fashion in the press, in resolutions by the
political parties, and in positions taken by church groups. This
belief that the dignity of our country and its standing in the world
would be besmirched if the tradition of the right of asylum were
frivolously discarded was very vigorously voiced in the Zürich conference for the discussion of the refugee problem.

The position taken by *Die Appenzeller Zeitung* was absolutely unam-
biguous:

All political considerations fall before the single certainty that
Switzerland will be a Christian Switzerland or else simply cease to
be, and that therefore, however hard it may be, we must live up to
the unmistakable commandments of Christianity.

*Die Schweizerische Kirchenzeitung,* a Catholic periodical published
in Luzerne, said on August 27:

Children are brutally torn from their parents, and there are scenes
that recall the massacre of the innocents in Bethlehem. Only one
purpose appears to be at the bottom of all this: the extermination
of Jewry.

*Le Démocrate* of Delémont said on August 22:

These practices have aroused and will again arouse in our country
an emotion as keen as it is profound. . . . It is one of our finest

traditions that is at issue here. One can be sure that the Swiss people will not view this problem lightly.

Taking account of possible pressure from abroad, *Die Neue Berner Zeitung* declared on August 28:

> It is absolutely out of the question to fall back on the solution of basing the operations of the right of asylum simply on the pleasure or displeasure of foreign governments. That would be a crime against the right of asylum and a break with our whole tradition.

*La Revue* of Lausanne said on August 25:

> To turn the refugees back or to order them to take up again their journey through the inferno seems unworthy of a country that so often—and, too, irrelevantly—makes a display of its Christian convictions and its obligation to set an example.

*Das Vaterland*, a Catholic publication issued in Lucerne, said:

> All the good Swiss traditions, the concept of Switzerland's Christian-humanitarian mission, seem to be imperiled or already gravely damaged.

*Das Luzerner Tageblatt*, an independent newspaper, was certainly correct in its interpretation of the protests when it asserted on August 27:

> Public opinion, that most sensitive of all control systems in a democracy, has angrily revolted against the increased severity of the police in their treatment of refugees, and under the pressure of that opinion the worst has now for the first time been averted for the unfortunate victims of persecution—and too, at the same time, for Switzerland's good name, which was in danger of falling into sorry discredit among all men of decent sentiment.

*La Gazetta ticinese* said on the same day:

> It is therefore an occasion for rejoicing if the decisions taken in Zürich mean what they say: the decision by the Alien Police to take

public opinion into account and to sacrifice some of the conditions
of our existence rather than the reasons for our existence.

Pierre Béguin asserted in *Le Journal de Genève:*

The letter of the law cannot be determining. It is much more
important to recognize the spirit by which it is inspired, and we
should draw our inspiration above all from a tradition to which we
are devoted.

From *Der freie Rätier* of Chur, on August 22:

. . . and, if a justified revolt has taken hold in widespread quarters,
and we say this quite openly, it is because of the heartless manner
in which the Federal Police Section and above all its head, Dr. H.
Rothmund, have chosen their major justification in artificial considerations of over-subtle reasons of state and treated the refugee
question in general in ways that the great majority of the Swiss
nation would reject as contrary to our tradition and to all human
decency.

From *Das St.-Gallen Tagblatt:*

The surrender of refugees who think that they are already safe
actually means the surrender of the right of asylum, and, with it, of
one of the noblest traditions of our democracy.

*Die Nation* of August 28 reprinted this from *Die Neue Aargauer
Zeitung:*

Whether Switzerland should grant asylum to those whom our time
has caused to suffer most, degraded and stripped of every right, is
not a question that should be settled in soundproofed conference
rooms on the basis of "considerations of *Realpolitik*"; this question
concerns the whole nation. With it the nation will decide on its
own moral existence and in addition on acceptance or dereliction in
the face of Switzerland's mission.

H. K. Sonderegger wrote in the Democratic *Landschäftler* of August 27:

> We are angry to the core at such barbarities of law and at the policy of force, and we must confess that with them our officials are performing the duties of jailers and hangmen. Whether it is Federal Councilor von Steiger's intention to cover up the actions of his subordinates will probably be revealed in the autumn session of the federal legislative and executive bodies. He has taken up a sinister inheritance from his weak and helpless predecessor: our refugee policy with its utter outlawry of the refugees and its total inhumanity. The worst item in the inheritance, however, is this Dr. Rothmund, whose removal from office is by now overdue. . . .

However great the differences in political interpretation and evaluation of domestic and international events might otherwise have been in the various newspapers, however graduated the form in which some of them had given—and were still giving—voice to their sympathy for or antipathy to the Jews: in the crucial moment when the nature and basis of Swiss existence were brought under discussion, when respect for human lives and recognition of human dignity were endangered, then all decent citizens and all decent newspapers were of one opinion. That was when what is called "public opinion" spoke through the best representatives of the nation and through its press. That was when the moment of life and death was faced with courage and honor.

# Quarrels Aboard the Lifeboat

Popular indignation at the Federal Council's refugee policy and especially at Dr. Rothmund's order of August 13, 1942, ran so deep that it had repercussions in the National Council. In a major and acrimonious debate on September 22 and 23 the principal electoral factions aligned themselves with the Federal Council through their spokesmen: National Councilors Theodor Gut, Radical; Thomas Holenstein, Catholic-Conservative; Rudolf Reichling, BGB; the Lucerne Conservatives, Heinrich Walther and Karl Wick; Antoine Vodoz and Georges Haldenwang, Liberals from the French-speaking cantons; and Konrad Bürgi, a Zürich Conservative. Ludwig Rittmeyer, Radical; Albert Oeri, Liberal; Albert Maag-Socin, Democrat; Walter Muschg, Independent; and Arthur Schmid, Walther Bringolf, Paul Meierhans, Pierre Graber, and

154

Henri Perret, all Social Democrats, bitterly attacked the Federal Council and Dr. Rothmund.

In the detailed speech with which he opened the debate, Federal Councilor von Steiger defended his policy.

## The Federal Council on the Defensive

Von Steiger said:

Permit me to introduce the statement that the presidential conference of the National Council has requested of me with a quotation from a wise Frenchman: "*La raison et le sentiment se suppléent tour à tour. Quiconque ne consulte qu'un des deux et renonce à l'autre se prive volontairement d'une partie des secours qui nous ont été accordés.* . . ."

This observation, translated into unadorned German, means simply this: one should never allow oneself to be guided by the heart alone or by the intellect alone. In dealing with the refugee question it would be and is a mistake to proceed solely in accord with reason or solely in accord with feeling. Both must guide us if we wish to arrive at the correct solution.

The Federal Councilor thereupon rehearsed the various decrees of the Federal Council, the demands of the army, etc. In practice, however, he said, there had been a great flexibility. Then word was received that the clandestine "black" immigration of refugees and other elements from Belgium and The Netherlands was being organized professionally in return for quite high payments, and thereupon it was decided on August 4, 1942, that the full power granted on December 5, 1939, by Parliament (the power to expel illegal immigrants) should again be strictly exercised.

Von Steiger continued:

That there were hardships in individual cases as a result cannot be denied. This happened in two or three instances. But the principle that had to be observed was open to no criticism, because it was the only way of seeking the proper course.

I have given very careful thought to the problem of examining what an influx would result if we did not enforce these regulations but allowed the black immigrants to remain. Night after night or day after day during September we have had black entries by fifty, sixty, seventy, a hundred thirteen, eighty persons, etc. If you take the average of sixty clandestine, unsupervised illegal entrants per day and project that over a year, you get a figure of twenty-two thousand persons, whereas the Federal Council has consistently expressed the view that a total of six to seven thousand would represent exactly what we could sustain without excessively serious consequences. . . .

Estimated conservatively, the total of "undesirables" in France whose influx must be reckoned with has been placed far over a hundred thousand. If we do not stop this influx, you can readily understand what this will mean for us. . . .

Any increase, such as was possible heretofore, is out of the question at present. . . . Our measures must therefore be executed on a broad scale. Switzerland today, under very onerous conditions, has about four hundred thousand more people to feed than in the years 1914–1918. Furthermore, we do not know what the postwar years may bring. The total of seventy-one hundred resident refugees that was reached before the war was increased between the beginning of the war and July of this year by about twelve hundred, so that at the end of July, as the Police Section's report pointed out, there were eighty-three hundred refugees in Switzerland. Today there are ninety-six hundred. Outlays on behalf of the refugees from the start of the war to the end of July 1942 have amounted to about 17 million francs, of which the Confederation has contributed 5.5 million and the rest has come from relief organizations, including some 1.7 or 1.8 million raised through the special relief tax. . . .

And now we come down to the illegal immigrants: between April 1 and July 31, 1942—in other words, in four months—we have received 664 clandestine immigrants; between August 1 and 31 there have been 561 more, and from September 1 to 17 there have been 733. You see how the curve is rising: the same figure of about six to seven hundred is reached first in four months, then in one month, then in two weeks. If we do not adopt measures, the influx will mount in such proportions that we shall be unable to control it. Thus developments indicate that, without certain counter-measures, a higher rate of increase and a decided growth in the total are inevitable. Clandestine and unregulated entry by foreign-ers, with the consequent evasion of frontier health examinations, is also not without significance with respect to the danger of the introduction of infectious diseases. . . . Therefore it is the duty of the authorities, even while in principle upholding the concept of asylum, to keep the influx within practical limits through special measures and as a consequence to prevent any increase that would exceed feasible proportions, even if this means that clandestinely entering refugees will have to be sent back. It is not admissible that on the one hand the state should require an official approval—the visa—for immigration and prohibit entrance without it, while at the same time it approves and rewards the violation of its own laws by tolerating illegal immigrants and thus making possible the oc-currence of what would happen if things proceeded in due and proper fashion. . . .

The conference of cantonal police commissions that was held in Altdorf on September 11 and 12 was therefore unanimously of the opinion that our frontier forces should be strengthened. The alarm-ing news that has reached us from our border guards in the past few days emphasizes the validity of this viewpoint.

Inasmuch as the border patrols and the local police forces of the cantons involved are not sufficient for the task, an increase in the military police is unavoidable. The money needed for this purpose must be voted. It may take until November to complete this reinforcement. If the influx does not abate, then special troops must be assigned to this duty. . . .

We are an unshakable island of justice and humanity, as I have been told in an open letter from Chur, and we want to remain so. But that does not exclude the fact that even on this island the fugitive cannot be helped unless certain principles of order and reason and certain measures for the protection of our domestic and international security are followed. . . .

Why, apart from reasons of domestic security and protection against dangerous elements, have we maintained so strict a border control for years? Well, simply to preserve the labor market for our

own fellow-citizens who even before the war could no longer establish themselves abroad, and not to allow that market to be flooded
and overrun by foreigners. If now the flow of supplies to this
unshakable island should stop, if no raw materials, or even if fewer
raw materials, should be available, if belts must be continually
tightened and the specter of unemployment, which has already
been forgotten, threatens again, is it so heartless and unreasonable
that the government should exercise foresight in its support of the
principle of asylum rather than proceeding without plans? I should
like any of you to spend just three days experiencing what a single
Federal Councilor, even if he does not head the Economics Department, goes through with requests from Swiss citizens who are
looking for jobs and work and other such matters. I wish you could
spend just a week at this. Then you would see why the whole
matter of regulating the entry of foreigners is so difficult a problem
for Switzerland. . . .

Whenever order triumphs over disorder, it is inevitable that
there should be certain hardships, however much we may grieve for
those concerned and however charitable we might like to be. Was a
Zwingli spared the necessity of ever being hard in his life, or a
Calvin before him? . . . .

How much that is good must be renounced because not everything can be accomplished, because the means and the possibilities
are not available for each and every man, because as a Swiss one
would rather do a little that is right than much that is bad and
because one believes that *non multa sed multum* is right, with full
awareness that those who lose out in the choice must suffer grief
and pain? We want to keep the level of help as high as possible,
but you demand the unreasonable and the impracticable of the
government. . . .

Not everyone who has been allowed into Switzerland is grateful
and content. . . . I have made an unannounced visit to a labor
camp and observed that two inmates were too lazy even to get up
in the morning; when the superintendent of the camp rebuked
them, there was an insolence in their facial expressions that clearly
showed that they did not deserve the asylum that had been given
them. When I went out of the camp into a field where a peasant
was plowing with two cows, and I spoke with him, he replied:

"And what about our unemployed, Federal Councilor? At least match every man you have here with an unemployed Swiss who will get the same amount of money that you are spending for these poor foreigners." You must look at conditions as they are in actuality. The news that is coming now from our border police is unfortunately not at all encouraging. It appears that some very arrogant and very unsatisfied elements are mingled with the poor and needy whom we should like to help, that there are people among them who think that, because they are bringing in dollars, sterling, diamonds, and everything else possible, it follows that they are entitled to some special consideration. . . . I want to avoid injustice to the poor and the deserving to whom we owe assistance—we are glad to help them—but there must be a clear differentiation in all cases, because we must operate intelligently from a long-range point of view. . . .

Today, however, everything is out of the question. Certainly we no longer have enough land and room even for our own people. So how can we serve as a country for colonization? Indeed, it costs us the greatest effort to find land that can still be colonized for the refugees and emigrants who have already come in, in spite of all the good will of the cantons and the communes. At the same time approximately twenty thousand refugees may have been cared for in the Evangelical establishments over two decades. This is less than the count of emigrants and refugees who are living here now, including the Poles. But hitherto Switzerland was not overpopulated and oversaturated with industrial and commercial labor as she is today; the contrary was the case. . . . The problem was that of helping these refugees to continue their emigration to other countries. Besides, these were refugees for reasons of conscience, and that must not be forgotten.

We do not examine whether the refugee brings anything in with him. What we take into consideration is how long we ourselves, from a broad-scale point of view, can share our resources with him. That is our mission.

. . . When you go back to the people after this session, try to make everyone understand that, in spite of hardships and mistakes that may have occurred, and other hardships that cannot be prevented in the future, . . . the Swiss nation can indeed say that in its willingness to help in the hour of need it has done everything within its power and that in any event it has no reason to fear any objectively based criticism. I am convinced that history will one day show that, all things taken into consideration, we have fulfilled the duty of humanity with independence and honor as in the past and with reason guiding our emotions.

## In Total Agreement

In the debate that followed Federal Councilor von Steiger's address on September 23, the leaders of the major parties expressed their groups' views one by one.

National Councilor Theodor Gut of Stäfa said:

I am authorized to make the following declaration on behalf of the Radical Democratic group: "The Radical Democratic bloc approves the Federal Councilor's report on the refugee question and the position adopted in conformity with it. The bloc supports the Federal Councilor in the view that for a variety of compelling reasons limits must be set on our capacity to absorb refugees, not least in the interests of humanitarian endeavors themselves, and the desirability of maintaining our potential in the long view to survive in this area as well.

"Insofar as the question of formulating estimates is concerned, it is the desire of our bloc that consideration be given to the honorable intentions of our people and to the refugees' needs to the extent compatible with the principles laid down by the Federal Councilor. The bloc further calls on the Federal Council to make provisions for uniform measures in dealing with the refugee and specifically the emigrant problem and so to apply them that in the future there shall be no regrettable and unnecessary hardships inflicted by the agencies involved in the execution of official instructions."

National (and later Federal) Councilor Thomas Holenstein declared:

In the name of the Catholic-Conservative bloc in the National Council I take the liberty of presenting the following statement with reference to the position adopted by the bloc on the refugee question: "The bloc stands firmly on the principle that the right of asylum shall be granted to political fugitives in our country. That right is the expression of the long-established liberal, humanitarian character of our national policy. But in addition the granting of the right of asylum—which does not represent an obligation to the individual petitioner for sanctuary—is subject to the superior principle of national concern for the preservation of the general welfare. The overall interests of one's own country ought not to be put in peril by the grant of the right of asylum to refugees, particularly in today's extraordinary conditions in which our country has been placed as a result of the current war. The admission of a large number of refugees means a heavy burden in a number of respects. The primary consideration should not be given only to the grievous financial onus that would be aggravated for the Confederation as the repository of the right of asylum.

"Our bloc has drawn from the Federal Councilor's report the conviction that the Federal Council and the instrumentalities of the Alien Police and the border patrol have made every effort, with the utmost good will, to give full consideration to the requirements of humanity in dealing with the press of worthy refugees at our western frontier to the extent to which this was possible and feasible without losing sight of the interests of our own country. Therefore the bloc takes cognizance of the Federal Councilor's report with approval."

National Councilor Rudolf Reichling delivered the statement of the BGB bloc:

The *Bauern-, Gewerbe, und Bürgerfraktion* (Peasant, Labor, and Citizen bloc) in the National Assembly wishes to express great satisfaction in acknowledging the information laid before our body yesterday on the question of the refugee problem by the director of the Federal Justice and Police Department on behalf of the Federal Council. Our bloc wishes to thank the Federal Council for the firm stand that it has taken since the outbreak of the war for the preservation of the traditional Swiss right of asylum with full provision against the danger of inundation by foreign refugees, and for its determination to continue this policy. The Peasant, Labor, and Citizen bloc proclaims itself to be in full and total agreement with the manner in which the Federal Council and specifically the Justice and Police Department have thus far fulfilled the obligations of the right of asylum, and we express the hope that in the future as well neither the Federal Council nor the Department will allow itself to be swayed from the carefully considered, definitive, and firm position thus far adhered to. The Peasant, Labor, and Citizen bloc shares the Federal Council's firm conviction that the safety, the reputation, and the honor of our country allow of no deviation from the line of action already laid down.

## The Voice of Conscience

One major departure from the official position came from Dr. Ludwig Rittmeyer, a Radical from St. Gallen:

> I must state publicly that I deplore the statements just presented, both that of the Radical Democrats and those of the Peasant and Conservative blocs, inasmuch as they present a false picture and to a degree lend themselves to the interpretation that the position of the Swiss people is now in fact as the various speakers have described it as being. Consequently it might be believed that the outcries that have been raised from both the Catholic and the Protestant churches, as well as the refugee organizations, since the closing of the border by the Federal Council arise in actuality from exclusively non-Swiss sources. This is completely false. These circles have not allowed themselves to be swayed in the interval. Unquestionably they are thoroughly steeped in the point of view that I am about to present here today. . . .
>
> I am absolutely convinced that, if after weighing all these problems of *pro* and *con* in the refugee question we can not make ourselves clearly understandable, then in the end we must allow the voice of conscience to speak, and we must say to ourselves that what has gone on thus far is wrong and henceforth we cannot give it our approval. . . .

As far as the physical aspect of the matter is concerned, Federal
Councilor von Steiger made it abundantly clear yesterday that he
regretted the instances that had occurred. I have taken due notice
of this acknowledgment of regret, but I cannot accept it. It would
be apposite and justified only if it came to use with the guaranty
that what has been done . . . cannot be repeated. Unfortunately,
however, we have no such guaranty. If you followed Federal Councilor von Steiger's statement of yesterday closely, you are compelled, on the contrary, to the conclusion that in fact nothing of
what has been done until now will be altered, that these regrettable
instances will be repeated, and that the only method of dealing
with the situation is through these regrets to disavow the Councilor's own subordinates, acting under his orders, who in fact did
nothing at the border but follow the instructions issued by their
official superior and refuse entry to expel these emigrants.

Next Rittmeyer attacked the inconsistency of the Federal Council,
which on the one hand admitted deserters and political refugees but on
the other hand closed the gates against victims of racial or other
persecution.

> . . . In actuality, what awaits them, the fate that they must face, is
> no different from that of expelled deserters or political refugees.
> . . . I can hardly believe that an increase in our admissions of
> refugees would damage us or work against us in any way with those
> powers that are our close geographical neighbors. If there is any
> desire to inflict damage on us from such quarters, sufficient other
> pretexts can always be found. . . . But, when one wants to get into
> international considerations, one should also do so from the point
> of view of the other side and ask oneself: "What shall we be risking
> if we sacrifice the other side's sympathies by taking too stubborn
> and ruthless a stand?" Let us bear in mind the constant diplomatic
> negotiations in London and Washington. Believe me, it will be of
> no advantage to our representatives if we are open to the reproach
> of applying varying criteria and being guided by overriding fear.
> Not even to mention the psychological consequences to be ex-
> pected after the war.

As for the contention, which had been more or less implied, that an excess of Jewish refugees in Switzerland might lead to anti-Semitism, Rittmeyer asserted that he considered this to be out of the question. In this connection he pointed out that the Swiss Jews had thus far been virtually the only persons burdened with the financial costs of the Jewish refugees. "And for once," he added, "I will agree that the limit of capacity has been reached in what the Jewish organizations can do: It is now the time when we as a people must lend a real helping hand."

Rittmeyer also rejected the argument that the frontiers must be closed out of concern for the nation's food supply. "Certainly," he said, "it is possible that the time might come when we would have to close the border because we had come to the uttermost limit. But this time has not come within view thus far."

## Stockpiling Inhumanity

Dr. Oeri, the Liberal National Councilor and editor in chief of *Die Basler-Nachrichten*, was no less critical in his attack on the Federal Council. He took exception to the fact that decisions on so high a political level as the instructions of August 4 could have been made by a departmental subordinate (Dr. Rothmund) when only the Federal Council could really assume such responsibility. Then he turned to the major question:

> How many refugees can we really admit? Aren't there already too many? I think there are not yet too many. We can take still more with a clear conscience. Against this view we have the statesman-like position of the Federal Council—the estimate given us yesterday by Federal Councilor von Steiger, on the basis of which a daily average of sixty presents the danger of a total yearly influx of twenty thousand. In his statesmanlike fashion he has insisted that this peril compels us to be cruel. . . . Assuredly I have no desire to ridicule the dangers that Federal Councilor von Steiger has described to us with statistics, but all this that he has put before us is merely a future contingency, not a certainty. So I ask: Must we be inhuman in the present for the sake of a contingent future danger —must we, so to speak, "stockpile inhumanity"? Must we thrust

fellow-beings into suffering and death when they flee to us for help, simply because there is a chance that later things may go badly for us too? At present things are certainly going undeservedly well for us; we are told so in every church sermon and in the utterances of the Federal Council as well. It is constantly repeated that everything is going underservedly well; and it is true. Hence we can in truth táke in many more refugees without any fear of hunger and unemployment for the present. It is, however, the right and the duty of the Federal Council to determine where the limit of our capacity lies. Today this limit has not yet been reached.

At the annual convention of the Youth Church in Zürich Federal Councilor von Steiger painted a clear picture of the situation: "One who has to command an overcrowded little lifeboat with limited accommodations and equally limited supplies, when thousands of victims of a shipwreck are crying out for rescue, must seem cruel if he cannot embark them all. And yet he is still being humane when at the same time he warns against false hopes and tries at least to save those persons already aboard." This is a very impressive image. We should like to develop it and add to it: our lifeboat is not yet overloaded, it is not even full, and, as long as there is room aboard, we will take on everyone for whom there is space; otherwise we commit a sin. The terrible moment can come when we are threatened with an overload. . . . But, to stick to the image: That moment has not yet arrived for us, and, God willing, it will not arrive. Therefore we do not wish to behave as if it had already come. May we never have to face the choice of offending against the duty of self-preservation or the obligation of help to our fellow-men! . . . Precisely because Christ knows how dreadful such a conflict of duties can be, he prayed in The Lord's Prayer: "Lead us not into temptation." May we Swiss be protected against such temptation in dealing with the refugee problem!

## In the Name of Humanity

The pronouncement of Dr. Albert Maag-Socin, a Democrat from Zürich, took proper statesmanlike form for its unequivocal development of the principles involved in the refugee question.

I have a few observations to offer on behalf of the Democratic bloc on the problem of assistance to refugees. We deplore the attitudes of the three government parties that were brought to our attention this morning in the form of statements, we deplore above all their heartlessness and the fact that these statements contained not one syllable of regret for the victims of our present conditions, not one word of protest against the revolting procedures employed. . . .

It is the view of my party that Parliament is not only entitled but obligated to devote every effort to the defense of those principles that alone are in harmony with the humanitarian tradition of our country and the violation of which must result in immeasurable moral damage to us. . . .

I cannot understand how it can be contended that a total of more than six or seven thousand refugees is beyond our capacities. We in the Democratic Party are of the opinion that the area of activity in this field can be very substantially expanded, to the point at which it would be legitimate to speak in the literal sense of the imminence of the sacrifice of our country and our people. I believe that we can serenely contemplate the duty of reckoning on an approximate total of forty thousand refugees as within the realm of what we can support.

It has been said, in reference to the procedures employed with these refugees, that there is a genuine desire to help in all really urgent cases and that the heavy influx must be curbed only insofar as it is advisable to keep out undesirable elements. This raises the question who in practice must make the decision. Supposedly the answer is the police forces on the border, which must act in accordance with specific instructions from Berne. What that leads to we have been able to observe in these terrible days of August. . . .

Again yesterday the head of the Justice and Police Department spoke impressively on this matter, saying that this onset of refugees was professionally organized and that these people were professionally transported, and from the whole tone of the presentation it was impossible to recognize that to a certain extent the subject in question was human beings. My party is of the opinion that these refugees who in the peril of death make use of whatever guides and means are available to them ought not to be calumniated on that account. It was equally bitterly distasteful to me that Federal Councilor von Steiger descanted yesterday on the "dollars" and the "jewelry" that have been brought in with the refugees. I must state that I cannot wholly shake off the feeling that this has produced a certain propaganda influence on his listeners that the director of the Justice and Police Department certainly could not have intended. . . .

Federal Councilor von Steiger has deplored the cruel events that occurred in August. We know that he did so from the bottom of his heart. The fact remains, however, that in August not a few persons but hundreds were turned back and that some at least were greeted by the hangman and all in any event were delivered into unspeakable suffering and peril. Therefore we find it particularly disquieting that yesterday the Federal Councilor announced that in recent days it had been decided once more to carry out Article IX of the Federal Council's decree of October 17, 1939, to the letter. Hence it seems imperative to me to demand a complete clarification from the Council as to what is meant by this. Otherwise, what we recognized in August as the evidence of the people's demand, backed up by the campaign in the press, for the relaxation of the restrictions would once more become an illusion.

. . . In the opinion of the Democratic Party it was a gleam of light in a period in which material cares have perhaps made far too heavy a demand on many citizens—a gleam of hope that now, in this at once spiritual and political matter, a surge of revolt against heartless procedures had swept through our people, or, let us say, through a large part of our people. My party is also of the opinion that naturally it is not enough to rely on paper protests and all possible speeches, but that in addition genuine material help must be given on the broadest scale. I ought to point out too that, next to the Confederation itself, it has been the canton of Zürich that has made the greatest sacrifices, in a manner deserving of the highest recognition, and it ought further to be pointed out that the Jews living in Switzerland have contributed altogether the sum of twelve million francs—an accomplishment that deserves our respect. But, if effective help is to be given, it must assuredly be an act of national assistance. . . . There should be no concealment, however, of the fact that some cantons that are reckoned among the most Christian have thus far made very little effort in this direction. This must be changed. . . . Horrible things are taking place in this uprooted Europe, things that concern us in ever growing measure, crimes against humanity in a form never before known, and it is our right to say in this connection that we feel ourselves intimately bound in infinite solidarity with the millions who are persecuted and oppressed.

At this point we must also raise the question whether it is not a *nobile officium* of the Federal Council to follow the example set by the Pope and speak out in its own fashion on behalf of humanity against the savageries that are taking place today. No one could denounce us on that account for meddling in others' business. Nor would it be a question of moralizing or being superior, but rather, very simply, the performance of a Christian duty. There are situations in men's lives and in peoples' lives in which silence becomes tantamount to the gravest injustice, to lack of character, and to faithlessness to one's own principles. I believe that today we have come to this point. In this era of unexampled betrayal of all the principles of human decency in our true federal tradition, our people and our government have the opportunity to prove their dignity.

## Sacro egoismo

A different tone was taken by National Councilor Dr. Heinrich Walther, a Catholic-Conservative from Lucerne. He argued that

> . . . no real right of asylum exists; rather, . . . the granting of asylum is an act of grace that is unilateral on Switzerland's part. This fact has its specific consequences. Since asylum is a matter of grace, each individual case must be exhaustively examined in order to determine whether sufficient grounds exist to warrant the exercise of such grace. . . . In every period such investigation has represented a conflict between reason and emotion for the Swiss nation. . . . I ought to point out that very often the heart has taken precedence over reasons of state in the Swiss nation, and at this

time this must be most emphatically stated, lest the heart impose its dominance at too great a cost. . . . Here, perhaps, is the source of certain differences in point of view between the people and the responsible authorities. The people allows its heart and its sentiments to speak too loudly, and it gives too little thought to national policy.

Then Walther turned to the continuing possibility of economic problems:

Give some thought to the coming year. Look ahead to September of 1943, and then surely you will weigh the question whether perhaps the people's attitude will be different. . . . Do you not think that at that time the same people who rely now on the dominance of the heart may make a strong appeal to reason and national security? . . . There exists a *sacro egoismo* that at certain times must be taken into account, and a certain influence on the exercise of the right of asylum must be permitted to this *sacro egoismo*. . . . Since . . . immigration has assumed such overwhelming proportions, would it not have been irresponsible on the part of the authorities involved not to have introduced timely measures that would prevent an excess intrusion of foreign elements into Switzerland? . . . There are not only pitiable victims who deserve our full sympathy but also a vast number of persons who are attempting to enter Switzerland but who for various reasons are in our eyes absolutely "undesirable." Of course we should be happy in our hearts if we could help them all, but an inundation by doubtful elements cannot even be considered by us. My honorable colleague, Mr. Rittmeyer, has discussed this, saying that the border can be kept open up to a certain point, and then . . . closed. But then we should probably face the consequence that the number of "undesirables" would be so great that we should no longer be in a position thereafter to admit those who deserve our compassion because the excess had put an end to admission.

. . . In the face of such grave problems one should have the utmost confidence in the responsible authorities. Without this confidence the solution of the problem would be doubly difficult.

. . . It can become our immediate obligation to allow our *sacro egoismo* sufficient influence to prevent serious harm to the welfare of our own people and our own country.

## Appeal to the Powers

National Councilor Walter Muschg, an Independent and a professor of literature in Basel, expressed the recognition by his group that "the painful agitation of the Swiss people at the latest occurrences on our national frontiers has also been understood by the government and given the serious consideration that they deserve."

He conceded the Federal Council's acceptance of its responsibility but he declared that its practices had "in part left a bitter taste." He criticised the cruelties and inhumanities that had become known, and he expressed the view "that in the establishment of the current limitations [on the number of refugees] the government should not act with excessive apprehension, because it was not yet a question of a mass invasion by hundreds of thousands of refugees, but rather a very small trickle that of course might possibly be the prelude to a mass invasion." He then added:

> . . . the Swiss Federal Council would perhaps conceive the bold but certainly not presumptuous notion of attempting intervention with the governments directly involved, specifically in Vichy and Washington, for the purpose of persuading these governments to make it possible for our Swiss refugees to cross the ocean and at least save their lives, and also, if possible, to initiate measures that would lead to a mass movement of refugees overseas. . . . This appeal could be launched and prosecuted through our International Red Cross Committee, and it should be made in the name of the entire Swiss people. Primarily we were thinking of what could happen to the children of the victims of the present measures in effect in France. Even the failure of such an appeal would be no danger for us, and certainly no disgrace, and to some extent it would alleviate the anything but negligible spiritual gloom that has settled on our people since these terrible things began.

## Switzerland's Mission

Dr. Paul Meierhans, a Zürich Social Democrat who was at that time
editor-in-chief of *Das Volksrecht* and later a privy councilor, launched a
sharp and pointed attack:

> By way of beginning his defense of the Police Section's policy
> Federal Councilor von Steiger quoted a French philosopher who
> had asserted that one should allow neither the heart nor the reason
> to speak alone. Now I should like to quote another French philoso-
> pher, perhaps even greater—namely, Blaise Pascal—who once said:
> "The heart has its reasons that reason does not know." Here indeed
> is the difficulty: that the heart has motivations that reason can
> never understand. It seems to me that the essential thing is that
> disharmony between the authorities and the people that has be-
> come a fact in these recent weeks. . . .
>
> Today the political parties have presented declarations of their
> complete endorsement of the statement by the director of the
> Justice and Police Department. When I run through the newspa-
> pers of these same political parties for the past few weeks, it
> becomes apparent to me that the Federal Council is playing the
> part of victim of a major misunderstanding here. For the state-
> ments of the press read very differently from the parties' declara-
> tions today. Let me offer you a few examples. . . .
>
> The newspaper of Mr. Walther, the Lucerne representative
> whose ancestors were refugees in 1848, said that "all good Swiss
> traditions and the concept of Switzerland's Christian, humanitarian
> mission are in danger or already violated." A Radical paper said:
> "Public opinion, this most sensitive of regulatory systems in a
> democracy, has revolted at the intensified police methods of dealing
> with refugees, and under its pressure the worst has now for the first
> time been averted for the persecuted unfortunates and at the same
> time for the good name of Switzerland." Even the Liberal-Conserv-
> ative newspaper in Geneva, *Le Journal de Genève*, declared: "The
> letter of the law cannot be determining. It is much more important

to understand the spirit that motivates it, and we ought to be inspired above all by a tradition to which we are dedicated." Or should I personally deliver to the Conservative group that declaration by a young Catholic study group that asserted: "Not only do the turning back—which now means the absolute expulsion—of many refugees and their abandonment to the agony that awaits them mean the death of belief in a humane Switzerland in their hearts; such actions put the entire world on notice that the best of Switzerland's heritage is being squandered here and a moral bargain sale whose consequences are inconceivable is under way."

This was how the press spoke in August. Certainly it stood in diametrical opposition to that complacency that came to the surface today in the statements of the political parties. . . . Or shall I shame the Catholic-Conservative group by reading the pastoral letter of the Catholic bishops, or the words of the Archbishop of Lyon or the Bishop of Toulouse, both of whom wrote: "The Jews are men like ourselves, their wives are women like our wives, foreigners are men and women like ourselves—part of the human race; therefore not everything is permissible against them; these men and women, these fathers and mothers of families, are our brothers; a Christian has no right to forget this." Nor should the Catholic-Conservatives of Switzerland forget it, even when it is the Jews who are in question. But look: Is it true that the activities of the Alien Police against the influx of Jewish refugees first came into conflict with the attitude of our Swiss nation in August? The practices of the Alien Police had long before given rise to well-founded protests.

I want now to tell you about the following instance, which will prove to you that for a long time there has been good ground to utter unequivocal words here in Parliament on conditions that cannot be opposed with weasel words—the question of Jewish refugees, about which we had no idea what was to be done if the flow should increase. At the end of April 1942 three Polish soldiers escaped from a German prisoner-of-war camp; they managed to cross the Rhine and flee into the canton of Zürich, where they were caught and imprisoned by the border patrol. After a few days, it seems, they were removed to the interior. Until then they had been put to work on a farm belonging to a captain in our army; this captain had nothing but praise for them, and he would have been delighted to be able to keep them with him and to help them. Nevertheless they were removed within a few days, with the explanation that obviously they could not be allowed close to the border: they would be taken farther away and interned in a camp. But what happened? This farmer who had taken in the soldiers was notified a few weeks later from a German prison camp that the three soldiers had been picked up by the Swiss Alien Police and shipped back to Germany. Thus, in spite of The Hague Convention and all the promises that had been made to us here in this Council, Polish prisoners of war, who had as such been able to flee into our country, had been sent back to Germany a few days later. I have the documentary evidence of all this here with me; I will turn it over to Federal Councilor von Steiger so that he can see the photostat of the card from the German prison camp that was sent to the man who had sheltered the prisoners. Moreover, it happened this way, that they were shipped back, only because they had managed to bring identity cards into Switzerland. You will understand that in the light of such events the distrust of the methods of the Alien Police—this case occurred in April 1942—is not allayed, but rather must of necessity be heightened by what followed in August of 1942.

Last night I learned of another case that I am also in a position to document. In April of 1942 two Jewish boys, one of them fourteen years old and the other sixteen, managed to get from France into Switzerland; they were thrown back across the border by our Alien Police. It was a deplorable scene, the way these two boys were sent back into Occupied Frence. That was the practice even then.

Meierhans declared further that his party could therefore not subscribe to a unanimous endorsement. He cited the example of Sweden, where the question was raised in Parliament whether the influx of refugees from Norway was within the country's economic and political capacities and the entire press replied as one: "Sweden ought not even to think of denying the right of asylum to any refugee, no matter who he is or where he comes from."

Meierhans continued:

This answer was understood and taken to heart not only by the Parliamentary questioner but by the government. Sweden, hence, is admitting tens of thousands of Norwegians now; Sweden too might thus be drawn into conflict with a foreign nation that has no legitimate concern with this flight of tens of thousands of Norwegians.

It has been said among us that it would be unjust now to treat those who have taken the trouble to obtain visas exactly the same as those who have come into Switzerland without visas and without police authorization. But they are actually not treated alike. Anyone who enters the country without a visa and without prior approval by our police officials, or manages to cross the border, is actually interned, actually placed in a camp. He can not move about freely like those who were in a position to get their visas.

And now one final word. There is so much talk about Switzerland's mission; we take such pride in the fact that we are fulfilling a humanitarian mission. We stage bazaars for the benefit of foreign children whom we take in. The Swiss Red Cross and the International Red Cross make every effort to assist in the fulfillment of this humanitarian mission. We are grateful to all these people here who sacrifice themselves. But this humanitarian mission must be supplemented by the government and by the government's attitude. It must be reinforced by practices that demonstrate that it is not merely a task for individuals or welfare organizations to fulfill this mission of Switzerland but that Switzerland as a whole takes this mission seriously. We thank everyone, and above all the nation, who has reacted as the Swiss reacted in August in aid of these unfortunates. Those who worked on behalf of the unfortunate then can indeed look back on a success, for in fact it was only as a result of this opposition among the people, of this vigorous reaction, that there has been that change, that relaxation in practice, that we wish to recognize. Unfortunately we cannot include the administration of the Alien Police in such thanks. It would have been preferable to us and the nation if we had been able to thank the Alien Police as well.

## The Lifeboat's Captain

At the end of the debate Federal Councilor Eduard von Steiger took the floor again:

Permit me too to address a few very simple words to you again. The daily report on clandestine immigration, which I received a half-hour ago, . . . contains the following figures for last night, September 22, 1942. Clandestine—that is, illegal—entrants amounted to a total of 175: 58 stateless persons, 79 Poles, 2 Russians, 26 Netherlanders, 6 Belgians, 1 Czech, 3 Germans. There is truth rising naked from the pit. These people did not take the legal route but traveled in secret: ninety into the canton of Geneva, thirty-six into the canton of Wallis, thirty-eight across the Lake of Geneva, four across the border in the Jura, and seven others slipped in somewhere or other and are now somewhere in the larger cities, without even prior medical examination or anything else. Make what you like out of these figures; there they are. "Nothing is more impertinent than figures." I have only one request: think about them. . . .

National Councilor Oeri has paid me the compliment of quoting from my speech in Zürich, which—as is proper—was not favorably received everywhere, my illustration in which I projected my vision of Switzerland as a lifeboat in a great sea disaster, with only very limited space and even more limited provisions. At that time, however, I also said the following, which National Councilor Oeri could not know because, even though we were in Zürich, the loud-speakers were suffering from a technical malfunction: "When, then, the captain of this lifeboat must choose whom he shall embark and for whom he wishes to reserve the space and supplies that are still available, while thousands and thousands have the same right and while he should and would like to help thousands and thousands, he faces the great spiritual torment of choosing whom he shall and shall not take aboard. Shall he take the women first, or the children, or the ailing, or the married couples, and say to himself: 'Perhaps the young and strong still have a chance to survive in spite of all dangers; but I have to make a choice!'" This is the painful task of the police agencies. And, if this produces mistakes that I regret—I should like to know who would not make mistakes in such a situation. I have been told of an incident at a border post where a guard made some inept excuse to someone whom he had to turn back; I defended him, explaining: "This was the tender heart of this Swiss, who was grieved at what he had to do and who, in his effort to comfort the man, used some pretext that was not very appropriate but that in truth came from his heart." In such situations many a man must keep close rein on his heart because in fact he does have a soft heart. That is a question of psychology. And it is not always the softest-hearted who speak softly.

All in all, everyone who has spoken today, with perhaps the exception of that great idealist, National Councilor Graber, has certainly drawn the proper conclusions, at least, and agreed: the border cannot simply be left open. When you concede that, however, the next question arises: How do we decide, when do we close the border, where do we open it? That is the difficult question. We organize and we must organize. . . . But at the same time we do not want to forget that in the exercise of the right of asylum we are facing a drama such as has not occurred in more than a hundred years, a drama of world history such as may not have been enacted since the Thirty Years' War. Consider that we must carry out this task with means that cannot be augmented. The Police Commissioners know this better than anyone. If I have appealed, and appeal again, for your help, I will also go yet a further step: If I encroach on the sovereign rights of the cantons and make unreasonable demands on the cantons, I should like to ask even the staunchest federalist to accept the concept of the central power without resistance in this crisis and not to raise federalist resistance. That clever National Councilor, Dr. Oeri, who is always so deliberate and so critical in his utterances, has employed the term, "certainty of the future." I am not trained in so sharp a logic as the people of Basel are in general; but I should appreciate it if, when the opportunity arises, I might be told how I should interpret "certainty of the future." There, gentlemen, is indeed the problem: to know how long a period we must reckon with. Even if we have plans, shall we now take in everyone, or can it happen that then we must also admit persecuted Swiss, or ration the facilities somewhat instead of exhausting all our capacities now?

It was proper to mention Sweden. I should like to point out here what great special respect the speaker feels for Sweden and what she is doing. We should be glad to allow Sweden and Portugal precedence over us in praise for aid to refugees. But what is in issue is the failure to praise Switzerland for her actions; on the contrary, in each case the situation is somewhat different, and it is not at all the same thing whether I admit people from my neighbor nation with which until a few decades ago I was united in a single state or whether I have to perform the task that now faces us. There is no differentiation of nations or of any races whatever in our operations; but there are certainly psychological postulates that are not always the same in the people's readiness to accept refugees. At this point I repeat: If we must come to the point of carrying out what the old Bernese and other cantons, but principally the Bernese, put into practice when they took the Huguenots from Geneva—that is, saying: "Let us distribute the people among families"—then I should like to see the degree of willingness, gentlemen, if I issue that appeal! Out of all the many documents that offered to teach me lessons (apart from declarations of cooperation from a few organizations, particularly the Swiss Federation for Women's Aid, in Basel), I have actually gleaned only two instances of practical help. One was a twenty-franc note from a simple Swiss and the other was a letter from a family certifying its willingness to take in a child. The letter came from Puschlav.

Do not forget that even we Swiss have been to a certain degree taken by surprise by these new developments. I am not ashamed to inform you that the entire organization that we ought to have had available for these changes is not yet in being. Hence we must all work together—the private relief organizations, which have already achieved so much and must be gratefully recognized, the cantons, the communes, and the Confederation. That the Confederation must lead the way with means of a financial and practical nature is obvious. But the Confederation itself has no land on which camps for the emigrants can be built. Land must be made available to it so that colonization can be undertaken. . . . The Confederation will be compelled in this area to do much more than it has done thus far.

Our efforts have been initiated with a view to maintaining means of further emigration and thus increasing our admissions of emigrants. But it goes against all my principles, and that is why I did not do so yesterday, to disclose anything in which there has not already been a positive result. In general, perhaps, we must take some pains not to talk too much about the good that we are doing. The upright man does good, but he does not talk about it. Therefore I should prefer to make my final report to you only when the whole first stage has been completed. I should rather present you in the meantime with a discouraging interim report so that you will not later be convinced that you had made a mistake.

The groundswell that has swept through the Swiss nation did not come as any surprise to me. I sensed it at the very time when on August 4 the Federal Council was compelled on principle to order the reapplication of Article IX.

We must make experiments. Here it is the delicate task of every police agency to find the requisite diplomacy and the right proportions. One must feel out who one can and cannot allow to enter. If a declaration were to be made that in principle everyone could come in, word of it would get about everywhere. As it is, hundreds of letters go out of Switzerland every day, saying: "Come here, everything is available." That is how things stand, and so this is a clear indication that now is the time to seal the door, of necesity, even if one must reckon with the reaction that will be aroused among our people.

I think I have a pretty good ear. In recent days I have learned to distinguish between the inflections of genuine human kindness, compassion, and honest anger in the petitions addressed to the Federal Council (in ignorance of the true situation) to do more and the tones of other voices that were not quite in tune and in which there was an obbligato of tactical, technical, and other orchestration in which I could not hear authentic feeling quite so loudly and clearly as I should have liked. So, if you discuss this difficult question with the Swiss people and explain that we completely understand the nation's compassion and emotions and that we honor its feelings, then quote as well, perhaps, the verse from the Epistle of St. James that *Die Zürichsee-Zeitung* cited one day in a Sunday sermon: "But let every man be quick to hear, slow to speak, and slow to be angry." Then we shall find our way in the refugee question too.

## Thoughtful Judgment

For all that the major parties approved the position taken by the Federal Council, it might still be said that broad sectors of the citizenry looked on the Radical Rittmeyer rather than on Federal Councilor von Steiger as the spokesman for their indignation. Felix Moeschlin, who was also a member of the National Council at this period, said in *Die Tat* on September 24, 1942:

> One is not always pleased at being a National Councilor. For now and then one has the feeling that one is playing the part of a supernumerary. Today one does not have this feeling. The debate on the refugee question has shown that the National Council is not yet superfluous.
>
> The comparison of Switzerland with a lifeboat—a comparison that goes back to Federal Councilor von Steiger's speech in Oerlikon—is gaining further interpretation today. I take no joy in this comparison, because it is false. The structure of Switzerland has not even the slightest resemblance to the structure of a lifeboat. If it is essential to draw a comparison from that oceanic world that nature has denied to us, then let it be that of a thoroughly organized, flawless, fully equipped ocean liner. We do not have to disclose its tonnage, but in any case it is no nutshell but rather, as I have said, a first-class ocean liner that is far from sinking even if it takes aboard a few more shipwreck victims in addition to its regular passenger list.
>
> It is not altogether pleasant when Federal Councilor von Steiger announces a vote of no confidence in the Swiss nation and implies that it would talk very differently if it were constrained to make personal sacrifices. Experience is demonstrably counter to this point of view. The Swiss have always been compassionate, beginning with Russian relief in 1922, when Switzerland sent three million francs to the starving Bolsheviki, and down to today's child assistance. Yes, the Swiss have a few national failings, but in the face of need they have never said *no*. Nor will they do so now if the Federal Council addresses an appeal to the Swiss people.

Dr. Markus Feldmann, also a National Councilor and at that time editor-in-chief of the Berne Peasant Party's *Neue Berner Zeitung,* said on September 27 at a meeting of the New Helvetian Society in Geneva:

> In every instance the outcome of these deliberations [in the National Council] bids us make thoughtful judgments in the invoca-

tion and employment of humanitarian rhetoric. More forcibly, more imperatively today than ever, we are summoned to the arduous yet splendid and proud task of increasingly reinforcing the outer appearance of our freedom-based national state with that substance that expresses the sense of federation in the true meaning of the word. . . . May every one of us do his part so that in the performance of this task we can stand self-respectingly before those who have preceded us and those who will come after us!

That was what was important in those years and in those days: the honorable realization of the special values that we had imposed on ourselves.

## Plebiscite of the Heart

Thus, with impressive accord, the will of the broadest circles of the nation was made clear through its representatives in Parliament, through the press, through the churches, and through leading citizens. Nor did it begin and end with words.

Under the title "Plebiscite of the Swiss Heart," Albert Oeri called in October 1942 for a demonstration of sympathy with the refugees:

> Today it is not enough to dispute who was right at that time [in the National Council's debate in September]; today it is obligatory to *act*. Therefore the relief organizations have set a national fund-raising drive in motion as quickly as possible and have received official authorization to conduct it during the period from October 17 to 31. This amounts to nothing more or less than a popular referendum on the question: Does or does not the Swiss people want help for refugees? This time, however, it is not a question of marking *Yes* or *No* on a ballot, but rather of writing a sum in francs and centimes on a green postal money order. Anyone who has even a vague notion of the dreadful sufferings that clamor for rescue at our frontiers will hope for a great-hearted popular decision.

The plebiscite was a success. In the midst of the difficult war years the Central Office for Refugee Aid collected the sum of more than one and a half million francs. A further indication of the nation's spirit was to be found, for example, in the fact that the sales of *Armor Has No Fear*, the Evangelical relief organizations' special publication for the benefit of their refugee fund, rose from sixteen thousand in January 1942 to forty-one thousand five hundred in December of the same year. An appeal from the Reverend Dr. Vogt quickly brought in several hundred offers of homes for refugees.

The Police Section and the Federal Council were compelled to reckon with this demonstration of the people's will. In September 1942, thirty-eight hundred refugees who entered illegally were allowed to cross a virtually open border. The Police Section arrived at an agreement with the clerical authorities under which the churches could submit to the police periodic lists of persons who were not to be turned back in the event of possible border violations. The frontier guards were given explicit instructions. Furthermore, the Swiss consulates in France were authorized to issue what was known as a "C" visa to everyone included in these lists—prominent persons were in the forefront—and thus to assure him of the right to cross the border unhindered. These lists ran sometimes to as many as eight hundred names. (See Ludwig, pages 224–225.)

## And More in the Old Spirit

Nevertheless there could be no thought of a basic liberalization of the refugee policy—Federal Councilor von Steiger had left hardly any doubt on that point. On August 29, 1942, under the headline, *On Guard!, Die St.-Galler Volksstimme* warned:

"Mr. Rothmund and the Federal Council have more assistants than may be readily apparent! If Switzerland is to prove her decency toward people fleeing from France and The Netherlands, a great deal of resistance must still be broken down. Keep watch on Berne, fellow-citizens!" The admonition was most decidedly needed.

On September 26, with the approval of the Federal Council, the Police Section sent new instructions by telephone to the various border forces, reminding them once more: "Refugees for racial reasons alone, under existing procedure, are not political refugees." And, further: "French Jews are to be turned back without exception because they are in no danger in their own country."

At the end of August the commander-in-chief of the army had expressed his opposition to any further increase in the refugee flow. In a letter of October 5 Federal Councilor von Steiger alerted him to the fact that, in the event that it prove impossible in the next two weeks to stem the influx of refugees with the means thus far employed, it would be necessary to call on the army. "As you know," von Steiger wrote, "I have delayed this request as long as possible and I have allowed considerable leniency to prevail even among the border guards. If, however, the tremendous tide of illegals does not abate, there must be a tightening of border controls. Therefore I am asking you in advance, *by way of preparation*, to give this matter your close attention."

Two days later Federal Councilor von Steiger forwarded to the general a letter from the Federal Military Department, dated October 2, in which it was pointed out that "the number of Jewish emigrants at the Swiss border is mounting in increasingly alarming fashion." Von Steiger's covering letter to the general concluded: "Hence it seems to us to be urgently necessary that you be at hand to assist us."

Thereupon, in a general order of October 9, the Army High Command instructed the commanders of the First and Fourth Army Corps to reinforce the frontier guard in the area between Lower Wallis and Geneva. At the same time the First Army Corps was ordered to erect barbed-wire barriers at the most important crossing points, particularly those places favored by refugees crossing the frontier illegally, in order to make entrance into Switzerland more difficult and the task of border control less arduous. (See Ludwig, pages 222–224.)

In October, consequently, the total of "illegal" immigrants fell to 1904—half the total for September.

# The Need Grows Greater

On September 7, 1942, *Die Tat* and other Swiss newspapers had published a British government report, received directly from France, on the persecutions of the Jews. On July 15 and 16 three hundred Jews, all identified by name in the report, had committed suicide. In actuality the number of suicides was much higher. In many instances entire families had chosen to die rather than face deportation and separation. In the *Parc du prince* and the *Vélodrôme d'hiver* twenty-eight thousand persons had been herded together, including many who were seriously ill, others who had been under surgery only a few hours before, and a number of women in the last stages of pregnancy. Many French policemen had refused to carry out his gruesome task. By the end of August three hundred Paris policemen had been dismissed on charges of "pro-

Jewish tendencies." The prisoners in the corrals included not only foreign but also numerous French Jews.

The British document described as well the persecutions of Jews in unoccupied France and the courageous stand taken by the Catholic and Protestant churches in particular against the anti-Jewish measures of the puppet government in Vichy.

On instructions from the Swiss government's press office the further publication of this article was prohibited. (From the Juna file.)

Also on September 7 *Das Ostschweizer Tagblatt* (published by Loepfe-Benz in Rorschach) published an article that said, in part:

> But do you consider how long a death these people must die when they are shoveled together today into the concentration camps of southern France and are loaded in the night, with all their agonies, into cattle cars? Fully conscious and totally aware of everything that is happening, they die by inches for weeks, until somewhere in the forests of the east the dry crackle of gunshots releases their broken bodies.

This extract was also distributed by the Juna agency. The press chief of Territorial Commando 6, Colonel Lindt, challenged it in a letter of October 26, saying: "We should like to call your attention to the fact that under present conditions articles of this kind are undesirable and their publication is not in the interest of the Jews. Therefore we request that in future you submit articles dealing with the refugee question to us before publication."

*Die Appenzeller-Zeitung* of September 10 said:

> Jews are torn out of their homes and deported. Their destination is not revealed to them. All that they know is this: Somewhere in the east an unspeakable agony awaits them. Somewhere far from France and their children. For even the ultimate right is denied to these people stripped of all rights: the right to their own children. . . . It is impossible to count the families that are thus torn apart. Are these human beings who commit such acts? They are not animals. Animals behave better. They respect motherhood.

A leading article in *Die Neue Zürcher Zeitung* of September 13 said:

> What has thus far become known from the accounts of these measures, whose unbelievable cruelty arouses a feeling of horror even in the midst of a world gripped by war, is still insufficient to establish a conclusive picture of what has happened; for every instance, however, we have evidence of an unimpeachable character, in the face of which any attempt at extenuation of the facts is futile.

In *La Tribune de Genève* for September 16 a Swiss physician who had just returned from France told of the desperate acts of Jewish mothers and of the deportations of Jews in cattle cars that he himself had observed with anguish. "Where are all these miserable people going?" he cried. "They do not know, but they can guess." This article, distributed by Juna, was also reprinted in various German-Swiss newspapers.

At the same time protests by high Catholic and Protestant dignitaries in France against the persecution of the Jews had also been made known in Switzerland, through documents such as the pastoral letters of Cardinal Archbishop Gerliers of Lyons, published in *La Tribune de Genève* on September 26, that of Archbishop Saliège of Toulouse, which was issued from his chancellory at the end of August and reported in *Le Courrier de Genève* on September 10, in *Das Volksrecht* on September 1, in *Die Thurgauer Arbeiterzeitung* on September 11, and in *Die Neue Zürcher Zeitung* on September 13; that of Bishop Théas of Montauban, printed in *Le Courrier de Genève* on September 11; and a petition by the cardinals and archbishops of the Occupied Zone in July to Marshal Henri-Philippe Pétain, published in *Le Courrier de Genève* on September 10, in *Die Thurgauer Arbeiterzeitung* on September 11, and in *Das Volksrecht* on September 16.

In a BBC broadcast from London on September 27, Thomas Mann asserted:

> In the past few days sixteen thousand Jews were rounded up in Paris, packed into cattle cars, and deported. Where? The answer lies with the German locomotive driver who is being talked about all over Switzerland. He fled there because he often had to drive

trains loaded with Jews; somewhere in open country the trains would be stopped, hermetically sealed, and pumped full of gas. The man could no longer endure it. But this man's experiences are in no way out of the ordinary. An accurate and authentic report tells of the deaths of at least eleven thousand Polish Jews by poison gas. They were taken to a special execution area in Konin, in the district of Warsaw, loaded into airtight sealed trucks, and turned into corpses within a quarter-hour. There is also a description of every step in the whole procedure, including the shrieks and prayers of the victims and the good-humored laughter of the SS Hottentots who carried the joke to its conclusion.

On September 30 *Der Führer* himself confirmed the inconceivable acts:

> . . . There was a time when the Jews in Germany too laughed at my prophecies; I do not know whether they are still laughing today or whether they have already lost their laughter. But even now I can assure you of one thing: They will all lose their laughter, and in the end I shall be proved right in this prophecy. [*Die Frankfurter Zeitung*, October 1, 1942.]

Of this *Die Thurgauer Arbeiterzeitung* rightfully observed on October 7:

> While it might have been possible hitherto to remain in ignorance of what the Jews deported to the east have to expect, now, after Hitler's unequivocal statement, there can be no further doubt on the subject. . . . Now that Hitler has shattered any illusion that anyone might hitherto have been able to foster as to the fate of the Jews, the assurance of asylum to the Jews emerges in a new light for us too, as Swiss; it becomes a duty of humanity that must be fulfilled.

Four days earlier, as we have seen, the Police Section's new instructions had been put into execution.

*Der Volksfreund* of Flawil declared on October 10:

Again and again trustworthy reports from eastern and northeastern
Europe contain news of mass executions, and recently a diplomatic
correspondent of *The Times* of London reported that in the Vilna
ghetto the original population of eighty thousand had sunk to
twelve thousand; these sixty-eight thousand persons by whom the
ghetto's population has been reduced were almost all killed by
hunger. In Lithuania, *The Times* further reports, these appalling
measures were aimed at the total extermination of the population
without differentiation among Lithuanians, Poles, or Jews.

On October 11 the United Press distributed a dispatch from its
Stockholm correspondent, Hubert Uexküll, which was reprinted by *Das
St.-Galler Tagblatt* and *Die Volksstimme*, among others:

It is now known that, in spite of the prevailing severe impairment
of rolling stock in Germany, regular shipments of Jews out of
Berlin—the only large city in Germany that still contains a sizable
number of Jews—have been got under way. . . . These "death
shipments," as they are known in Germany, are dispatched first of
all, as a rule, to an overcrowded, unsanitary ghetto. This is the first
stop, from which the Jews are sent to primitive, unhealthy labor
camps in the Polish or White Russian swamp areas, if not directly
to the places of execution, most of which are in the vicinity of large
cities such as Warsaw, Lvov, Minsk, Riga, etc.

As has been reported from Berlin, only physicians and midwives
can escape death, as well as a few specially skilled workers, since not
enough qualified Aryans in these three categories can be found.

The press chief of Territorial Commando 7 rebuked *Die Volksstimme*
for its "sensational headline"—"DEATH TRANSPORTS TO THE
EAST"—and the publication of "no less sensational" dispatches of
"unverifiable content" originating from "obviously unreliable sources."
The newspaper, it was charged, lacked the necessary caution. The
editors replied: "The matters discussed in the dispatch have long since
been known to us. They are identical with what the Swiss Red Cross has
ascertained regarding the deportations in the eastern states."

In his call for a day of prayer in October, the Reverend Dr. Paul Vogt laid special emphasis on what we in Switzerland were in a position to know, and ought to know, of the fate of the Jews in France.

In *Die Reformierten Flugblättern*, published by the Evangelical relief organization for refugees in October, it was stated:

> Uncounted refugees are dying in loneliness today. They die in flight through the forests. They die in freight cars carrying them into deportation. They die beneath the wheels of railway trains, like H, who was plunged into despair in Switzerland by the news of his mother's deportation. . . . A vast pall of death has settled over the peoples of Europe. A vast pall of death has settled over God's people, the Jewish people. Europe is aroar with death rattles. Europe is filled with the screams of the dying as they are shot and gassed. . . .

Were these sounds unheard in Berne?

On December 4 *Die Thurgauer Arbeiterzeitung* reported that Sidney Silvermann, director of the British section of the World Jewish Congress and a member of the House of Commons, had revealed that up to the end of 1942 some two million Jews had lost their lives as a result of persecution based on racial policies.

But "refugees on racial grounds alone are not victims of political persecution."

## Appeal to the World's Conscience

On December 17 the League of Nations issued a declaration that was read in the British Parliament, the American Congress, and similar bodies and was also made public in Moscow. It said, among other things:

> The attention of the governments of Belgium, Czechoslovakia, Greece, Luxemburg, The Netherlands, Norway, Poland, the United Kingdom of Great Britain and Northern Ireland, the United States of America, the Soviet Union, and Yugoslavia, as well as the French National Committee, has been directed to

various authenticated reports from Europe, according to which the German authorities are not content with destroying the most elementary human rights of persons of Jewish origin in all areas over which they have extended their barbaric rule, but are now putting into practice Hitler's reiterated and explicit threat to exterminate the Jewish people. Jews are being herded eastward from all the occupied countries with the most revoltingly ghastly and cruel methods. In Poland, which has become the largest of the Nazi slaughterhouses, the ghettos set up by the German invaders have been systematically emptied of all Jews except a few skilled workers who are required for the armaments industry. No word is ever heard again from any of the deported. Those still able to labor are worked literally to death in labor camps. The ailing and the feeble are left to die of cold or hunger, or destroyed in carefully planned mass executions. The number of victims of this bloodthirsty insanity has been estimated at many hundreds of thousands of utterly innocent men, women, and children.

The above-mentioned governments and the French National Committee condemn to the utmost these bestial methods of cold-blooded extermination. They declare that such incidents only harden the determination of all freedom-loving peoples to overthrow Hitler's barbarous tyranny. They reinforce their unshakable resolution not to allow those responsible for these crimes to escape punishment, and to expedite all requisite practical measures to this end.

This proclamation, which was read aloud to the Commons by Foreign Secretary Eden, was also published in the Swiss press.

Not long afterward, under the leadership of the Archbishops of York, Canterbury, and Wales, the Anglican bishops issued an appeal to the Allied and neutral powers in these words:

The bishops of the Church of England are deeply distressed by the government's statement of December 17, 1942, on the Jewish question. They confirm the fact the number of victims of this cold-blooded extermination runs into the hundreds of thousands. They further state that Hitler has adopted for the accomplishment of the goal outspokenly proclaimed by himself—the extermination

of the Jews—measures that mean the extinction of six million
Jewish human beings who exist today under Hitler's rule. The
bishops of England declare that the sufferings of these millions of
Jews and their condemnation to death impose an obligation of
humanity that no one can any longer evade. Rescue must be
provided without delay. The bishops believe that it is the duty of
the civilized nations, regardless whether Allied or neutral, to devote
all their energies to the provision of sanctuary for these victims.
Therefore they call on the British government to provide leadership
for the world by declaring its readiness, working in cooperation
with the Dominions and all Allied and neutral governments, to at
once establish havens for refugees in the territory of the British
Empire and anywhere else for all those who are threatened with
annihilation and are able to escape from the Axis countries, as well
as for those who have already fled, so that room can be made for
the others who thus far could not escape.

*Die Tat, Die Neue Zürcher Zeitung,* and other Swiss newspapers
reported the indignant address delivered by the Archbishop of York in
the House of Lords against the extermination of the Polish Jews. His
speech was described as one of the most moving ever made in the Lords.

The Labor Party issued a summons to the whole of civilized mankind
to "raise its voice against the bloodiest crime in the history of the world,
which has now begun with the extermination of the Jews in Europe." It
also called on the neutral nations and their Parliaments to lodge a
solemn protest in the name of humanity. (See Ludwig, pages 240–242.)

This call brought forth no echo at all from official Switzerland. In the
Federal Council, for example, no word was ever uttered in connection
with the Allies' proclamation of December 17. It was publicly stigma-
tized with the epithet of "atrocity stories."


## . . . Thrown Out Without a Hearing

A short time after these urgent appeals to the conscience of the world,
and only a few days after Christmas, the Police Section, acting in accord
with the Federal Council, issued new instructions to the border forces.
These were some of the provisions:

I. 1. Foreigners who are seized by border or police forces in illegal crossings of the frontier or in the immediate vicinity of the border are henceforth to be sent back across the frontier. . . . The term "vicinity of the border" for the purposes of this instruction means a belt approximately six to seven and a half miles deep along the frontier. For example, this includes the entire canton of Geneva, that part of the canton of Wallis west of Martigny (including that town), the Pruntrut peak, the entire canton of Schaffhausen, the Rhine valley in St. Gallen, etc.

2. Expulsion is to follow immediately and without exception, unless an interval of a few hours appears to be necessary because of the lateness of the hour, weather conditions, or the physical state of the refugees; when necessary the refugees are to be given such care as is possible in the circumstances.

*In every case precautions are to be taken so that refugees who must be sent back are prevented from having any communication, direct or indirect (specifically, by telephone), with anyone (relatives, friends, lawyers, diplomats, consulates, refugee organizations).*

3. The expulsion should be so carried out, in principle, that the refugee receives the opportunity to cross the border in the same fashion and, if at all possible, at the same place as the manner and place of his entry. When this is not feasible for technical reasons, the refugees are to be handed over to the border patrols on the other side of the frontier. The same procedure is to be followed even if the refugees resist being sent back after they have been warned that they will be turned over to the foreign border forces. In each case the refugee is to be warned that he will again be turned over to the foreign border forces if he attempts another illegal entry. . . .

II. 3. Refugees in flight solely on racial grounds are not to be regarded as political refugees within the meaning of these instructions. . . .

Following this ominous sentence, Section III provided that the police chief of the appropriate Territorial Commando should review all cases of refugees reported to him and submitted for his decision after prior arrest "by the border forces in conformity with Sections I and II," and that he should forthwith order the prisoners sent back. In addition, refugees who had made false representations on essential matters to him or to the border patrol, refused to answer questions, attempted to smuggle in money or other valuables, or in some other major respect behaved improperly were to be expelled forthwith. (See Ludwig, pages 229–232.)

These orders were strictly enforced. In January (1943), 460 refugees were admitted; in February, 857; in March, 818; in April, 662; in May, 612; in June, 616; in July, 708; in August and September, after the collapse of Fascism in Italy, the number of civilian refugees admitted rose to 903 and 4907 respectively.

The records of the Central Office for Refugee Assistance emphasized the fact that refugees who had already crossed the Swiss border were prevented from entering into communication with friends or relief organizations in Switzerland. Their expulsions were supposed to be carried out with as little publicity as possible. The officials of the Police Section were still suffering from the aftereffects of the storm of indignation in the summer of 1942. When the Central Office for Refugee Assistance held its meeting on March 1, 1943, Dr. Regina Kägi-Fuchsmann reported that even persons who held exit permits as "recognized political fugitives" had been thrown out. In violation of Federal Councilor von Steiger's express promise that refugees would be permitted to communicate by telephone with assistance organizations, the border forces prevented this.

Requests from the Swiss Central Office for Refugee Assistance that the refugee policy be eased in view of the unprecedented emergency, embodied in a letter of March 18, 1943, were denied, almost without exception by Federal Councilor von Steiger in a reply dated August 5. Apparently he persisted in the opinion that any concession would mean a catastrophe for the country. Rigor was the constant in his policy.

## Obvious Death

In January 1943 Julius Streicher published an article in *Der Stürmer* in which he said that Hitler's prophecy had now begun to be fulfilled and that world Jewry was about to be exterminated; he added that it was glorious to know that Hitler was liberating the world from its Jewish sufferings. In November of the same year Streicher quoted verbatim an article from *Das Israelitische Wochenblatt* of Zürich in which it was reported that the Jews were in truth disappearing from Europe, and he commented: "This is no Jewish lie."

Various Swiss newspapers, including *Das St.-Gallen Tagblatt* of January 21 and *Die Volksstimme* of the next day, printed the protest launched by the Catholic organization, the Poland Reborn Front, against the extermination of Polish Jews, which said:

> Inside the Warsaw ghetto, behind the walls that separate them from the rest of the world, thousands of miserable men and women are waiting for death. Their persecutors patrol the streets and fire at everyone who shows himself in the window of his home. The total number of victims has risen to between eight and ten thousand every day. The Jewish policemen are compelled to surrender the victims to their persecutors. If they refuse, they themselves are shot.

The protest then described details of the liquidation of the Warsaw ghetto, the forced evacuation of children, the reactions of their mothers, and the loading of the deportees into freight cars. Few of the persons shipped out by rail survived the journey. Many Jews, it was added, preferred a quicker death. For this reason all poisons in ghetto pharmacies had been confiscated. The only means of suicide left was to leap from a window. The number of Jews who availed themselves of this death was great. What was happening in Warsaw was only a repetition of what had been going on for six months in hundreds of small and large cities in Poland:

> Everyone must go into hiding, rich and poor, old and young, Catholics who die with the names of Jesus and Mary on their lips and orthodox Jews. . . . Everyone who comes from a Jewish family is condemned to death. The world watches all these crimes, worse than any to which history has hitherto testified, and the world keeps silence. The massacre of millions of defenseless persons goes forward in a doom-laden universal stillness. This silence can no longer be tolerated. Whatever the origin of it, it redounds to no one's honor. Therefore let us raise our voices as Catholics and Poles. We do not wish to follow the example of Pilate. We have no

means of preventing the massacre, we cannot help, we can rescue no one. But we can protest from the depths of our hearts, which are heavy with compassion, pain, and desperation.

On February 5, 1943, Dr. Regina Kägi-Fuchsmann made a speech before the Lyceum Club of Zürich on the refugee question. "It can be stated without contradiction," she declared, "that at least 90 per cent of those who are now trying to get into Switzerland will be sent back, even if they manage to remain in this country for a few days." She described in detail how the deportations in France were carried out. She added,

> Now you understand why people try to cross our borders, why, haunted by the fear of being deported, they risk the greatest of dangers in order to reach Switzerland, the land of asylum. What does deportation mean? We know only one thing: Whoever crosses the demarcation line [between Occupied and Unoccupied France] is swallowed up by night. No slightest word of such persons is ever heard again by us. . . . If one wishes to be honest and say exactly what happens to them, one can say only: We do not know, but we must conclude, from what we know from Theresienstadt, from the ghettos of Warsaw, Lublin, Cracow, etc., where the imprisoned Jews are shot by the tens of thousands, that sooner or later every deportation is the equivalent of a death sentence for those involved.

Exchange, a news agency, reported on February 14, 1943, that thoroughly reliable reports from the SS showed that entire ghettos had been liquidated in the cities of Warsaw, Lvov, Lodz, and several other places. It was feared in government circles that not one of the inhabitants had escaped. The latest confirmed information had made it clear that, of Poland's former Jewish population of 2.8 million, only six hundred fifty thousand were still alive. More than half of these survivors lived in restricted ghettos, the rest in labor camps, where they were subjected to a dreadful fate. "A ghastly catalogue is in preparation," Lord Selborne had told the House of Lords (*Die National-Zeitung*, Basel, February 15).

In his speech in the Berlin *Sportspalast* on February 19, Josef Goebbels once more dissipated the last doubt as to what was happening to the Jews:

We regard the Jews as an immediate peril to every country. How other peoples protect themselves against this danger is a matter of no concern to us. How we defend ourselves, however, is our own business, to which we will tolerate not the slightest objection. Jewry represents an infectious presence that contaminates everything. If our enemies abroad lodge sanctimonious protests against our anti-Jewish policy and shed revolting crocodile tears over our measures against Jewry, that cannot stop us from doing what it is necessary to do. In any event Germany has no intention of yielding to these menaces; on the contrary, she will oppose them in good time and, when ·necessary, with the most radical counter-measures. [*Die Frankfurter Zeitung*, February 20.]

"Deportation means the most brutal annihilation of the innocent," the annual report of the Swiss Labor Relief Agency for 1942–1943 declared.

## Report from Poland

Under the title, "The Modern Pogroms," *Der Aufbau* of Zürich published on March 19 an extraordinarily sensational report that had appeared two months earlier in *The National Review* in England and that was based on information provided by the Polish government in exile and the Polish National Council:

The following frightful report of unprecedented murder came from a German who had been confined in the extermination camp of Belzec. The camp is situated near the railway station and is completely surrounded by barbed-wire barricades. When a carload of Jews arrives, it is switched to a spur line that leads to the electrical execution place. The men are placed in a barracks on the right, the women in another on the left. There they are required to undress. "After they have stripped, both groups go into a third barracks, where there is an electrified platform. Here is where the executions are performed. The corpses are then taken by train to a grave . . . that is some hundred feet deep. This grave was dug by Jews who were subsequently executed without exception. The Ukrainians

who are on guard duty are likewise executed as soon as their job has
been completed."

The effect of these mass butcheries, from which there is no
escape, on the Jews themselves is described in an appendix to the
book issued by the Polish government. Its source was a Polish
policeman, who reported that the Jews were completely passive;
they were in a state of such thorough psychological disintegration
that they allowed themselves to be deported ahead of the scheduled
time simply in order to put a quicker end to their suffering. "Many
Jews went insane. . . . Children who were not strong enough to
walk were simply loaded into the cars. They were loaded in so
brutal a fashion that few of them were still alive when the train
reached the siding. Mothers went mad when they saw the hellish
spectacle. The number of those whose sanity was destroyed by
desperation and terror is quite as high as the number of those who
were shot. . . .

"Freight cars stand waiting on sidings. The brutes cram as many
as a hundred fifty persons into each. The floors of the cars are
thickly covered with chloride of lime, which has been washed down
with water. The car doors are sealed. Often the train leaves the
siding immediately it has been loaded; but equally often it remains
there for a few days. . . . No one pays any further attention to it.
Of all these people who are packed in so tightly that those who die
cannot even fall but remain standing shoulder to shoulder with the
living, these people who die lingeringly in the fumes of the chloride
of lime, without air, without water, without food, not one in any
event can hope to survive. Where and when at last the death trains
reach their destinations, their contents are only corpses. . . ."

The Polish government and the Polish National Council have
published this account because they hope that their report will
"arouse the conscience of the world." We too hope so.

In *Die apologetischen Blättern,* published by the Apologetics Institute of the Swiss Catholic People's Union, the following appeared on
April 12:

Archdiocese of Lvov. The German occupation is known by its
blood baths. In Lvov fifty thousand Jews are known to have been

killed, but Poles are not immune. The Jan Casimir University has been closed, as well as the seminary. The professors have been deported to an undisclosed destination. . . . In Vilna the Germans' persecutions are even worse than anywhere else (among other things, sixty thousand Jews have been killed).

## Questions to the Federal Council

On June 1, 1943, Dr. Eduard Koechlin, a Basel physician, posed a number of questions by letter to Federal Councilor von Steiger in connection with the orders issued on December 29, 1942. He wanted to know whether as a result of these orders a number of excluded refugees had not been killed in Germany; whether there was not a violent contradiction between these orders and the demands of many Christians in the preceding autumn, as well as the promises that were made at that time; whether it had not become possible to admit a much larger number of refugees; whether the position taken by Swiss authorities had not made us equally guilty; whether the definition of "political fugitive" had not been made too narrow; and whether Federal Councilor von Steiger was not prepared, in the light of these considerations, to revise his orders and grant asylum in Switzerland in the future to racial and political refugees alike.

Federal Councilor von Steiger wrote his reply on July 27. The Police Section's orders, which, moreover, had been submitted to the Federal Council, were intended primarily to guarantee the admission of those refugees whose return would create special hardship, persons who either must expect particularly severe persecution or, as a result of their lack of resources, had only the barest possiblity of somehow surviving. The Police Section's orders had been thoroughly thought through and were founded on the experiences of the preceding months. Since this was a matter of orders to and from experts, it should be no cause for surprise if they were not always properly understood in the circles of the uninitiate. As events had certainly shown, these orders served as a useful instrument to the border forces that had to execute them. "In practice the orders have thoroughly justified themselves."

By all means!

"What is of the first importance is not the problem whether this or

that category of refugees is to be treated as political refugees but rather
whether and in what numbers the Confederation can admit refugees in
general."

It was obvious, von Steiger continued, that at present no more
refugees could be allowed to cross the border than the daily rate already
established.

Dr. Koechlin published this exchange of letters in Der Aufbau of
August 6. He added:

> In the light of the fact that between two and three million Jews
> have been killed in Germany . . . , we regard the admission of
> eleven thousand refugees since last summer as a most inadequate
> rescue effort. If ten or twenty times as many had been admitted,
> then perhaps it might have been possible to speak of a sufficient
> sacrifice by the Swiss nation.

To this the publication's editors appended their own opinion:

> When anyone has managed, in spite of the innumerable hazards
> and snares that beset him in his flight, to reach the Swiss border, he
> has already experienced all the terrors of fear and desperation, and
> he has the right to expect that he will not be thrust back into the
> jaws of death by a state that makes so great a display of its
> humanitarianism.

Once more, too, the Basel clergymen, the Reverends Rudolf Schwarz
(in Die Arbeiterzeitung of June 17) and Samuel Dieterle (in Der
Aufbau of June 25) threw the light of truth on the fateful construction
of "political fugitive" by the Police Section, which was prejudicial to
precisely those persons most exposed to persecution and bodily harm.

> The whole policy of the Axis powers is based on the concept of race
> and looks on the elimination or extermination of the Jewish people
> as its most important task. . . . In the eyes of him who can see,
> therefore, the Jews are victims of a racial policy and hence they are
> collectively political fugitives. . . . Consequently this sentence in
> the orders ["Refugees on the grounds of race alone are not political
> fugitives within the meaning of these instructions" (and hence are

to be refused admission—author's note)] is in itself a repudiation
of a universally recognized fact and its intent is a dangerous accommodation to un-Swiss thinking. [From Rudolf Schwarz files.]

Dieterle raised questions.

. . . Now the Federal Council is in a position to issue a declaration
that the great mass of the victims of political persecution consists
of nonpolitical refugees! How can such a thing be proclaimed?
Perhaps because anti-Semitic sentiments have already erupted
among us? Or must we see in this, actually, the inception of a
certain racial legislation? Or is it merely no more than an exaggerated regard for the anti-Semitic power on the other side of the
frontier? Any one is as bad as any of the others!

In his reply to the Central Office for Refugee Assistance in August,
which has already been cited, Federal Councilor von Steiger refused the
requests for increased admissions of refugees with the implication that it
was impossible to guess from which direction a sudden torrent of
refugees might come and also with the observation that in fact our
capacity for assistance was not so great as we had been encouraged to
consider it by press reports and comments in August and September of
1942. On July 27 the southern border had once more been completely
sealed against all illegal immigrants.

From then until the beginning of 1944 such things as the incident
that follows could occur frequently. The source for this instance is a
letter sent on February 22, 1944, by the Association of Swiss Jewish
Refugee Agencies to the Evangelical Association for the Rescue of
Refugees:

A twenty-five-year-old man who had been engaged in refugee work
in Italy arrived at the Swiss frontier with his mother, who was
about fifty-five. Both were turned back with the explanation that
Switzerland did not have enough rice for its own people and
nobody needed foreigners in addition. A few days later, mother and
son tried again, and again they were turned back. When the
mother collapsed in an attack of nerves, the son's luggage was
seized and it and he were thrown into a ditch. Four customs guards

or soldiers laid hold on the mother in order to carry her back across the frontier. The result was that the mother went back alone. She did not know that her son had been arrested by the SS. Nothing is known as to his fate.

In a short time even more such cases may become known to you. We know that there are a great many border troopers who behave wholly admirably toward the refugees, but what is lacking is actually the order that in general, at least for the present, no more expulsions shall be made. Now only very few people can cross the western border because the French as well as the German supervision is unusually strict. Those persons who are sent back can expect an unimaginable fate. [From Dr. Vogt's records.]

Of course there were some refugees who were not so harshly treated. The Reverend Max Gerber wrote in *Der Aufbau* of January 28, 1944:

In the major debate on the treatment of refugees, Federal Councilor von Steiger at one time [when he was defending the expulsions] made the ominous remark that it must be borne in mind that in the course of time refugees of an undesired kind might begin pounding on our doors. The day seems now to have come. Some time ago Contessa Edda Ciano and former Minister Dino Alfieri requested asylum in Switzerland. They are being treated quite differently from the "undesirables." For such people there are no reception camps. They are not separated from their children. They sleep in soft beds. No one makes any difficulties for them over private accommodations.

The official announcement refers to the commandment of humanity, which forbids sending back those whose lives are in danger. This commandment of humanity is invoked for criminals such as these while thousands of innocent persons are sent back to certain death without a moment's ceremony. That is how things are with us.

## We Knew What Was Happening

On June 20, 1943, in a lead article, *Die Neue Zürcher Zeitung* took up once more *The Fate of the Jews in Poland:*

Hitler's and Goebbels' speeches leave no doubt that the road marked out for the deportees and the established Jewish population of Poland leads in one form or another to destruction and annihilation. . . . It is obvious, from a long series of dispatches and announcements over the past months and weeks, that the battle that the National Socialist system was waging against the Jews by means of outlawry, deportation, and imprisonment in ghettos has been accelerated in Poland and given the form of elimination by force.

On June 27 in Zürich the Jewish organizations held a widely observed demonstration of mourning. The Reverend Dr. Paul Vogt, Professor Oskar Farner, and the Reverend Ernst Hurter sent an outraged letter to be read at this ceremony, once more citing in detail the horrors of the deportations from Germany, France, The Netherlands, Rumania, and Greece, and adding: "We combat any resignation to these sufferings and any apathy in our Swiss fellow-citizens in the face of such need."

In *Armor Has No Fear* a letter was quoted from a soldier whose duty it was to accompany and guard the refugees aboard the horror trains: "From time to time, when my job gives me the chance, I have to go away a little in the silence and just howl out everything. What I see in front of me is too terrible."

In a fiery sermon in Thayngen on August 29, 1943 (it was not published until later), Dr. Vogt once more dealt in minute detail with the abominable events taking place on the borders of our country and in eastern Europe. "We shudder at the death of the Jewish people. But we shudder equally at so much coldness and cruelty and stubbornness among Christians, chilled to the freezing point." At the same time, as *Das Israelitische Wochenblatt* reported on September 3, he spoke before a regional branch of the National Independent Organization; his subject was the death trains to the east. On September 14 the Lyons correspondent of *Die Neue Zürcher Zeitung* sent his paper a long dispatch describing the shipment of foreign Jews from southern France to "labor service" in Germany, where a large number of them, if indeed not all, were exterminated.

At the end of September a number of Swiss newspapers, including *Die Arbeiterzeitung* of Basel, printed an Exchange dispatch from New York concerning an official memorandum—based on carefully compiled reports from the official German press, statements by the governments in exile, and reports from the occupied countries—that showed that, of the 8.3 million Jews who lived in Europe in 1933, five million had died by the end of August 1943.

The Church Synod of the canton of Zürich appealed to the Reformed population on October 22 and urgently stressed the sufferings of the Jewish people. *Die Neue Zürcher Zeitung* and other Swiss newspapers printed this Church Council document. On the occasion of the opening of the Zürich Church Synod in October, its president, Superior Judge Dr. Max Wolff, once again spoke of the extermination of the Jews of Germany.

On November 16 the Juna Agency distributed an appeal from the Social Studies Committee of the Swiss Reformed Pastors' Association that denounced the "monstrous attempt to exterminate entire races and peoples." The appeal continued:

> We therefore adjure all responsible persons in the whole world to save those who may still be saved. We call on the Swiss government, which maintains diplomatic relations with every government in the world, to develop a plan with them and with the International Red Cross. In the name of Jesus we call on our own officials not to send any more refugees back to death pending a definitive program but rather to offer them Christian asylum in the fullest measure.

Eyewitness reports from rescued victims and from Swiss citizens who had observed the ghastly occurrences in the ghettos were made public on November 18 at a press conference of the Central Office for Refugee Assistance under the chairmanship of Privy Councilor Robert Briner.

At the end of November the Central Office published a pamphlet, *Refugees in Grievous Need*, which contained a number of documented accounts as well as an eyewitness account of the uninterrupted succession of deportations in France and other occupied countries. There were descriptions of suicides of mothers with their children. The report pointed out that later children under sixteen were officially exempted from deportation provided that their parents voluntarily accepted separation from them. "What mother or father would not sign if she or he could save a child from certain death!"

But, the account continued,

. . . an hour later huge buses drove into the courtyard of the camp. Now the children were snatched out of their mothers' arms and piled into the buses. The engines began to roar. . . . Only now, it seemed, did the parents really understand. . . . As the buses slowly moved off with their children, their natural emotions overcame all rational considerations. The women screamed. Shrieking, they seized the wheels of the buses and tried frantically to stop them. But the horsepower of the engines was stronger than women and mothers. Women's and mothers' arms and hands were broken in the courtyard of the camp. But their hearts were so much more crushingly broken that they were not even aware of their broken members.

In the early morning the survivors of the camp were loaded aboard cattle cars. There were twenty-two such cars, forty persons in each. Then the sliding doors were closed. The train set out. It was as if twenty-two red iron coffins were rolling right through Europe. . . .

## A Twelve-Year-Old Girl's Story

"Shattering" is the only word for a twelve-year-old girl's story, which the Swiss Relief Agency for Emigrants' Children communicated to the Central Office for Refugee Assistance, which in turn made it public.

When Austria was occupied by foreign troops I was six years old. They came looking for us because they wanted to put my father in the concentration camp of Buchenwald. So Daddy fled to Belgium, and a month later we followed him there. We lived in Brussels until I was almost eight. When the war started we fled to France. In Toulouse we were unloaded from the cattle car in which we were traveling and we were taken to the camp at St.-Cyprien. Later we were transferred to Gurs. Daddy came too, but we were separated from him by barbed-wire fences. The camp was very dirty; we slept on the floor because rats were living in the straw. One time, in fact, a rat built a nest in our clothes. After eight months we had to go to another concentration camp. One evening all the people were called into the courtyard together and a man with a long list called out almost all the names and said that these people must get ready to go away the next morning. Almost everyone just collapsed in weakness. Mama was there too. It was awful the way she came into the room, weeping and completely weak. In the morning a big truck came and we were pushed into it. Daddy, who was loaded on it too, was weeping because he had hoped that Mama and I would be saved. That was the first time I ever saw Daddy weep. The other men looked like death too. We spent the night in a camp near Marseilles. In the morning we could hardly recognize one another because we were all swollen from bedbug bites. Our names were posted on a wall, and under them it said that we were going into our final deportation. Again many people collapsed. I had to go from one to another with water. I did this all day long. Later a number of children, including me, was taken away in a relief-agency truck. This was the worst thing in my whole life, because I knew I would never see Mama and Daddy again. First I was sent to a children's home in Savoy, and later a man showed me how to get to Annemasse. That was how I came to Switzerland, where at first I had to answer a lot of questions. Then I got into the children's home, and I'm very happy there.

James Schwarzenbach wrote in *Die Neue Zürcher Zeitung* of December 2: "The Jewish question has become a Jewish slaughter. There is no other word for this brutality, which has no precedent in all history. Shootings of hostages, deportations, forced labor, extermination, hatred. A battle of life and death. Without mercy. That is the reality of 1943."

On December 15 *Die Volksstimme* in St. Gallen and other Swiss newspapers published the dispatch of Paul Winterton, chief correspondent of *The News Chronicle* of London, from Kiev; it was distributed by Exchange. This report told how at the end of September 1941 all the Jews of Kiev—men, women, and children—had been rounded up by SS *Sonderkommandos* (Special Task Forces) and assembled near the city in groups of a thousand each, which were mowed down by massive machine-gun fire. In one day twenty-five thousand of the city's total of seventy thousand Jews were butchered. When the Russian forces approached in the beginning of August 1942, the Germans issued an order that the bodies were to be exhumed and burned. Winterton had found evidence that convinced him of the authenticity of the massacre.

Because of its publication of this dispatch *Die Volksstimme* was made the object of a public warning by the Press Office. The Press Inspection Division of the Press and Radio Section unanimously found the newspaper guilty of "furtherance of foreign propaganda. . . . This is a matter of foreign atrocity propaganda of the sorriest kind." On December 17 the Press and Radio Section sent a circular letter to the editors of all Swiss newspapers and the press officers of the Territorial Commandos, in which it referred to the fact that some newspapers had published Paul Winterton's story. They were therefore reminded that dispatches of this kind might be accepted only if they came from "reliable sources" and hence might be published only if they originated from "official sources." This was eight months after the Allies' statement on the German massacre of the Jews.

These are only a few of the many documents that appeared at this time in the most prominent and important newspapers of our country and that were also read over the radio. Federal Councilor Eduard von Steiger, however, wrote in his comment on Professor Ludwig's report:

The approximately four hundred Swiss newspapers . . . dealt only very occasionally with all news of military events, war atrocities, National Socialist and Fascist policies, reports of refugees' fates and the refugee problem. . . . As far as reports on events in the east were concerned, they did not in fact seem so worthy of credence as they deserved to be. The news of the declaration made to the House of Commons occupied hardly any great space in the Swiss newspapers and for the most part was barely noticed.

# The Manifesto of the Merciless

With all the precision that could be desired, the negative sentiment of pure defensiveness was expressed in November 1942, in a document entitled *Declaration on the Refugee Question*, published by the Fatherland Front. The Fatherland Front was brought into being in 1919 with the goal of "contributing to the preservation of the free and independent Swiss Confederation on the foundation of democracy and federalism and, among other things, with the purpose of combating spiritual and physical dangers that may emerge to threaten the life of the state and the people." The Front's membership included influential conservative leaders in industry, politics, and the higher military ranks. Some of them were men who certainly did not identify with the spirit of the 1942 *Declaration*. Unfortunately, however, they left the field open to the demagogues at the head of the Front. Federal Councilor von Steiger was also a member of the Fatherland Front. In the *Declaration*, which was submitted to the delegates' assembly on October 24–25, attention was first drawn to the gains made by the Front in its fight against anti-militarism and for national defense. Then came this:

## SUBMERSION BY REFUGEES IS A NATIONAL PERIL TO SWITZERLAND

This statement, the supporting evidence for which will follow, is not intended to impugn the *right of asylum* insofar as it is exercised as a right of the state in the spirit of the Swiss tradition, freely and independently as a duty of humanity, but not as a juridical obligation.

Humanity must not be placed above the national interest; for, just as a soldier's human feelings toward the enemy must be thrust into the background because that is required by the defense of the fatherland, so with respect to emigrants the human aspect of the question must be subordinated when higher national interests are at stake.

For the moment there is not yet any difficulty of food supplies, but the problem cuts much more deeply: Specifically, it is the question of inundation by foreigners, which in our present economic situation entails particularly severe political and cultural dangers.

Unfortunately, propaganda on behalf of aid to refugees and partisanship for emigrants deal exclusively with these hardly challengeable questions of humanity and food-supply capacities, without even discussing—consciously or unconsciously, that is beside the point—the economic, political, and cultural aspects of the problem.

What is specifically involved, therefore, is whether and to what extent those foreigners who in recent years and particularly in the past months have sought sanctuary in Switzerland can be tolerated by and also absorbed into the body of our nation without long-term harm to Swiss interests and without creating a tide among our people that will turn against those elements that are alien to it in spirit.

This capacity, on the basis of the experiences and observations available to us, has already been exceeded. Indeed, the *total of refugees who have entered our country* in the immediate past has risen in terrifying fashion. In 1938 a large influx entered from Austria, so that by the beginning of the war there were some seven thousand refugees in Switzerland.

Further immigration raised the total to eighty-three hundred at the beginning of August 1942, and in a few weeks in August and September—that is, up to September 22—this was increased to ninety-six hundred. By the middle of October the figure of thirteen thousand emigrants had been exceeded.

In addition to this, there is an uncalculated number of illegal immigrants, foreigners who have not yet registered as of today. That the number of "black" immigrants living in this country is high can reasonably be taken for granted in the light of previous experiences, because even in 1938, with the cooperation of certain political organizations, hundreds of refugees were harbored for months and years after having come in under false names and, as has only recently been confirmed, also used forged travel papers or arranged to have expired documents revalidated.

Hence it is high time that the responsible officials, and with them the entire Swiss nation, recognize the danger and come to grips with it before even greater damage is done and the refugee question gives birth to a catastrophe for our Fatherland.

*Various Comparisons*

The advocates of unlimited admission of refugees think back with nostalgia to the open arms with which Switzerland welcomed the Protestants driven out of France, the *Huguenots of the seventeenth century*, and the blessings that our land derived from them in abundance.

But one must ask oneself why a comparison is not made with those refugees who *a few decades ago* and then again since 1933 and 1938 crossed our borders, and who in their origins and their characteristics have much more in common with today's emigrants than with the Huguenots.

If comparisons are desired, however, it seems indeed essential to us to think back first of all to the period of the First World War, through which our generation lived, and to remember that at that time the emigrant, *Lenin, with his retinue* of Russian refugees, was living in Zürich and preparing the Russian revolution here, that a Radek-Sobelsohn was envisaged as the Soviet commissar for Switzerland, that only thanks to the vigilance of our authorities and the loyalty of our troops was it possible to prevent the overthrow planned with the support of emigrants and the creation of a Soviet Switzerland, and that again and always foreigners make themselves conspicious by such preparatory maneuvers, such for example as the organizer of the Young Students and the Socialist Youth, Münzenberg. Let it also be noted, moreover, that a whole array of political leaders was able to acquire Swiss citizenship and even win election to the National Council, and they made themselves prominent in not exactly desirable ways in the expected left-wing circles; and let it be noted too that a large number of newly naturalized lawyers behaved in discreditable ways. The Helphant-Parvus case, as well as the parts played by racketeers and usurers who came across our frontiers with nothing and soon emerged as owners of houses and businesses, should still be alive in the memories of many Swiss.

The fact that unpronounceable names from those days adorn our business directories and, unfortunately, in many places our voter lists as well, to the extent to which accommodating officials have not yet authorized changes in surnames—so that for instance a Madowsky becomes a Mandeau in the canton of Berne or a Mandoni in Grisons (official announcement in the Board of Trade publication, October 10, 1942)—should likewise open our eyes and inspire us to stand vigilant guard over our Swissness.

## The Necessity for Defense

In the light of these experiences during and after the First World War, the present commands us to be viligant and to avert threatening dangers from our country and our people.

*Our defense* lies in this, that the borders be completely closed and that this action be followed by the universal confinement of all refugees in the country, without exception, in camps.

We are well aware that such thoroughgoing measures entail great hardships for those affected. But our officials should not shrink

from their application if the lifeboat is not sooner or later to
founder in the vortex under its burden and go down with it.

*Either Or*

Should the war develop in one direction or another, even when
our country has been assured of its safety and of its food supply, the
inundation by foreigners that has already begun will become an
unbearable burden.

Either foreigners will dictate to us how we have to treat the
refugees, and as a result our right of self-determination, the country's national independence, and our honor must be lost, or else
those who scurry for asylum today will dictate and dominate after
the war because they are striving to fasten their grip on the body of
our people and our economy and to supplant the Swiss and Swissness.

*Concerning Economics*

It is of course hardly to be wished that similar conditions again
obtain as was the case after the other war. . . . Hence it should
neither now nor later come to pass that unwanted refugees infil-
trate themselves into our labor system, and it is also necessary to
prevent the possibility of unpaid labor, because such activity can
give rise to serious employment problems. If the emigrants must be
put to work—and they ought to be—this raises the question of
their employment in farm work, and of course there can be only a
very restricted scope in the area of the camps, from which the
entire requirements for the feeding of all the refugees ought to be
met without putting Switzerland under the obligation of special
thanks to them.

But, even if this type of occupation is put into effect, it should
not be forgot that at the same time the many "black" refugees—
that is, those who have not yet registered with the authorities—
must also work somehow in order to stay alive, and from time to
time this can lead to improprieties—exclusively economic in character, of course—that can be overcome and prevented only through
strict measures. The foregoing, moreover, applies equally in the
fullest measure to the academic professions, and there it seems to

be particularly undesirable that special efforts should be exerted in order to enable the young emigrants to pursue their educations in Swiss institutions of higher learning; the obvious consequence of this would be a further oversaturation of the academic professions, and furthermore this would not be restricted at all to the economic domain. To be specific, it is very gravely to be feared that *in the realm of culture* too—first of all, naturally, in academic circles, but then spreading into everything—an influx of refugees would wreak harm that could not be prevented if we were unsuccessful in averting the danger in time.

In every respect, then, the refugees are totally alien in spirit to our nation. They do not speak its language, nor do they follow its customs and usages, and in many ways of thinking and expressing themselves they deviate from our ways. Their assimilation, however, cannot be expected in the light of all our prior experience, but rather, at best, some adaptation for the sake of material advantages or because it is required by legal prescriptions. As long as the contamination of our body politic can be avoided by preventing further immigration and, in particular, illegal residence, these considerations can take a somewhat secondary rank. They are all the more legitimate, however, when direct cultural influence is exercised by circles that are already busy in the press or otherwise—as writers, in the theater, in the cabarets, in film, and in radio—or even working as teachers of children or as professors in the higher institutions, as well as writing Swiss history, as for example in the case of Valentin Gitermann, who is teaching in the girls' upper school in Zürich and who, in spite of his Russian origin (he was naturalized here in 1929 as a former stateless person), has published a history of Switzerland with a character of its own. When one contemplates such possibilities it is certainly not an exaggeration to regard the saturation of Switzerland with refugees as a peril to the country, and surely therefore in this respect too there is sufficient reason to be on guard and apply measures before the situation gets out of our control. In view of the bitter experiences with emigrants and unwanted foreigners that I have mentioned and that accomplished their pernicious effects in Switzerland during and after the First World War, it is imperative to come back once more with special emphasis to the *political aspect* of the refugee question.

Without any desire to launch a fresh discussion of foreign policy, let it be pointed out in this connection merely that it appears at least noteworthy how unimpededly, in actuality, the thousands of refugees were able to leave their homelands and swarm across our borders, so that there is good reason to ask on what grounds flight to Switzerland was more or less encouraged.

But we are far more concerned with the fact that, even in the great flood of refugees from Austria in 1938, flight to Switzerland was particularly fostered by Marxist quarters. Not only were support provided and hideouts furnished at that time through the Communists' Red Relief under the pretext of political activity, so that hundreds of emigrants were able to reside in this country under false names or aliases, some of them "black" until very recently; in addition, it can be proved that provision was made by official Socialist quarters, through the cooperation of public officials who were members of the Socialist Party, not only to prevent the exclusion of refugees at the border but to enable them to proceed at once to the interior of the country.

It is equally demonstrable that, under the leadership of emigrants, political-education courses were established, that even the Chancellery of Protestant Churches sponsored lectures by emigrant women who made insulting references to other countries, that political tracts were written and distributed that not only dealt with foreign affairs but also were critical of our officials. Only recently, however, was it also confirmed that emigrants were writing political articles for the Swiss press that are not in the best interests of our country, and that—in so-called closed meetings, to be sure— distrust of the Federal Council was expressed by unassimilated elements who accused it of having neglected the spiritual defense of the country. These are facts that should not be omitted from the complete picture of the situation. And, finally, it would be dangerous to overlook the fact that even in the refugee camps political activity has been initiated that is extended during the refugees' leaves from the camps and whose illegal machinations have brought it to the attention of certain Swiss organizations.

*What Does the Total Picture Teach Us?*

When one analyzes and weighs the range and significance of all these experiences and points of view, one is compelled to the logical conclusion that, even if one wished to avoid generalization, an overall picture takes shape that gives rise to justified apprehension.

But, when one recognizes the dangers, which are growing greater daily, it follows that they must be averted by all the means at our command, for we wish no inundation by foreigners from whom our nation and our people can expect only spiritual and material misfortune.

In addition, however, we wish through timely steps to prevent the refugee question from being the source of a Jewish question, which would inevitably further the interests of those whose policy is fundamentally based on such a question and which would lead to the end of our existence as a democratic-federalist state.

To the populace and the authorities of the entire Confederation, to all who love our homeland and wish to preserve it free and independent but also firmly rooted in the soul and spirit of our ancestors for a better future, therefore, we address this clarification dictated by our concern for our Fatherland.

*Our Requests*

We appeal to our readers to stand with us in demanding that the frontiers of our land be more tightly closed,

that all emigrants who have entered "black" be required to register with the authorities under the penalty of expulsion for violation of such requirement,

that all emigrants everywhere in the country who lack personal reputation and financial means or personal sponsorship be placed in special camps without permission to leave them, as is currently granted, until their final departure from Switzerland,

that emigrants be required to perform joint labor in the national interests,

that, if required for the validation of the appropriate legislation, foreigners entering as refugees be forbidden at any time to obtain residence or settlement permits in Switzerland and also that they be excluded from naturalization; and that those already naturalized be forbidden to change their names; and that the re-emigration of refugees be furthered with all available means.

Fellow-citizens! We count on your comprehension and your support, because only through them can the economic, cultural, and political perils with which the influx of refugees threatens our country be dammed and eliminated.

The *Declaration* was followed by *Dispassionate Conclusions on the Emigrant Question*, which included the following:

At one time Geneva granted asylum to many thousands of Huguenots because those Huguenots cherished a fanatical love for the same religion and the same ideas. Today we must once more state that there is not the slightest ideological bond to link us with the emigrants who flee to our borders. What we feel for them is only sympathy.

Never yet has a healthy, life-loving people done more out of sympathy than was permitted by the interests of the state and the people. Sympathy ought never to permit a surrender of ourselves or a rash endangering of our people and our state.

Many who assert that they are not in sympathy with Switzerland's refugee policy because they profess to think and feel as persons of great generosity, prepared to sacrifice, criticize the Federal Council and its policy only because they seek to undermine its authority, divide our people, create perils for our country, and fish in troubled waters. What interests them is not the emigrants but their own policy that menaces our country.

In our country it is customary to say nothing when one is in agreement with the government's policy. Today, when clamorous opposition groups pretend that the Federal Council is adopting a position on the emigrant question that is contrary to that of the majority of the Swiss people, it must be loudly proclaimed that this is not true and that our people understands and approves the Federal Council's position.

The Swiss Fatherland Front's *Declaration* was distributed to the nation's newspapers, a number of members of the National Council and the Council of States, and other prominent figures, as well as cantonal and communal officials.

The document is its own commentary. This was an unequivocal appeal to the "anti-Semite in us," to envy, malice, hatred of the Jews. This was consequently an anti-human philosophy wrapped in the flag of the Fatherland and in that other symbol of Switzerland, the Red Cross. And this in the very moment when a horribly oppressed minority was being handed over defenseless to a government of murderers. These were shabby heroes who with the stance of patriots vented their spite on the emigrants under the wing of the Third Reich.

What an honorable ring there was in those days to such names as "Union of Loyal Patriots," "Federation of Socialist Workers' Party," "Union for Nation and Homeland," "National Movement," "National Assembly," and what smugness in such newspaper titles as *Swiss People*, *National Notes*, and the rest. They had as little to do with the Confederation's democracy as the concept of people's democracy has to do with a freedom-loving state.

## The Echo

The Fatherland Front's *Declaration* did not go unanswered. Dr. Arthur Frey, the director of the Evangelical Press Service, wrote:

> The manifesto of the Swiss Fatherland Front was dictated less by concern for our country than by a much more intense and unequivocal anti-Semitism. As Christians we must combat this anti-Semitism frankly and resolutely, and urgently bid the Christian Swiss people not to follow the Swiss Fatherland Front along this false and evil road. . . .
>
> If the Swiss Fatherland Front wants to frighten our people out of its duty to the refugees, the poorest of the poor, and hold up the refugees as a menace to our country, then we cannot avoid the impression that the Swiss Fatherland Front is trying to divert our people's attention from the real danger that threatens our country. It is obvious enough from the large number of treason trials where the real threat to our country lies. If it were the business of the Swiss Fatherland Front to protect our country against perils, then it

would be obliged above all else to warn against those movements that maintain ideological relations with the traitors. The Swiss Fatherland Front, however, does not regard this as its mission; it would prefer to stigmatize as a danger to our country those who are already the victims of that unholy spirit! This state of affairs should make it sufficiently clear to the Swiss people what is to be made of the Swiss Fatherland Front's *Declaration*.

Federal Councilor Eduard von Steiger evaluated the Fatherland Front's *Declaration on the Refugee Question* quite differently. In his answer to a brief interrogatory submitted on December 9 by National Councilor Jacques Schmid, a Social Democrat of Solothurn, von Steiger discussed the pamphlet, saying:

> In recent months the refugee question has been actively discussed in the press and in meetings. In both areas there has been sharp criticism of the authorities' measures for the stoppage of an unending and uncontrolled influx of refugees, as well as attacks on the temporary internment of the refugees in reception camps. Very often these critics have overshot their targets. . . . It was inevitable that other voices would be raised against these protests.
>
> The Swiss Fatherland Front's *Declaration on the Refugee Question* of November 1942 is familiar to the Federal Council. It is unquestionably the product of concern for the preservation of a free and independent Confederation.
>
> In the opinion of the Federal Council, any vigorous espousal of position in public for or against the refugees is out of place.

With all due regard for freedom of expression, von Steiger added, this view had been brought to the attention of the Swiss Fatherland Front. "On the other hand," he continued, "it should not be forgotten that excessive activity on the part of those very persons who champion the refugees, and in part as well the behavior of certain refugees themselves, can evoke a hostile reaction and indeed even lead to consequences."

Various newspapers gave space to the Fatherland Front's *Declaration*. It was hailed by *Die Neue Glarner Zeitung*, for example, with editorial comment:

> We must bear in mind not only the refugees' entry but also their return home—in other words, what our situation will be in the

event that some of them remain here, and indeed probably most of them: the businessmen, those whose financial means have enabled them to buy a partnership somewhere or who have acquired our nationality with solid cash. Above all we are thinking of *the Jews*, to whom it makes no difference where they settle down. . . . The Jew's basic attitude makes him a corrosive element. We have in mind especially those Jews who go into politics, as well as the journalists, the editors, the poets, the theatrical directors, the film people, all of whom have put down roots in the economy and are repugnant to our Swiss customs. So now it is time for us to protect ourselves. For after the war a great deal that is unhealthy and sick will come to the surface again; there will be new tides directed against our national entity; perhaps it will come to major political conflict. If we have at that time an active class of Jewish emigrants, even, perhaps, enjoying the protection of major political leaders, would that not create a grievous burden on our existence as a state? in other words, would not their mentality, as vastly different from ours as it is, still further enlarge the schism among Swiss that already exists, would it not naturally lead to venomous, personal, unbridled conflicts? Is it not reasonable to anticipate their influence in the newspapers, the films, and the theater, an influence that would be comparable in its effects to what the Weimar Republic and the French Third Republic had to suffer to the limits of their capacity?

"In certain parts of the country," the Swiss Central Office for Refugee Assistance said in its *Bulletin No. 11 to Cantonal Committees* in the autumn of 1942, "rumors are being circulated that refugees have found jobs in the federal government and are taking the bread out of Swiss mouths, or that bread and milk are about to be rationed as a result of the mass influx of refugees."

In actuality the Fatherland Front lodged a formal complaint against the Reverend Dr. Paul Vogt with the Zürich Church Synod because of his appeal for contributions for bread for refugees. The president and the secretary of the Front appeared at the formal hearing, where the secretary testified, in a long-winded statement, that refugees were a national threat to Switzerland and that they were literally getting more food than the Swiss soldiers on the border!

No means, not even outright lying, was too low for the "sound,

upright, decent" patriots when it was a question of arousing the populace against the refugees.

A year later the Federal Office for War Economy declared:

> We are now harboring approximately sixty-two thousand refugees,
> who are naturally costing the Confederation a great deal of money;
> the refugee total, however, represents only 1.5 per cent of our
> population, so that the care of these unfortunate victims of the war
> does not really create much of a burden for us if one remembers
> that the food supply for our people should still be reckoned as more
> than adequate. Our present rations are larger than those of most of
> the belligerent nations and occupied countries. Should we not pay
> for the blessing of peace with a modest sacrifice? [Ludwig, page
> 221.]

The same bulletin also said:

> In the first half of this week [the end of October 1942], two large
> newspapers in St. Gallen published an anonymous advertisement,
> paid for by the St. Gallen section of the Fatherland Front, that
> called on the people of the canton to support the winter-relief
> drive, miners' relief, etc., and added: "These are more valuable and
> deserving tasks for the Swiss people than the support of interna-
> tional, unwanted elements of dubious convictions. Let us remem-
> ber 1918."

In its fifteenth bulletin on November 30 the Swiss Central Office for
Refugee Assistance asserted that the Fatherland Front was supplying
the press with both long and short articles in which its previous conten-
tions were elaborated. The Front also summoned its followers to attack
the refugees in letters to the newspapers. "Hence we have to deal with
an organized propaganda campaign," the bulletin said. (Later, at the
end of 1945, the Fatherland Front's anti-Semitism became the subject
of judicial notice. Hans Schwarz, a journalist, had published an article
in Die Nation accusing the Front of anti-Semitism and propaganda
against refugees and Jews. The secretary of the Fatherland Front filed a
lawsuit, the dismissal of which was upheld by the First Civil Section of
the Superior Court of Berne, even though, objectively, there was no

question that the charges were damaging. "It must be recognized," the court said, "that the Front's attitude was described as anti-Semitic because this adjective embraces all gradations of anti-Jewish thinking, including the Front's . . .")

It should not be surprising that the Swiss Press Service joined the *Declaration* battle and distributed articles attacking "undesirable elements" to the two hundred fifty newspapers that subscribed to it and that printed a large number of the articles; nor should it be any more surprising that, after a four-month suppression, *Die Front* resumed publication and lent a powerful hand.

On November 27, 1942, *Die Innerschweizer Bauernzeitung* made the Fatherland Front's appeal its lead story and commented editorially: "If indeed further efforts should be made to stigmatize every criticism of the presence of refugees among us as a sin against humanity, this could easily bring about the creation of a movement that should not be very welcome either to the emigrants or to those who now play the part of their special protectors."

Earlier, on October 20, H. M., a constitutional lawyer, had contributed "Switzerland's Right of Asylum" to *Die Neue Zürcher Nachrichten*, advancing a conveniently contrived thesis:

> In this connection it must also be remembered that very often in the past streams of refugees have flowed into Switzerland, refugees who already had something in common with the Swiss, whether it be religion, as in the case of the Huguenots, or political convictions, as in the case of the German refugees of 1848. Today, however, Switzerland is getting many refugees who are utterly alien to us and thus unassimilable, and whose permanent *settlement* among us is *absolutely undesirable*. It is not unjust to point out here, for example, that the great influx of Jews can one day give rise to a Jewish question for Switzerland too, with all its unhappy consequences.

## The Refugees Are Guilty

Before some thousand persons from central Switzerland attending a farmers' fair in Muri (Aargau), Dr. Eugen Bircher, a divisional colonel, physician, National Councilor, and director of the Fatherland Front, returned to the refugee problem. He said,

> In connection with such manifestations, the refugee question is to be pointed to as a major danger. There are already thirteen thousand who have crossed our border. Obviously one can be sympathetic toward them. But in 1917–1918 the same elements tried to turn our nation upside down. And again today inflammatory articles are already appearing in certain newspapers. The emigrants want to acquire an economic grip for themselves among us. We will not permit any more of them. They will scatter their poison. They constitute a foreign body in the nation that must be rooted out.
>
> Currently a relief drive for the emigrants is under way. But have people of this kind ever done anything at all for our poor miners, for our winter relief, etc.? We have already gone so far that soldiers have to clear out of their good barracks to make room for the emigrants. Yes, indeed, they get double rations of meat, butter, etc. Is this right? These people bring us lice that we cannot use. So now it is time to be tough.

Eugen Bircher, the fire-eater, had run away with Eugen Bircher, the physician, whose first duty was to save men's lives.

In the National Independence Day edition of *Das Aargauer Tagblatt* in 1941 he had published a long article, "Contemplation and Outlook," in which he addressed himself forcefully to the Swiss conscience and called on his compatriots to do justice to the reality of the "new era" that was beating with all its strength on the gates of our ancient and honorable national being. He had been especially disturbed by freedom of the press:

"Loud-mouthed nonsense, spattering the sublime with mud, suspicion, boastfulness, self-glorification—these today are the language of intellectual contention. No summons to men's higher inner values, only the appeal to the lowest instincts is supposed to bring us out of these difficult times!"

Obviously part of the "summons to men's higher inner values" was propaganda against the refugees: "It is impossible to deny that for all these miseries very many—in the nature of things, not all—emigrants,

with their coffee-house intellectualism, their biased, pathological, but
nonetheless unpardonable busy-bodying in their erroneous appraisal of
the situation, are guilty; they have abused the privileges of a guest and
thereby damaged the host country."

Bircher's admiration went out to "the venerable Marshal Pétain,"
who had laid bare the "deep-lying reasons" for the French collapse
"with complete candor, which would also be useful for us." Among
these basic causes, according to Bircher, was the "decline in the desire
for large families, particularly in the upper classes."

Bircher had his own interpretation of democracy. He called for a
"toughening of the people" and the abolition of those outmoded usages
of which the Federal Council had spoken in June 1940: "It is time to
prepare ourselves, with clear vision and strong will, so that we shall be
armed and capable of taking an active part in a new order in Europe.
We can wait no longer; instead it is time to go over to deeds. . . ." The
deeds that he envisaged? "The leadership of the state will be reinforced.
Parliamentarianism, the National Council will be reorganized as a
professional order. The Council of States will be revised. The honor and
worth of the individual will be guaranteed, an end will be made to
disturbances of the public peace. The criterion of quantity will be
replaced by the criterion of quality."

And furthermore: "Absolute neutrality in international affairs will be
maintained, and irresponsible demagogues will be brought to book."
Bircher's democracy could be "authoritarian, yes, even aristocratic. Both
forms are in full harmony with the true essence of democracy."

These excerpts are taken from *Die Schweiz vor neuen Aufgaben*
(*Switzerland Faces New Tasks*), published (without a date) in 1942 by
Polygraphischer Verlag AG, Zürich.


## The Devils' Chorus

On March 15, 1943, *Der Morgen* of Olten carried an article saying:

In the past as in the present the Jews have so abundantly and
unashamedly, insolently and unjustly, spread themselves at the
expense of Christians over all the key positions in private and
public life, in the economy, the press, literature, the theater, poli-

tics, that it has become an act of the most elementary self-preservation to hold them back and prevent them from exploiting their insolence. Jewry itself is responsible for anti-Semitism. . . .

In a variety of ways the thousands of Jewish immigrants represent tremendous dangers to our people and our country. The gravity of our supply situation is known to every one of us. Where in the beginning the refugee was content and thankful, very soon he reveals his drive for freedom and the relaxation of the laws. The sly, crafty Jew tries to reach his desired goal by side roads and back doors. Hence we understand the strict military supervision of these foreigners. Every exit is closed to them without a military escort. Outgoing and incoming mails are rigorously watched. . . . The most meticulous supervision of the Jews, punctilious observance of our military ordinances, the tightest border control: These are the order of the day. . . .

The Pharisee said: "God, I thank thee that I am not as other men are, extortioners, unjust, adulterers, or even as this publican." Thus it is written in the Gospel According to St. Luke, 18:9. *Der Demokrat* of April 21, 1943, treated its readers to this:

But, when I saw these mostly "intellectual" refugees, the majority of whom consists of Jews of various nationalities, busy with root stocks or potato peelings, when I watched a writer pushing a hoe here and a professor working with a kitchen knife there, I could hardly suppress a heretical delight. Is not this "back to nature," this enforced return to the simple, basic things of life that necessary school of experience that was lacking in European education, to its own undoing?

"Love ye therefore the stranger," the Lord commanded (Deuteronomy, 10:19). And the Reverend Dr. Vogt reiterated the commandment in one of his sermons at this period:

And a chorus of devils all round responds with a thundering *No!* . . . And they do not see that in this very rebellion of their wills against God's will they are digging the mass graves, and driving the deportation trains with their tragic human freight, and building the concentration camps, and earning the guilt for the five million Jews who have died in Europe.

These were strong words for a Swiss Protestant clergyman. But were they exaggerated?

A Swiss wrote to Dr. Vogt: "I will certainly have to stop contributing to the refugee fund if one centime of it goes to help Jewish refugees!" Dr. Vogt remarked that "anonymous and other letters complain in every possible tone about the foreigners, who are so completely different, so much more wicked, so much more immoral, so much more unpleasant, so much more uncongenial."

The letters contained such things as these: "Are you really not ashamed to place us Swiss Protestants in the second rank and in general merely use us as your tools and always and only stir us up? Sure, we know very well that you are very richly paid for your Jewish propaganda!" Or: "Send me a child, please. But it must not be a Jew child. A Jew child I won't accept." Or: "As much as I abominate Hitler and the methods by which he rids himself of the Jews, I wholly and completely accept his basic idea that the Jews have created misery." The annual report of the Evangelical relief agency contained this account:

> It was learned that a pastor sought out those members of his community who were willing to accept refugees in their homes, and then urged them not to do so. He predicted that the refugees would make problems for the community. It was also disclosed that an alderman forbade the admission of any refugees in his district because he wanted to be certain that all of them were safely herded together in camps without any risk of obligation toward the ill, the weak, and the infirm.

The report also observed:

> We must sorrowfully admit that our greatest disappointments in refugee work have come from precisely those religious persons on whom we thought that we could rely and from whom we expected patience and understanding. The police have received all kinds of complaints and accusations from religious circles with respect to the refugees. . . .
>
> "From the first minute when I saw the refugee come out of the railway car," a Christian woman said, "I found him unpleasant. . . ." A Jewish refugee reported: "The hand that I offered in conciliation was not taken." A member of a religious community

said: "A Christian who can live in peace with a Jew under the same roof is no true Christian." A nurse wrote of a Jewish couple with whom in the beginning she had been completely at one: "These crazy German Jews."

This was the Christianity of the Fatherland Front.

The October 1944 issue of *Armor Has No Fear* offered another example:

> Poison-spreading is the word for what was said by an official Independence Day speaker during a break in a card game in a hotel: "*Ach,* Hitler might at least have done a real favor for us Swiss if around 1940 he had demanded the expulsion of all the Jews from Switzerland. Switzerland would have had to give in at that time, and in this way all the Swiss and non-Swiss Jews would have been got rid of at one stroke." A refugee woman told how an official in a communal war-economy office had shoved a food-ration card at her with a sneer: "To think we still have to feed the Jews!" A clergyman who had offered to house a Jewish refugee found this notice on his door, signed by Swiss: "Please watch out for yourself, you dirty fraud. The same law ought to be made for you Jews in Switzerland as in Germany: 'Bury them alive.' "

# The Price of Humanity

The records of the privy councilor for the canton of Aargau for July 4, 1941, contain this proud statement:

> The canton of Aargau has no obligation whatsoever toward these foreign emigrants and therefore it is unnecessary for the canton to share in the expenses of their re-emigration. The cantonal Alien Police has made it its business from the start to keep penniless emigrants out of the canton's jurisdiction. In this way we have succeeded in saving money for the canton. At present there are only very few penniless emigrants in the canton's territory. But the re-emigration of emigrants with means is also being expedited so that our canton will not have to bear any great burden. [From Dr. Vogt's files.]

In August 1942, Dr. Vogt had launched the movement to provide sanctuary for refugees. When Privy Councilor Briner asked him how many more refugees the church was prepared to take in, he had said three hundred. It was a bold undertaking: the cost was 120 francs per month per refugee, or 432,000 francs per year in all; and it was followed in short order by offers not for three hundred but for four hundred refugees. But unfortunately these offers could not be taken up, because the legal and technical regulations of the Police Section, as a result of the cantons' hesitations, could not be issued until the spring of 1943. The cantons made difficulties because they either did not grant the necessary permits or demanded such high security bonds that in most instances these could not be found. The privy councilor of Thurgau, for instance, stated in his annual report to the Great Council:

> In 1941 a total of 142 permits was granted: 39 to deserters, 18 to emigrants, 57 to Jews, and 28 to other categories of foreigners without papers. The following security bonds were posted: 384,000 francs of cash deposits in commercial banks and 83,981.50 francs in savings accounts.

A total of 468,000 francs for 142 refugees!

When Dr. Vogt made an inquiry concerning a Dr. Heinrich Mayer, the cantonal Alien Police replied on October 17, 1942:

> In reference to the immigration application forwarded to us from your office, according to which Miss M. F., a teacher in Gebenstorf, offers to sponsor a refugee named Dr. Heinrich Mayer, we regret to have to inform you that such requests cannot be granted. Our country has reached the limit of its capacities and is already harboring too many foreign emigrants. The burden of refugees on Switzerland is disproportionately heavy and therefore the utmost caution in the issuance of entry permits has been ordered. . . . Hence we must reject the above-mentioned application on behalf of Dr. Heinrich Mayer. . . .

The town council of Gebenstorf had already approved the admission of Dr. Heinrich Mayer, refugee.

On November 1, 1942, the Reverend Dr. Paul Vogt wrote to the Reverend D. A. Koechlin of Basel, then president of the Swiss Church

Union, violently attacking the shameful haggling of the cantons over the admission of refugees:

> The cantons' bargain-driving in the matter of granting residence to refugees is growing constantly more disgraceful. . . . Places for them have already been found in sufficient number. The camps cannot be liquidated and these places cannot be taken as long as newly arriving refugees are prevented from regularizing their status in a canton of domicile. And this regularization can never be achieved if the cantons continue to refuse the applications. As a result, women, men, and children must remain in the reception camps, members of the same family often being distributed among various camps. This is a simply vile state of affairs and it is all related to the different cantons' refusals to grant permits. The refugees cannot be admitted to central Switzerland for military reasons. Zürich, however, refuses to accept all those who are thrown out. In spite of good harvests and the willingness of the populations there to accept refugees, Aargau and Thurgau are closed to refugees. What is to happen? Are we in Switzerland approaching the time of concentration camps? [From Dr. Vogt's files.]

## The Confederation's Business

The attitudes of many cantons were in complete harmony with the views of the Fatherland Front. On September 4, 1942, in a circular letter to police commissioners, the Federal Council asked them "whether and to what extent their cantons were willing to admit refugees, construct camps or prepare other facilities for their group existence, and assume a share in the monetary costs of maintaining the refugees." The police commissioners' replies, insofar as there were any, were not very encouraging to the federal authorities. One exception, as Dr. Rothmund informed the conference held on September 11–12, 1942, was the canton of Basel (city), which, in spite of the large number of prewar refugees whom it was still housing, stated its readiness to accept more individually and to reopen and enlarge a camp system for them. Zürich also pledged itself to construct a labor camp for fifty persons at its own expense, but, of course, only if the other cantons committed themselves to similar endeavors within their own jurisdictions. Freiburg announced that it could provide facilities for fifty persons if the Confederation assumed the expenses.

A certain degree of willingness, though of course with reservations, was manifested also by St. Gallen, Solothurn, Zug, and Appenzell-Innerrhoden. The other cantons either replied with resounding negatives or did not respond at all.

The same adverse reaction was produced by a second circular letter, containing specific questions, that was issued after the police commissioners' conference of September 11–12. By the end of 1942 fifteen cantons had answered. The ten others replied either too late or not at all.

Willingness to grant domiciliary permits for refugees—which were required for the occupation of the homes offered in the cantons—was expressed in isolated instances in which the support of the refugees was guaranteed. Almost all the cantons refused to assume any financial responsibilities.

One of the questions in the circular letter was: "How many refugees can you admit in your canton?" Berne evaded this question; Luzerne was prepared to accept fifty to sixty able-bodied men; Uri and Schwyz refused because of their geographical situation (fortifications); Basel (city) was prepared to accept refugees who had entered the canton and had family or other connections in Basel; Schaffhausen was willing provisionally to admit as many refugees as families or organizations could take in; Appenzell-Ausserrhoden would grant temporary domicile to approximately twenty-five refugees if it was absolutely necessary; Appenzell-Innerrhoden would take individuals; St. Gallen would admit new refugees only if all the other cantons agreed to accept an equal number of refugees and emigrants; Aargau would take only a limited number because of prevailing housing problems; Thurgau too would accept only very few, provided that they proved that they had close connections with persons in the canton; Ticino refused because as a border canton it was in no position to accept; Neuenburg was prepared to consider applications from individual refugees with favor if they were sponsored by Swiss citizens and bonds were posted for the applicants; Geneva did not wish to allow the number of refugees in its jurisdiction to mount beyond four hundred.

Another question asked whether the cantons were prepared to participate in the support of the refugees. Berne said no; Luzerne said that this was the Confederation's affair; Uri suggested that, to the extent that the Confederation did not meet the costs, they should be distributed among all the cantons equally; Schwyz was negative; Basel (city) found the question academic, since the refugees either had means of their own or were supported by individuals or relief organizations; Schaffhausen wanted the Confederation to assume the expenses or else allocate them among the cantons on the basis of size and economic potential; both Appenzells refused; St. Gallen, Aargau, and Thurgau also wanted to foist the monetary burden on to the Confederation; Ticino declared that it was absolutely incapable of contributing anything toward the costs; Neuenburg's reply was ambiguous, and Geneva did not wish to be burdened.

A third question dealt with the possibility of placing refugees in private families and making the required police checks. This drew varied replies from those cantons that answered. To the extent to which any of them saw any such possibility, it was also very limited. Police supervision would be possible only if the number of refugees was not too large. "No canton was ready to undertake any special activity at all on its own."

The question whether the cantons might be able to provide collective quarters for refugees revealed that the most to be hoped for in such facilities would be a capacity of six to seven hundred persons. Analysis of the replies compelled the recognition that only one such facility could be considered; anything else was out of the question. One canton, for example, objected to the creation of a military reception camp within its jurisdiction. Only Basel (city) was prepared under certain conditions to levy a special tax in order to provide cantonal financing for such quarters. All the other cantons contended that these costs too must be borne *in toto* by the Confederation.

By the deadline of December 10, 1942, the Police Section had listings of 448 homes for refugees, including 193 for children. The registrants' names were communicated to their respective cantons for investigation of their qualifications, accompanied by the question whether the canton was prepared to grant domiciliary permission. Up to the deadline this permission had been assured in four instances. In 14 others the registrants had been found to be unqualified, in 105 they were qualified. No answers had been received as to 325 others.

A few months later, when the question arose of adopting a position on the pilot draft of a final decision on the accommodation of the refugees, the response from the cantons was as unsatisfactory as before. In the police commissioners' conference of February 8, 1943, sixteen cantons reiterated their complete refusal to share in the costs and only seven expressed their willingness to participate: Glarus, Solothurn, Basel (city), Basel (region), Schaffhausen, St. Gallen, and Thurgau. All, however, emphasized their determination to accept no allocation of refugees—not even as internees—without prior approval by them in each individual case. (Abstracted from the report issued by the Police Section: *The Handling of Refugees in Switzerland During the Second World War and in the Immediate Post-War Period*, pages 61ff.)

The request of the Swiss Central Office for Refugee Assistance to Police Section on July 6, 1943, for permission to be more liberal in granting domiciliary and internment permits (except in Wallis and central Switzerland, which were out of consideration for military reasons) evoked an affirmative response from only eight cantons.

What friendly relations prevailed among the cantons of the federation when it came to the removal of the refugees could be seen from a report prepared for Professor Ludwig by the municipal police commissioner of Basel:

> Innumerable refugees have been moved into Basel. Very often they were simply deposited in the market square. For a long time it was the practice of the canton of X to expel refugees with the warning that, if they were still within the canton's borders after sunset, they would be arrested and handed over to the Germans at the border. Result: flight to Basel.

Equally informative was the letter that Police Commissioner Vodoz of Vaud wrote on December 23, 1942, to Federal Councilor von Steiger, urgently requesting the adoption of special measures to halt the constantly increasing flow of refugees from France:

> In the face of the substantial influx of refugees coming from France and entering the cantons of Vaud and Geneva, I find myself compelled to demand that you be good enough to take the requisite measures to prevent this flow from continuing.

The police forces that we have assigned to the frontier for security duty are overtaxed. At one point on the Vaud border, La Curé, thirty-one refugees entered today. If they are added to those who crossed at other places along the border, the total comes to about a hundred. For several days the rate of border crossings has been the same. In other words, this amounts to seven hundred refugees a week or twenty-eight hundred a month, which is intolerable and dangerous to the national security.

But it does no good if we reinforce our constabulary posts unless the instructions given to them by the federal authorities are revised from top to bottom. I therefore request that you modify in a more limiting sense the instructions given earlier to the frontier posts with reference to the categories of refugees whom we can allow to enter.

It may seem strange that so many refugees are coming to us from France when that country's border is now occupied by German troops along its whole common length with ours. Nevertheless this fact is understandable if it is true, as the conclusions of recent days have repeatedly indicated, that the German troops do not hinder clandestine crossings into our territory or at least close their eyes to them. This is a point to the importance of which it is certainly not necessary to draw your attention. [Ludwig, page 244.]

*Die Neue Zürcher Nachrichten* of September 11, 1942, was not so very wrong when it asserted:

There are cantons that in no circumstances permit the establishment of even temporary residence by emigrants who have registered in other cantons and received domicile there on the basis of the right of asylum. This is true even when such other cantons agree to take them back after the expiration of such temporary residence. . . . In this connection there have been really scandalous incidents. On this aspect of the matter, which is of the greatest significance and which was not at all considered in the latest discussions, we refrain from investigation on the pretext that these are individual cases. At the same time we ask everyone who is angered by the measures taken by the Federal Alien Police and who denounces its harshness and lack of comprehension to cooperate in eliminating the real cruelty and lack of understanding on the part of many officials; for this is a prerequisite to a better solution of the whole painful refugee problem.

## 650 Years After the Founding of the Swiss Confederation

This was how, one or two years after the 650th anniversary of the founding of the Confederation, the governing authorities of the nation and the cantons fulfilled the world-famous Swiss tradition of asylum in the spirit of the Fatherland Front's appeal.

At every possible opportunity—in the National Council, in lectures, in letters—Federal Councilor Eduard von Steiger cast doubt on the Swiss people's willingness to help. "The people's readiness to admit refugees, which manifested itself spontaneously last summer in many circles under the pressure of events abroad," he told the Central Office for Refugee Assistance on July 27, 1943, "has become noticeably less evident. . . . Of the approximately twelve hundred refugees recently listed as unable to work, not many more than a hundred twenty have thus far been provided with accommodations."

Unfortunately he never mentioned the frequently all too fraudulent difficulties that the federal and cantonal authorities created for the refugee-relief organizations, particularly in the matter of finding homes for the refugees, thus incidentally—and perhaps not always unintentionally—discouraging and eroding the spirit of helpfulness.

Unfortunately, too, an appeal from the Federal Council to the people for humanity, for help, for sacrifices on behalf of the persecuted was never once uttered during these sinister years of apocalyptic inhumanity. The guideline for official action and inaction was always and only that *sacro egoismo* expounded and espoused by Dr. Heinrich Walther of Lucerne in the National Council.

# The Jews Must Pay!

For a long time this was both the principle and the practice of Switzerland's refugee policy, in the federal government and in the cantons.

Georgine Gerhard, the self-sacrificing founder and director of the Relief Agency for Emigrant Children in Basel, has told me of a meeting of the Swiss Central Office for Refugee Assistance during the 1930s to which Rothmund had been invited. When he was informed that it was hoped that the Confederation might provide financial assistance for the endeavors of the relief organizations, Rothmund declared that the necessary funds must be found from private sources. To this he added: "If I had a check in my pocket for a hundred thousand francs from the Federal Council for your relief activities, I would keep that check in my pocket."

A press release on a conference of cantonal police commissioners on August 17, 1938, said: "Switzerland is prepared to admit the refugees from Austria *after* the Federation of Swiss Jewish Communities has assumed the obligation of paying the expenses of their maintenance, etc."

Answering a question in Parliament in December 1938, Dr. Johannes Baumann, President of the Confederation and also director of the Federal Justice and Police Department, said that, in accordance with its pledge, the Federation of Swiss Jewish Communities had assumed the responsibility for the refugees and was providing maintenance and care for some twenty-three to twenty-five hundred penniless Jewish refugees. The outlay for their food, clothing, housing, and medical care amounted to approximately 250,000 francs per month, which was provided by Swiss Jewry.

This meant a burden of three million francs a year for a religious minority that embraced somewhat more than ten thousand persons: in other words, about three hundred francs per person, including children, the aged, and women. No other sector of the population had to shoulder such a burden on behalf of refugees. Nor was any other sector expected to do so.

The Jews must pay! After all, these were "their" refugees, who were no concern of ours.

In a survey of the growth and activities of private Swiss aid to refugees, the Central Office for Refugee Assistance said on May 10, 1955:

> It must be emphasized here that the admission of this increased influx of refugees [after the annexation of Austria] to Switzerland and their temporary sojourn here were made possible, just as the hermetic sealing of our borders after the introduction of the visa requirement could be prevented, only because relief agencies and above all Jewish agencies undertook to assure the authorities that they would be supported. At the same time they had to exert every effort for the quickest possible re-emigration of individual refugees.

It was certainly understandable that the Swiss Jews assumed to a special degree the burden of the Jews persecuted by National Socialism. But the fact that for years the admission of these victims was made contingent almost exclusively on the Swiss Jews' ability to pay and willingness to sacrifice attested to a questionable way of thinking. It testified to a dilution of the concept of the right of asylum and revealed a highly sinister attitude when Dr. Rothmund said so often, as he had even in Evian in 1938, that Switzerland ought not to admit too many refugees because they would overtax the financial capabilities of the Swiss Jews!

When Dr. Rothmund was asked, at a meeting of the Swiss Central Office for Reguee Assistance on March 4, 1940, what was to become of the newly impoverished refugees, he replied that the Confederation would be forced into extravagances if it began to help. "The burden of supporting the newly impoverished refugees," he said, "must be imposed on the people who brought them here." They had sown human kindness, so let them now reap it.

Not until the summer of 1942, when the entire burden of the care, control, and maintenance of the refugees could no longer be borne by the Jewish and non-Jewish relief organizations alone, did the Confederation make up its mind to take over the responsibility for quarters for the refugees.

Then too the cantons refused to take any part.

# The Millstones

The official attitude toward those emigrants and refugees who were admitted was, as we already know, inordinately cool and callous. They were the unwanted. They were—the word stood black on white in official documents—tolerated. Where peace and quiet at home and an undisturbed daily routine are the highest ideals, foreigners who unintentionally, merely by reason of their presence, unsettle the well-ordered pace of life can be only a burden. All too many officials' minds lacked the imaginative capacity to recognize the human destiny that lay behind each "case remanded and closed." All that mattered was to be tough. Making life in Switzerland so miserable for the refugees that they would leave of their own volition was a widely favored method of getting rid of them as rapidly as possible.

The term *emigrant* was reserved for those who had found asylum in

Switzerland before October 17, 1939. In the official meaning of the word, all those who entered after that date were *refugees*.

These were the restrictions imposed on emigrants and refugees alike: They must abstain from political activity and not disturb the policy of neutrality; they must obtain official permission to engage in any kind of economic activity and to leave their official places of residence for any purpose; those interned in private homes must report periodically to the police; they were subject to a house curfew between ten o'clock at night and seven o'clock in the morning; they were forbidden to go to bars and dance halls; they must obtain official permission for any public utterance, such as lectures, newspaper articles, publication of books.

The cantons had to concern themselves only with those refugees interned in private homes; the refugees interned in camps were the responsibility of the Confederation.

These were the rules under which the everyday practice went on. Their inspiration was the mentality of the Police Section. They were applied by human beings, dependable functionaries who performed their duties exemplarily—and to the letter. Behind the desks of the federal, cantonal, and communal functionaries sat men who had families, who were good fathers, who on Saturdays went fishing or tended their garden plots, who played cards every week, who were members of choral societies or bowling clubs. From eight in the morning until noon and from two until six in the afternoon they had to decide cases within the scope of the instructions given to them. Many of them knew the conflict between heart and reason. Others were spared the temptations to human decency. They were citizens of this nation, men of utter honor and rectitude. Their papers were in order. They were no burden to anyone.

In front of their desks stood the others—the stateless, the banished, the outlawed, the downtrodden. Their papers were not in order. They did not enjoy "normal relations" with the governments of their countries.

Between the two sides of a desk there was a distance of a yard—and yet the men on either side were worlds apart.

## The Minor Anguish

We should like to try to depict for a moment what could ensue in the nation of Switzerland from a "minor anguish."

There were, for instance, Julius and Berta J, whose case was favorably decided only after long-drawn-out protests. The wife was born in 1880 in Zürich, where her parents had lived since 1878. In 1888 her family moved to Basel. In 1900 the family went back to Germany. But the country of her childhood was Switzerland. The husband, born in Germany in 1883, worked in a shop in Freiburg im Breisgau. He served with distinction in the First World War. In 1937 he and his wife were put out into the street. Their daughter married in Zürich and was naturalized. Both she and her husband worked. Though they were not rich, they lived quite comfortably.

In Germany Mr. and Mrs. J were in danger. They were deprived of every means of survival. On April 7, 1937, they went to their daughter in Switzerland: an uncle of Mrs. J lived in Adliswil. So they had close ties with the country in which they had often spent their vacations.

When their residence permit expired at the end of April 1938 they moved on May 13 to Liechtenstein. After three months—so the Alien Police had assured them—they would be permitted to reenter Switzerland.

On May 30 their lawyer filed a petition for a new residence permit. On July 13, exactly three months after their departure, they went back to their daughter in Zürich, relying on the assurance given to them by the Alien Police.

Two days later the lawyer was advised of the decision on the petition that he had filed on May 30: Denied. Immigration forbidden before July 12, 1940. Grounds: too many foreigners and poor-law considerations.

The J's returned to Liechtenstein, where they had to live in a boardinghouse.

On August 12, 1938, their lawyer appealed the refusal of the petition. He offered to post a bond of ten thousand francs in order to satisfy the "requirements of the poor-law." At the same time the daughter filed a petition for an entry permit to be granted when the bond had been posted.

In November 1938 the J's were expelled from Liechtenstein. On November 18 they arrived in Zürich. They registered with the Alien Police three days later and were granted permission to remain in the city for ten days.

Four days later the bond of ten thousand francs was posted. The municipal and cantonal Alien Police recommended the issuance of the residence permit.

On December 7 the lawyer's appeal was dismissed. That did not matter, however, he thought, inasmuch as in the meantime the municipal and cantonal Alien Police had forwarded their recommendations to Berne.

On January 12, 1939, he himself filed a new petition with the Federal Alien Police in Berne. This required the J's to disappear again into Liechtenstein for two or three weeks. They left Switzerland on January 15 but were immediately sent back from Liechtenstein. Now they had to wait in Zürich for Berne's decision.

The lawyer's petition said: "In extraordinary times, . . . when thousands of people must try to enter our country in order merely to protect life and limb, such considerations [excess of foreigners] must be waived, especially when a Swiss citizen wishes to fulfill his family obligations by accepting such refugees."

The Federal Justice and Police Department's decision said: "The governing point of view . . . is that of population policy. The contention that the inundation of our country by foreigners cannot prevent the readmission of the petitioners is invalid. . . . The excessive foreign population of our country [some seven thousand persons] compels the Federal Alien Police to oppose any further immigration by foreigners."

A letter from the J's to a relative in the United States on June 27, 1939, said:

> Since we have no other connections anywhere in the world who could make it possible for us to emigrate to some other country, we turn to you with the heartfelt plea that you will sign an affidavit for us for the USA and at the same time we beg you from the bottom of our hearts for God's sake to take us in. We would gladly accept any kind of work in order to support ourselves. . . . Again we beg you, help us, save us, make it possible for us to go to the USA, take us in until we have found work there. The good God will reward you.

On July 22, 1939, their son-in-law received the reply:

> Your latest letter was the bitterest of disappointments; because, after all our efforts to bring your relatives to safety, I have to tell

you that we are at the end of our resources and can do nothing more. I can do nothing. An affidavit would be useless. No one can enter here for the next five years, and there is no work here for emigrants. Thousands are without jobs or homes because so many have come here. There is only one other possibility: I am sending your letter to a big organization in New York that has plenty of money and power, and, if anything can be done for you, it is in [illegible: perhaps *other*] hands. I am two thousand miles from New York and completely helpless here in the west: old and almost blind. Perhaps you will hear from this organization if anything can be done for your relatives. With deepest sympathy, Clara S. R.

Letters of this kind were going back and forth by the thousand in those days. Hard-working, upright, simple people in the closing decades of their lives, driven out of their homelands to be treated as millstones in the country of the Red Cross, vermin to be got rid of as quickly as possible. Hopes were aroused and again destroyed. Understanding, sympathetic officials were rebuked and repudiated by Berne, lawyers were dressed down like schoolboys, helpless people were pushed across the border by iron fists. Decisions and orders were issued as if for merchandise or animals or criminals. Almost never did a single word of human understanding wander by some chance into an official document. In no letter from the police authorities did anything from the heart find its way into the cold, tempered phrases. The innocent were treated as if they were guilty, while the Swiss did business with the criminals as if they were men of honor, and even made plain the Swiss sympathy with their inhumanity.

Nowhere is there any record of the physical and spiritual strength that was eroded by degrees through the heartlessness of bureaucrats, of the energy and time that had to be expended in order to rescue men and women and instill reason in obdurate policemen.

In 1941, when a central Swiss canton made temporary domicile for the A.-H.s, who were old and penniless, contingent on a bond of ten thousand francs, even though the commune where they planned to live had set no such requirement, Dr. Paul Vogt wrote to the Police Commissioner involved:

Neither of these emigrants has any assets. They will be supported by monthly payments of 160 francs from our refugee organization.

Our organization has no capital out of which bond can be posted. In this anniversary year of the Swiss Confederation we urgently implore the Privy Councilor of your ancient canton to waive the requirement for a bond. Our organization guarantees to you that we will send the emigrants money every month and also, to the extent of our abilities, perhaps provide the financing later for their complete departure. Both these people want nothing more than a quiet refuge until some little door opens for them in another country. It ought to be a matter of honor for Switzerland to grant asylum to such hard pressed fellow-beings, especially when church institutions offer to guarantee their support.

It must be said, to the credit of this canton, that the bond was waived. Others were harsher.

In one canton, for instance, a guaranty pledge from the Evangelical relief agency was not enough in the case of a fleeing German cleric whose family had remained in Germany. Personal sureties had to be found. The authorities first approved and then disapproved, because, among other reasons, one of the sureties, a Protestant clergyman of Jewish ancestry, a Swiss citizen and a public official, had been denounced as an "emigrant who could not pay."

It was a crushing battle of permits, francs, and people.

## A Dangerous Woman

There was the case of S. A., a Christian woman of Jewish stock. In her youth she had had tuberculosis. The combined pressures of her illness and the National Socialist persecutions in Germany had made the Christian faith a profound, living experience for her. To testify to her mission of love, the solacing and succoring of others had become a spiritual necessity for her. After she had been compelled to leave Germany she had been admitted to the University of Basel as a student of theology.

In 1941 she delivered a series of lectures on the Bible in various places in Switzerland, mostly to exclusively religious groups. Taking as her text the twentieth verse of the eleventh chapter of the *Epistle to the Romans*—"Because of unbelief they were broken off; and thou standest by faith. Be not high-minded, but fear"—and "When *one* member suffers, all the members suffer together; when there is joy in *one* member, all the members rejoice together," she spoke of the fate of the Jews and of the affiliated churches in Germany. Where God was no longer the lord, other hands, she said, seized power: force, arrogance, pride. Therefore the question was posed for us as for every people, for every human being: Who is your Lord? By whom are you guided? To whom do you acknowledge responsibility?

The Jews and the churches had very often stood opposed to each other. Now, however, they were sufferers in the same anguish: they stood on God's side together against unholy powers.

The lecturer, who was in her forties, cited examples of outstanding humanitarian behavior toward the victims of persecution in Germany. She spoke, too, of Prior Grüber's office in Berlin and others who stood by the churches. The churches had found a new life in God, joyousness, serenity, the power to testify, love, and devotion. Now it was time for physical suffering in imitation of Christ. From this she went on to talk of the collaboration between Christians and Jews that had led to a deepening of religious life.

On August 20, 1941, Miss S. A. delivered a similar lecture in the church of Zürich-Altstetten. Her audience was struck by the spiritual strength that emanated from this tiny, delicate woman scarred by persecution and illness. As the Reverend H. Zollinger observed in a letter written six days later: "In her description of her experiences as a non-Aryan Christian in the persecutions of Jews in Leipzig and Berlin, she in no way allowed her theme to be tainted by words of hatred; on the contrary, we admired her noble, truly Christian attitude."

One of her listeners, however, was a woman who construed the Biblical quotations as anti-German propaganda and therefore de-nounced Miss A to the head of the Police Section, Dr. Heinrich Rothmund. As a result she was forbidden to give any lectures, even before closed groups. The charges lodged by the National Socialist-ori-ented accuser were deemed sufficient proof of the speaker's refractory nature. When she tried to defend herself, friendly clergymen exerted all their gifts of persuasion to induce her to remain silent: Dr. Rothmund was already angry enough.

That gentleman had to be handled like precious crystal. When the Christian refugee, devoted as she was to truth, nevertheless explained the content of her speeches to him in order to convince him of the groundlessness of the accusation against her, he wrote to her on December 18:

> In your letter of November 5 you submitted the text of the speech delivered by you on August 20 in the New Reformed Church in Altstetten, as the result of which charges against you were lodged with us. I have the honor to inform you that permission to enter Switzerland was granted to you, as to all other emigrants, only on condition that you make immediate preparations for re-emigration. When, on the insistent pleas of the Reverend S, the Alien Police gave you permission to take an active part in a church function, this was conditioned on your restricting yourself to purely religious remarks. Your text compels me to conclude that the accusations made to us are justified, because in your speech you discussed the treatment of the Jews. Consequently, even if it had a religious basis, your lecture could serve as a political speech, and this was the effect that it had on your accuser. Hence you have engaged in an activity that we must regard as a violation of the terms of your residence here.
>
> I find myself therefore obliged to inform the Federal Alien Police that an extension of your tolerated presence for the purpose of preparing for re-emigration is to be granted only on the strict condition that you pledge yourself on your honor not to leave your commune of residence without the express permission of the Federal Alien Police and in future to abstain from every activity of every kind in speech or writing.

Miss A could still call herself lucky, for there was a moment—as was shown by a letter from the Reverend S to Miss A—when this man in Berne who was so strong against the weak was insisting on the expulsion of this contumacious Christian from Switzerland.

What, one wonders, would Mr. Rothmund have done about Christ?

In August 1941 National Councilor G. B. Rusca, a Ticino Radical, told Parliament:

> Those unhappy people who are persecuted elsewhere for their political convictions or simply for their racial origins and who must flee and flee again in secret in order to avoid suffering and death

represent no special threat to our country, even if they do not possess proper travel documents. They may be even less dangerous than certain dashing, well-dressed gentlemen who book themselves into luxury hotels with all the passports and visas that one could desire but of whom one must often wonder what purpose really brings them into our country.

As has been remarked before, Mr. Rothmund took a different view of the matter.

## Rich and Poor Guests

The refugees were a burden, and they were made to know it. But we loved foreigners and treated them with the utmost hospitality when they came to Switzerland for their vacations and brought adequate supplies of money.

In *The Refugee and Humanity*, a pamphlet published in 1945, Dr. Hans Zbinden remarked trenchantly:

> Many a man who comes to us today as a refugee would have been welcomed by us with our world-renowned servant obsequiousness, for all his unlovable qualities that perhaps one would like to throw in his face, if he had arrived as a tourist, of his own choice, and been able to walk as a free-spending foreigner into the hotel that now grudgingly admits him as a beggar. If in the past, in the good old days of tourist invasions, we could treat even undesirable, unwanted visitors with the patience of angels because of their obviously well-filled purses, then surely it will not hurt us now to demonstrate a tiny measure of this patience (and no more than that is required) for the benefit of the wretched and the suffering.

The Reverend Dr. Paul Vogt once telephoned the owner of a famous luxury hotel in one of Switzerland's best-known health resorts in order to ask the owner for a small contribution to the emigration of an Austrian refugee who had formerly been a regular customer of the hotel. Dr. Vogt was indignant when the talk was over: "I shall never forget the sneering laughter at the other end of the line and the hotel owner's remark: 'No, I have no money for this fellow. Even good-heartedness, Reverend, can be carried too far.' "

## In Prison

A most especially dark stain on our honor was the internment of political and other civilian refugees in prisons such as Witzwil and Bellechasse. It is easy to imagine what a shock it was for Hitler's victims when, having barely set foot across the border of the proverbial country of freedom, they were hauled off like criminals to Swiss prisons.

The matter was raised in a letter of December 22, 1939, from the Central Office for Refugee Assistance to the Justice and Police Department: "Commitment to penal institutions should be ordered only in cases of refugees who violate our normal laws or endanger the safety of other persons."

Federal Councilor Baumann pointed out in his reply, on January 20, 1940:

> Like other foreigners, refugees are interned only when the conclusion is inevitable that their support is impossible or appears to be too difficult. A refugee who has laid himself open to no charge is interned only when no one will assume the responsibility for him and his maintenance would otherwise become a burden on the community; in addition, this penalty is invoked for serious violations of regulations laid down by the Alien Police, such as illegal entry, clandestine residence, prohibited economic activity, or other behavior contrary to public order—for instance, resistance to discipline in an emigrant camp, fraudulent procurement of assistance by giving false information, etc. Obviously, too, foreigners who have serious criminal records are interned, as well as those who have been politically active in Switzerland or whose political activity must be reckoned with in the future, such as Communists. This enumeration, of course, is not complete; it is intended merely to show the direction taken by the practice of internment. . . . Emigrants whose moral characters are not under major attack are interned in Witzwil or Bellechasse. They are subjected to a special discipline, of course go out to work together with the other inmates

of the institution, and receive normal prison food; but in their leisure time and at night they are allowed to be together. They also enjoy certain privileges—for example, in entertainment, reading matter, mail, etc. . . . Naturally their internment is not made a matter of criminal record.

This was unarguably big-hearted. But it did not alter the impairment of Swiss nobility arising out of the fact that, when noncriminal persons sought protection in Switzerland, they were sent to prison. Refugees who entered Switzerland "black" had no rights under the law. Juridically their existence was not envisaged. As Professor Zbinden emphasized in his brochure, their only recourse against measures and regulations that appeared to be unjust was to complain to the Police Section—which was a party in interest.

It was possible for refugees to be condemned to several months in prison, wearing prison clothes and undergoing the same discipline as convicted criminals, even though they had not been convicted in any regular trial but merely because they had escaped from camps whose living conditions were demonstrably unbearable: this breach of discipline, however understandable to anyone with any human feeling, was sufficient ground for imprisonment. Any criminal tried and convicted with the protection of due process of law knows why and for how long he will be in prison; disciplinary cases are informed of neither the one nor the other. [Zbinden, pages 72–73.]

The treatment to which many refugees were subjected in certain punishment camps was shameful and a disgrace to a democratic state. In Witzwil—and this could happen to ordinary Swiss convicts as well—the infamous wool-blanket technique was often used. The punished prisoner was bound in a wool blanket from neck to feet; in many instances this produced a complete panic reaction. Bellechasse was notorious for its frequent reliance on deliberate malnutrition and the consequent physical and psychological exhaustion that it produced in refugees and Swiss criminal inmates alike. I was reliably informed by a Freiburg businessman and his wife, who had regularly supplied food, clothing, and shoes to the refugees in Bellechasse during the war, that without help from outside the prison's regimen would have been absolutely inadequate:

I remember one sumptuous lunch to which we were invited by the prison officials after we had completed our regular visit to the inmates. The table was abundantly laden with fresh-smelling bread, cheese, butter, bacon, ham, sausage, and so forth. There was cream for the dessert and the coffee—Bellechasse was really set up like a farm estate. Normally during the war it would have been impossible to eat so well in any restaurant. But I could not get any of the food down when I thought of the miserable state of the refugees in the same place.

Referring to a visit made by his wife, he added:

Contrary to all previous practice, she was driven up from the station. When she asked the reason, she was told: "The Swiss inmates wanted to welcome you with a volley of stones because you bring packages only for the foreigners and never for them." It made a deep impression on my wife, because she could never have imagined that the Swiss inmates' food too was so bad and so inadequate.

How bad the food was may be further deduced from the fact that the refugees in Bellechasse, each of whom received a monthly allowance of fifteen francs from the Jewish refugee-relief organizations, asked that instead of the money they receive the equivalent in food. The prison food was mixed with bromine.

Dr. Emerico Galocsi of Milan, an Italian physican born in Hungary in 1905, wrote a vivid description of the ways in which the refugees were disillusioned by the Swiss authorities. Having been compelled by the racial laws to leave Italy, he had gone to Brussels and wanted to reach England; in furtherance of this aim he had come to Switzerland and, on the advice of the British Embassy in Berne, registered with the police authorities, who saw how exhausted he was and told him: "We'll give you a bed"—whereupon they put him into a cell. He wrote:

In this cell I underwent the most paradoxical experience of my life: Through the barred windows I could hear the bands and the songs celebrating Switzerland's Independence Day. After all the years that I had spent under Fascism and German occupation, I had to spend Independence Day in free Switzerland in a cell for the first time in my life.

He was later informed that he would be transferred to a refugee camp near Sugiez, where he could work as a physician—and he wound up in the Bellechasse prison. "For the second time I felt that I had been betrayed in Switzerland." He added:

> I went through a great deal of hate and horror in Bellechasse. It was not only what happened to the refugees but also the inhuman, barbaric treatment of the convicts that appalled me. Many Swiss with whom I later discussed these ghastly conditions had no idea of their existence—and yet this was right in Switzerland. Why were we placed in this prison and thus made eyewitnesses of these disgraceful things that we can never forget? We had no "good" nationalities. We were pariahs from Hungary, Poland, Rumania, not "first-class" citizens protected by their embassies and consulates like the British, the French, the Dutch, and others. This was unfortunately the fact. This is not the place in which to describe the mistreatment to which the prisoners were subjected. Only one thing: I was interned in the punishment barracks for juveniles, and thus I could see how these underfed boys were sent out in all kinds of weather from early morning until late in the evening to perform arduous land work. When an inspector came from Berne, never without the advance knowledge of the superintendent, the superintendent always ordered slices of bread and pieces of cheese to be placed in the drawers of the dining tables, and he then promptly discovered them and cried out triumphantly: "Again the kids left their food because they get too much of it!" The refugees were always kept so far away from any such visitors that they could not make any contact with the investigators.

And another former refugee told me:

> There were very bad things in Bellechasse, but we also saw some examples of the highest humanity there. One of the prisoners was a real saint. And there was a German prince, a professor in Freiburg. He visited us regularly. He was the most perfect Christian I have ever seen. As for the superintendent—he had terrible stomach trouble.

# Camp Life

The Federal Council's decision to establish labor camps for refugees was made on March 12, 1940. On December 22, 1939, the Central Office, on behalf of all refugee organizations, had itself suggested the establishment of internment camps because of the current emergency and as a result of the ominous experiences with the cantonal police officials.

Even before this time there had been loud demands for the removal of the emigrants from the larger cities, and from the border towns above all. As Professor Ludwig reported, a northwest Swiss city canton had complained that the refugees were marring the beauty of the landscape. In other areas they were forbidden to go into railway stations, cafés, and other public places. Naturally, too, they were most harshly forbidden to engage in any gainful activity even if they were left without means as a result. Dr. Vogt told of one instance in Ticino in which a refugee who happened to be in an office answered a ringing telephone in the sheer spirit of helpfulness. He was fined fifty francs, and he was not allowed to appeal. A refugee-relief organization had to pay his fine because he had no money at all.

On April 12, 1940, the Federal Council officially notified the cantons of its labor-camp decision and prescribed the living conditions and rules for the inmates of the camps. The refugee's travel to and from the camp would be paid. He would be provided with insurance against accident and medical and hospital expenses for illness, he would be paid one franc for each day's labor, and some of his working clothes would be furnished to him.

The organization and administration of the camps was entrusted to the headquarters of the Voluntary Labor Service under the direction of Otto Zaugg, an engineer. The military training of the refugees in the labor camps, however, was turned over to the Federal Police Section. (See Ludwig, pages 177–178.)

"The creation of the refugee camps was motivated by the belief that the emigrants should perform useful work for our country, which was granting them temporary asylum," the Justice and Police Department explained in a press release dated February 22, 1941. "At the same time such labor should strengthen them physically and psychologically so that later they would be able to embark on new lives across the ocean. This result would be furthered by the discipline made necessary by camp life and the community spirit that would be fostered by their stays in the camps."

The task was anything but easy. Even if all the proper preparations had already been made for the collection of thousands of refugees for a considerable time in camps, even if they had been received with open arms and genuine fellow-feeling, the problem would have been many-sided and complex. When men and women who were complete strangers to one another, who came from different countries and different social and cultural backgrounds, who belonged to different religions, sects, and nationalities, and who spoke different languages, were suddenly gathered together under one roof and made to eat at the same table, it was for the most part extremely difficult to create a true community together.

"We are not welcome guests," one refugee wrote to Dr. Gertrud Kurz in Berne; "we are harassed, persecuted, 'looked after.' *Persecution could do no better job.* You must be patient with us—patient until we can become what we want to be: human beings who have found themselves again and *feel love for their neighbors again* and are allowed to reciprocate it in the deepest, trusting thankfulness." (*Judennot* [*The Jews' Need*] page 34.)

A social worker described her first visit to a Swiss reception camp:

The camp is primitive in its arrangements, but very well managed. It houses about 230 inmates, including 80 children, of whom more than 40 are less than five years old. There are about 80 women, many of them old and ailing and 4 pregnant. I counted 13 nationalities: Turkish, Yugoslav, Serbian, Rumanian, Bulgarian, Hungarian, Austrian, German, Polish, Italian, French, Belgian, and Luxemburger. The inmates are intellectuals and artisans; 220 are Jews, eight are Catholics, and two are Protestants.

Their histories are shattering: Husband and child in the camp, mother deported. Mother and small children here, husband deported. I held in my arms a three-year-old girl with whom, as well as another child, the mother made her way over the barbed wire—the father was deported. And shall I help now? The FHD* was a tremendous help to me. The camp supervisor, a first lieutenant from St. Gallen, was very glad that at last someone from a welfare organization could come. . . .

Much love, much good will, much devotion were invested in the refugees in the camps, and undoubtedly good will was dominant in the labor-camp administrative headquarters. It would be unjust and inaccurate to ignore that fact. And it was impossible, even with the best will, to do everything properly. Among the refugees, as in any other group, there were selfish, conniving, difficult persons, egotists who thought only of themselves and never of others. Perfection could never be achieved under even the most ideal conditions.

There were camp directors like First Lieutenant Girard in Grand-Saconnex and Monachon in Varembé. They were rich in human understanding, they talked with the refugees, they explained Switzerland's difficult situation to them, they appealed to their reason—and the discipline in their camps was excellent.

* Frauen Hilfs Dienst (Women's Auxiliary Army Corps)

But there was also Captain Q in the Champel camp, who made no secret of his own anti-Semitism and distributed the notorious anti-Semitic French publication, *Gringoire*, as camp reading. His disciplinary methods, such as deprivation of food for trivial offenses, were dreaded. A Jewish mother who had approached the barbed-wire fence of the camp "in an unauthorized manner" in order to exchange a few words with her son, whom she had not seen for some time, was sent to St.-Antoine Prison in Geneva for five days to expiate her crime.

All attempts by Armand Brunschvig, chairman of the Jewish refugee agency in Geneva, to obtain Captain Q's dismissal were fruitless. As a result, the authorization issued to Brunschvig on October 8, 1942, to visit the reception camp was withdrawn, on the demand of the Army High Command, on October 26, 1943; it was not reissued until the end of January 1945. Those who were critical had a difficult time. They were not kindly regarded. They were menaces to "peace and quiet." Military discipline was the alpha and omega of many camp supervisors.

There was also Captain R in the Charmilles camp, who never rationed his anti-Semitic insults of the refugees. His disciplinary techniques were cruel and arbitrary. He threatened to use the horsewhip on little Jewish children, until the commander in chief ordered him henceforth to leave his horsewhip at home when he went to visit the camp.

There was also Brigadier P of the Charmilles camp police, who roared denunciations at the Jews as the instigators of revolution and war and who told them that Switzerland knew what to expect of them.

We Swiss had our own SS characters.

Only specially authorized persons such as clergymen were allowed to visit the camps. The conditions imposed on their visits were these:

> It is forbidden to act as an intermediary for refugees' correspondence. Violations of the basic rules for the handling of refugees in reception camps after December 30, 1943, will be punished by the immediate withdrawal of visiting permits. The visitor must report at once to the camp commandant and religiously follow his instructions. The visitor is authorized to get into touch with the refugees and to speak with them. The camp commandant will provide opportunities for this. The visiting permit must be shown voluntarily when the visitor enters the camp.

Clergymen and lawyers were treated in the camps as potential accomplices of criminals. Regulations can reveal a state of mind. Here they did so.

A Swiss officer who at this period was serving as a young lieutenant in a camp under military command and who was outraged by the brutal, shameful treatment of the refugees told me that he had made a report to the camp commander's superior officer. He was thereupon sent for and informed by the higher officer that he should not meddle in matters that were none of his business. Since it seemed hopeless to try to effect any amelioration, the lieutenant had himself transferred from camp duty.

In cold fact people were often appointed as camp supervisors who had no qualifications for the post and accepted it only because of what they could get out of it.


## Rationed Human Kindness

In *Das Volk*, the Olten Social-Democratic newspaper, the following letter was published on December 30, 1942, under the title, *Jews' Camps*:

> We wanted to send a couple of jars of preserves to a hungry family that had fled from France . . . and was now in a camp. The package came back to us with some of the glass broken and leaking. And today we got a postcard with a printed message: *"The sending of rationed or quota products to refugees is prohibited."* So the parcel that we prepared must stay where it is. Jews do not need to get anything. There can be only one explanation for this prohibition: the desire to make the Jews feel their convict existence as bitterly as possible.

Not only food but human kindness and helpfulness were in those days rationed by the government.

The jealous minds of the Fatherland Front did not want to acknowledge what *Die Neue Zürcher Zeitung* had described on October 28, 1942:

The help given to the refugees has not, however, gone unremuner-
ated. Far more than a thousand labor-camp inmates are busy on
improvement projects or agriculture. In Ticino they have planted
more than two hundred acres of potatoes and harvested a crop that
filled eighty freight cars. Elsewhere they are employed in cutting
peat and have already brought in some seventeen hundred tons.
The refugees are also employed in important highway and reclamation work. Projects of national importance are carried forward by
their labors; projects for the execution of which we previously
lacked the required manpower. Thus both we and the refugees are
at once givers and receivers, and both parties have reason to be
grateful.

However much acknowledgment must be given to the good intentions of the central labor-camp headquarters, there was in many respects
an equal adherence for far too long to rigid theories that were unjust to
the persons whom they affected and that led to avoidable errors. Federal
Councilor von Steiger calculated, from Professor Ludwig's report, which
fine hotels and what fine places contained refugees. That some did was
certainly true. But the most luxurious hotel becomes a prison when the
spirit of understanding is lacking. Residence in neither Celerina nor
Lugano could erase the anguish of arbitrary separations of families, or
idleness, or lack of liberty.
A refugee wrote (in the 1943 annual report of the Evangelical Relief
Agency):

I will never forget the first step that we took on Swiss soil when we
had managed to cross the border after a three-hour trek through the
mountains and the surrender of the last penny of our savings to the
Italian border patrols. We laughed and wept, we wanted to kiss the
ground beneath our feet, we wanted to hug the whole world. A
totally unreal ecstasy of joy sent us reeling: Here you are human
beings again, free, upstanding people like anyone else. Here I hope
I can recover my spiritual balance, my peace of mind and heart.
Then came the camp in A. About 550 persons gathered for a meal
in a single hall. An unbearable din. One did not speak, one shouted
in order to be understood; children yelled, benches were thrown,
dishes rattled. Every ten minutes there was a new order, a warning,

a reprimand from the camp officials. I could not eat, there was only one thing I could do: lie down on my straw mattress and let my tears pour out. But even there I was not alone. And I did not want to let anyone see my tears. . . .

Of course a person can collapse when his nerves are taut, when he has allowed himself to indulge in overroseate pictures of asylum, when he has not understood or does not yet understand that it is difficult to support and accomodate hundreds of persons without preparation, that it is impossible to prevent mistakes. Is he to be condemned on that account? Must he be told—as so many were so often: "If you don't like it here, go back where you came from"?

This was the sort of thing to which the refugees had to listen. Having visited a camp at the request of the refugees—one of their bondsmen told the chairman of the Jewish refugee agency in Geneva—Dr. Rothmund said publicly, in French: "Let them huddle on their straw as long as possible, so that of themselves they will be led to ask permission to leave; let them see for themselves that Switzerland is no paradise, so that those who want to come in will be discouraged."

A police official countered that Dr. Rothmund had said only that no complaints about the straw mattresses would be heeded; Swiss soldiers also had to be satisfied with straw and the refugee should be grateful that they were allowed in at all. (See Ludwig, page 257.)

Professor Hans Zbinden took up arms vigorously against this kind of thinking:

If a refugee made a specific charge, or, losing some of his control, uttered a criticism, or worse, at the end of his nervous strength after years in a camp, expressed his anger in a letter to the authorities or before the camp commander, often enough he heard in reply that classic argument against which there is obviously no appeal: "Just be glad that you're allowed to be here. We didn't send for you; and, if you don't like it, you can leave again." It was not always people who were giving vent to their irritation or contempt who talked like this. Whatever the motive, however, it can never erase the shame of such a reply. Obviously this shuts the mouth of every helpless man and silences every complaint.

How must it have sounded to a refugee when he was told: "You ought to be glad that you're alive at all. Without Switzerland you would long since have been in a mass grave"?

"How are we going to get rid of the refugees?"—that seems to have been the unspoken question that expressed the Swiss state of mind, instead of endeavors to provide not only physical but emotional security, Professor Zbinden said, adding: "Now we have, somehow, really got rid of them. Often, unfortunately, at the price of ridding many refugees of themselves: of their nerves, of their hopes, of their will to live."

## The Shattered

One David D wrote to Dr. Paul Vogt in November 1943:

> I have been in Switzerland as a refugee for eleven months. When I crossed the border with my wife, who was in the last stages of pregnancy, and our two-year-old daughter, Claudette, my wife began to feel labor pains. I had to go into Switzerland alone with my little daughter, and since then I have been shifted from one camp to another. Fortunately, in Burgdorf I found a family that took in my child as its own, and she is still there.
>
> Three weeks after her confinement my wife came into Switzerland with the new baby, Jean. The baby was so ill that he was sent at once to the Geneva children's home, Grange Canal. Now he is quite healthy and he is still in Geneva.
>
> Since I am unfit for a labor camp, I am in a home in V and my wife, who does not have her baby with her, is in the labor camp in B. So here we are, a family of four, each of them in a different place! My wife and I are going *mad* because we see no hope of being together again, particularly with our newest child, who is still in Geneva.
>
> I implore you to help us *at once*, because my health is rapidly deteriorating, I suffer from nervous crises that almost proved fatal a few years ago. My wife's care helped me to improve, but now I am at the end of my rope, and in terror I see the time coming when I can no longer be cured. You know, Reverend, that nervous ailments

have emotional roots, and that only spiritual peace can heal such a condition. Save me, I implore you!

On the same day a letter was sent by a mother in the camp of Langenbruck:

Forgive me if I disturb you, but there is so much in my heart that I must tell it all to someone. We can regard this camp at Langenbruck as a Swiss camp, but at the same time one has the right to ask what crime we have committed that we should be sent to such a camp. So often we are told: "You have certainly saved your life! What more do you want?" Of course we have, but why go on with this life if one must live *like this?* Many people say: "No, we can't any more." This is now my seventh camp. Never, I assure you, have I suffered so much in my soul as in this camp, never has an army officer allowed himself to leave me standing so long in a silence of death before he told us to sit. In no other camp have we been formed into ranks and columns of two to wait to be called like little children. The camp commander should not forget that there are many old people among us. Switzerland has already done a great deal for us, and unfortunately she will still have to do more during this war, which seems to have no end. But one thing I do not understand: Many camps are like paradise and others are like hell. Everyone here feels that it is *dismal* here, everyone has the impression that a cloak of ice has been thrown over his shoulders and that we are freezing to death.

Today, Wednesday, we are allowed to have our children with us from two o'clock until five, but already the thought of the imminent separation weighs us down, we go for walks, we hold our children in our arms like suffering souls, we press them to us, because they are immediately going to be taken away from us again. We are told that in France it would be even worse for us than under the Germans. Quite so, but we are in Switzerland!

My husband is in the camp in Andelfingen, my son is in W (in Aargau), my little daughter and I are in Langenbruck, she on the second floor, I on the third. I wake up at night and wonder whether the child is sleeping, whether she has kicked off all her covers. So many torturing questions that haunt my sleep!

All the mothers here are very deeply concerned. It is good that
our children are taken care of while we are at work, but then is it
not possible for us to be allowed to have them with us at meal
times and to sleep with them? That was the case in other camps in
which I have been, and it worked very well. [From Dr. Vogt's files.]

The November 1943 bulletin of the Central Office for Refugee
Assistance quoted this letter:

It is exactly five years since I fled like a hunted animal from Austria
through Belgium and northern and southern France and finally
arrived in Switzerland. I was interned for forty-one months, and
more than thirty of those forty-one months were spent behind
barbed wire. I know that the past five years have not passed over
me without leaving some trace and that my heart disease is very
bad.

There was also a letter from Champéry:

I received your letter of March 6 [1944] and read it carefully.
Unfortunately it was God's will to take my little daughter on
March 6. As a clergyman you will certainly understand best. After
we had already gone through so much suffering, God has now put
us through the worst test. As a result of this tragic event my wife,
my six-year-old son, and I were immediately placed in the family
camp in Champéry. Unfortunately we had to pay much too high a
price for this. Most unhappily our six-year-old son was immediately
taken away from us here and put in a building with all the other
children about five hundred yards from here. You will understand
what this child means to us now, and, since we can see him only
three times a week, it is very, very hard for us, because now this
child is everything to us, the solace of our souls. . . .

Individual instances? We have them documented in dozens of filing
cabinets. No special, particularly grievous cases have been singled out;
there are always those. These are, rather, the daily run. Heartfelt letters
of thanks side by side with appalling accusations.

The separation of married couples was for a long time arbitrary, cruel,
and unnecessary. It was required by the police, the administrators, the

bureaucrats. The persons concerned, for the most part, were neither consulted nor heard. Only rarely was it possible to avert or reverse the senseless orders. A leaflet issued by the Swiss Labor Relief Agency in the spring of 1943 said:

> It seems to us unthinkable for our country that couples must live separated for months in different camps—not because there are only sexually segregated camps: No, the camps are mixed. And yet in a great many instances couples are placed in different camps without permission even to see each other for four to five months. We consider it unthinkable too that, as is the case in certain camps, men, women, and children who are strangers to one another must live and even sleep together in the closest quarters; this is a situation that certainly does no honor to Switzerland and has very little in common with "protection of the family and of children". . . .
>
> Hygienic conditions, too, in many camps leave much, if not everything, to be desired. Is this necessary? Most of these people have lost everything in repeated flights, their families have been partly exterminated, partly scattered over the world; must we further degrade and terrorize them by insisting that they live under conditions unworthy of a civilized nation? How can we answer for the fact that women, children, the aged, and the ailing are still sleeping only on plain straw, with insufficient blankets, when there are plenty of quarters available for them where they would be welcome? . . .
>
> Six thousand refugees—men, women, children—crawl into their cold straw every night after a worse than frugal meal; after an idle, wasted day in a tiny space overcrowded with people; with their hearts overflowing with fears for relatives threatened with deportation or already deported; with all their dread of the unknown future—does anyone still think that such conditions do not play havoc with people's nerves and have no influence on the thinking of the internees?
>
> Anyone who has any dealings with them, however, knows something else as well: How grateful they are for any sign of understanding of their situation, for any contact; and how the respectable persons among them—who constitute the overwhelming majority —themselves suffer from the fact that they are lumped together

with the less admirable in the same heartless, uncomprehending, presumptuous accusations and condemnations of unthinking observers.

The people who thought that they had evolved a masterful solution to the admittedly difficult problem of designing the camps unfortunately forgot only too often what Prof. Zbinden rightly emphasized: "The mass camp is above all an un-Swiss solution in so far as we recognize the ideal that is the opposite of all mass concepts. If people want to talk about inundation by foreigners in these times, the idea of the mass camp unquestionably testifies to such a transition to alien notions." (Zbinden, pages 42–43.)

Why, for instance, was another method possible in Sweden? Why did the Swedes abstain as much as possible from the establishment of camps? Why did they make every effort, within the limits of feasibility, to let the refugees work in their original or related occupations? Was it really merely because Sweden was in a more comfortable position than Switzerland? Or was it not also at least in part the result of a more human attitude toward the stranger? In my opinion this was the case.

*Der Schwyzer Demokrat* of Siebnen reported on March 3, 1944:

> A Dutch refugee couple was separated after entering Switzerland, and, in spite of all their pleas, it was never possible for the man and his wife to make specific arrangements to spend their three-day vacations together. In a period of one month there were six other instances of the same kind in this same camp. In another camp the commandant made a spectacle of his unbridled hatred of Jews. Two inmates whom his predecessor had appointed as labor and camp officials were immediately dismissed by him for no reason other than "aversion to Jews." In other camps there were shortages of physicians while in still others physicians had to peel potatoes and cut wood.

## Received into Grace

*Die National-Zeitung* reported,

> In March of this year [1944], a Jewish boy barely sixteen years old fled over the Swiss border, was seized by the frontier patrols, and

gave his age as ten days less than the truth because this would save him from being sent back across the border to certain death. He was placed in an educational institution of his own faith, and there, of his own free will and in spite of the fact that it would have been impossible to unmask his lie, he revealed how he had cheated death. Any teacher would consider him a fine lad and wish that all his pupils might have so great a concern for truth. This was not the view of minds illuminated by the spirit of the policeman. On the contrary: the boy was informed by the Federal Justice and Police Department that as punishment for his offense he was to be put into a labor camp and denied leave for two months: it was only because of his extreme youth that the government refrained from imposing the harsher penalty of expulsion (read: condemnation to death in Maidanek). The department's highly memorable letter to him said, among other things: "We hope that through your work, as well as your behavior, you will make every effort to be worthy of the *leniency and hospitality* that Switzerland has extended to you in spite of the fact that your age would have justified your expulsion." I am afraid that not all the refugees who are treated with the same leniency and hospitality will entertain so high an esteem for the police mentality that inspired both these mercies as the highly placed officials seem from their own words to anticipate.

And what did National Councilor Walter say to the National Council on September 23, 1942? "The right of asylum is an act of grace unilaterally bestowed by Switzerland."

The spirit of the warm-hearted act of grace also infused a document dated "Berne, June 1944," which was handed to every refugee who was allowed to enter. Its very first paragraph reminded him that "the right of asylum is the right of a state, to be granted to persecuted foreigners who for political or religious reasons have crossed its borders in search of haven and protection from the violent acts of a foreign state. Every independent state is free to accept refugees or send them back."

Then it added:

And now you [using the familiar rather than the polite second person] have been admitted to our country. You have sought refuge in Switzerland in order to save yourself and your life from persecution in your country of birth or residence. We know that you and many of your fellow-victims have lived through many arduous sufferings and hardships. We know what unspeakable pain many of you have experienced. Hence we understand your great need and your grief. We know that it is not easy for you to comply with the many rules and regulations that must be imposed in order to preserve proper discipline. Many of you undoubtedly thought that in the land of freedom you would be allowed to do or not do whatever you pleased, and perhaps you are disappointed when you are immediately placed in quarantine camps that are often very simply furnished and for the moment you can not yet breathe the scent of a freedom that is frequently wrongly interpreted. . . .

Since able-bodied refugees must be assigned to various kinds of work, it is unfortunately impossible to keep husbands and wives in the same camps and institutions.

The document continued in this same confidential tone of the familiar second person. But the style was that of the director of an orphanage setting forth the rules of the house in a paternal manner to "his" adolescent, unfortunately shipwrecked charges, the children of alcoholics and broken homes. Now the new arrival knew what he must and, above all, must not do. And finally he was assured: "The refugee is not without rights in Switzerland. Complaints lodged by him in proper form and based on accurately documented facts will not subject him to any penalties." The leaflet was signed: "Federal Justice and Police Department."

The truth, unhappily, bore a different face.

When the press was invited in the spring of 1943 to tour various camps, J. B. Rusch of *Die Republikanische Blättern* refused the invitation, writing:

I will not take part in any whitewashing mass visit. Thus far the model for these camps has consistently been the concentration camp with all its degradation of the inmate. And *this* is simply *unworthy* of our traditional right of asylum. We call on the Justice and Police Department to turn over the entire matter of the refugees to a commission of *human beings:* teachers, physicians, clerics, women; and *absolutely* to exclude mere police officials.

It was not until February 1944 that a fact-finding commission to study the refugee question was created in the manner proposed and composed in part of women—exclusively Swiss. And it was not until the end of 1944 that the refugees were granted the right to be heard on matters that concerned them.

By the time their authorized representatives were allowed for the first time to take part in a conference for the discussion of their problems, it was March of 1945. Two months later the war ended. We Swiss had had a marvelous opportunity to demonstrate to foreigners who had sought asylum among us the true essence of our democracy, our national development, our federalism, our multi-lingualism. Discussions, lectures, readings, theatrical representations, where these had been offered on the initiative of camp directors or relief agencies, had afforded the most satisfactory results. But, as Professor Zbinden pointed out, for a long time the central camp headquarters would not issue permission for such activities. Proposals to this end were left unanswered for far too long a time. "A modest attempt was first made in 1944 with a monthly credit of five thousand francs. Swiss speakers were to travel from camp to camp delivering lectures on Swiss problems, democracy, etc." But by and large it was now too late. "The refugees have in the meantime learned about Switzerland from experience." And this experience—in spite of praiseworthy exceptions, such as the establishment of a hospice for intellectuals in Frontenex-Geneva, permission to publish the magazine, *Über die Grenze* (*Across the Border*), and its similarly entitled series of pamphlets, as well as *Les Cahiers de Frontenex* (*The Frontenex Notebooks*), "all of which publications were produced at the expense of the federal government," as Otto Zaugg pointed out in Professor Ludwig's report—was in all too numerous instances not such as to have been able to compensate for what was left undone.

# Democratic Coordination

## The Example of Jakob Haringer

The situation of the intellectual refugees—scholars, artists, writers—was particularly painful, and, in numerous instances, tragic. Accustomed to creative, intellectual, or highly specialized work—for example, as singers, violinists, pianists—they were thrust into camps "without respect to persons" and assigned to farm labor, road-building, land reclamation, maintenance. Hypersensitive persons thus psychologically imperiled could be destroyed in this way.

Let us take the example of the famous lyricist, Dr. Jakob Haringer. Granted that he was a difficult man, frequently intransigent and anything but adaptable. His sometimes almost unbearable manner and his often extravagant letters of complaint were too much even for some of the patient refugee workers, so that in the end only Dr. Kurz was prepared to go on dealing with him. But nevertheless let us take this instance of the sensitive, highly gifted man accustomed to fame and recognition—and now thrust out of his intellectual and physical "living space" into a strange world that saw no longer the poet but only the burdensome, refractory emigrant, Haringer.

As for so many others—and in spite of the fact that Haringer often flooded him too with unjustified accusations—Professor Hans Zbinden undertook various interventions, by letter and word of mouth, with the authorities in search of greater understanding for the poet. But the Police Section made its judgments on the basis of the "record," and this was its judgment:

> Our latest re-examination of the record has not been able to provide a foundation for any amelioration of the impression of Haringer that was formed earlier. In his case it appears that we are dealing with a man who is unquestionably highly intelligent but utterly asocial and, to a certain extent, dangerous. Most of his former advocates have obviously turned their backs on him. Haringer's assignment to Leysin already signified a concession that was granted solely on the ground of his literary reputation. Any further compromise, such as would be represented by his release from Leysin and his placement in compulsory residence, seems to us unjustified with respect to a man who, on the abundant evidence of his proved lack of responsibility, requires strict supervision. It is impossible for us to grant Haringer the respect as an artist that he has not earned as a person. We regret that we cannot give you a more favorable decision in this matter.

Professor Zbinden did not allow the official decision to discourage him. In a detailed letter he set forth the reasons why Haringer should be released from the camp. The grounds that he adduced applied equally to many others in the same circumstance.

> I do not know Jakob Haringer's record and hence I cannot assess the merits of the charges against him. I must assume that they must be unusually grievous if they justify the subjection of a man

in great physical and mental anguish and on the brink of despair to measures that otherwise would hardly be envisaged for someone of his type and position. I cannot altogether rid myself of the impression that in this instance a man of absolutely extraordinary sensitivity, suffering under the burden of a need for solitude, is being judged far too rigidly after a pattern and is being made to pay for his inability to follow that pattern even with the utmost good will. What is described as "asocial" and "of bad character" in him is basically nothing more nor less than the consequence of the fact that an intellectually productive and highly talented man is compelled for years to live in the midst of conditions that deprive him of every possibility of quiet, concentration, and solitude and thus finally arouse his unpleasant aspects. He is forced to live permanently under conditions that constantly aggravate precisely those things in him for which he is reproached by the authorities, and then this aggravation is thrown back in his face as justification for the refusal of any other kind of treatment and for even greater severity against his reactions.

If we force a naturally harmless and gentle dog to live constantly under conditions that are completely contrary to his nature, he is bound to become snappish and even hostile. Is this a reason for punishing him for his hostility and intensifying the conditions that are largely responsible for his state?

I fear that even many very respectable members of the Swiss Writers' Union and indeed our officials themselves, if they had to live for years as a Haringer, among others, has been compelled to live for years in our country, would in the end manifest highly unacceptable and indeed "dangerous" aspects of their characters. That Haringer, in his present state of extreme exacerbation, is spiritually (even more than physically) weakened, that his nerves are damaged, that his sensibilities are rubbed raw, that his faith in mankind has been destroyed, seems to me, in the circumstances, not to be wondered at. I am the more surprised that, as I have been told, Mr. Hänni, the director of his camp, speaks of him as a companionable and quiet man, just as Dr. Kurz has expressed a substantially similar favorable opinion. Professor Egger in Zürich and Hermann Hesse esteem him highly. Hugo Marti [former fiction editor of *Der Bund* in Berne] and Max Rychner, both reliable witnesses, who knew him in normal times before he was driven to despair and collapse, held him in high regard not only as an artist but as a man.

I know something of the conditions in Leysin, and, on the basis of my own impressions and the reports that I have had from other sources, I can well understand that a man like Jakob Haringer suffers unspeakably in such circumstances and, in his utter inability to enjoy any quiet and solitude in the midst of a human environment that frightens him (and certainly this is not because of his guilt), feels himself driven into increasing inescapable bitterness and contempt for his fellows—sentiments that originally were not part of his being and that are something very different from the denigrating epithet of "asocial" that the police record apparently casts at him as an accusation.

It seems certain that a humanely conceived solution would prove in the long run to be more practical and more advantageous also from the point of view of the police authorities, because the continuation of the present conditions can only substantially aggravate the situation and create more difficulties for the authorities. It can hardly be to the interest of the authorities to drive a man to the limit of his endurance if another way proves feasible—in that case offenses must be so heinous that every effort in that direction is foreclosed. In any event it cannot be a matter of indifference to us —and on this you will surely share my opinion—whether a man such as Haringer is driven insane. . . .

I should be pleased if, as a result of my letter, . . . the matter could be reopened, perhaps with more attention to psychological considerations rather than in reliance on the record alone, and an acceptable solution could be sought.

What for a long time was regarded by the Police Section and the central administration of the labor camps as democratic—identical work assignments without respect to persons: for instance, farm labor for professors as well as for farm workers, for pianists as well as for lumbermen, for singers as well as for masons—came down in practice to a coordination of employability and talent. The "job training" that certain bureaucratic minds had conceived for men and women who were persecuted and driven out not because of their inability or unwillingness to work but because of the desire of a government of racially pure scoundrels to be rid of "alien-minded elements" proved to be the destruction of many extremely valuable and intellectually preeminent persons.

The officially imposed ban on activity in specific occupations, of course, was no less damaging. With full understanding for the principle that the refugees should not deprive Swiss citizens of employment, a little good will would have made it possible to find some more humane procedure. In a speech on November 4, 1936, to the general meeting of the Central Office for Refugee Assistance in Olten, Dr. Heinrich Rothmund had emphasized that "work is the pillar of the inner man, and without it he disintegrates morally"; on April 3, 1937, he had told the delegates' assembly of the NHG in Zürich that "for a man of working age unemployment means a major misfortune, and for a youth it can destroy his whole life!" Obviously, these truths were not equally valid for refugees. The consequences of this attitude are attested to by uncounted instances in the files of the Police Section, the refugee-relief organizations, and other welfare groups—evidence provided not only by whiners and unthinking refugees but also by highly endowed, formerly respected persons of impeccable character. A highly educated, sensitive, cultivated lady, a scholar from an eminent family of scholars, who had survived the camp at Gurs, France, with her sisters and brothers, told me that after her arrival in Switzerland in 1942 she had often felt almost a nostalgia for Gurs. It was not the sanitary arrangements, not the hunger, not the living conditions that appalled her. All those things were immeasurably better in Switzerland than in the French camps. What wounded her was the heartless, bureaucratic, tactless attitude of so many functionaries in the police and refugee administrations, their terrifying incapacity to put themselves even to the slightest degree in the place of the outcasts; it was the power of the minor bureaucrat that everyone had to endure, the utter dependence on the good intentions or the irritable temper of some official potentate who was a zero at home and in his private life, that often made living in Switzerland a misery for persons of any feeling.

## A Song Goes Round the World

The fate of Joseph Schmidt, the singer, cannot be forgotten. The sudden death of this internationally known and loved artist, who starred in the film A *Song Goes Round the World* (*Ein Lied Geht um die Welt*), among many others, was reported at the end of November 1942 by Dr. Fritz Heberlein in *Die National-Zeitung, Das St.-Gallen Tagblatt, Die Glarner Nachrichten*, and other newspapers. Joseph Schmidt was removed on October 27, 1942, from the Gyrenbad camp to the cantonal hospital in Zürich, where his illness was diagnosed as a minor laryngitis and tracheitis. He was then discharged as cured, although he complained of chest pains. He was very fearful at the thought of returning to the camp, because he dreaded—and certainly not without reason—the serious damage to his most precious asset, his voice, that might result from the extremely bad hygienic conditions and the dust of the straw pallets in Gyrenbad. A private physician was prepared to accept him into his own clinic after his release from the hospital, give him a thorough examination, and treat him. But the camp authorities, without any malevolence, refused permission—in fact, on the ground of democracy—because even refugees of means were supposed to be treated only in cantonal hospitals. So the thirty-eight-year-old singer finally went back to the camp. As a concession, the camp commander billeted him in the inn that adjoined the camp.

The next morning Schmidt died of a heart attack.

Granted that his death cannot be simply ascribed to the functionaries. But if they had been somewhat less bureaucratic and thus avoided agitating the singer, at least they would not have been vulnerable to the charge of contributing to his death.

The story did not end with Schmidt's death. Dr. Heberlein wrote a newspaper eulogy of the singer, in which he described the circumstances surrounding his tragic death, and sent a copy of it to Privy Councilor Robert Briner of Zürich with a request that the conditions in Gyrenbad, which Heberlein did not of course know personally but of which he had had highly unfavorable reports, be thoroughly investigated. Privy Councilor Briner sent the eulogy and the letter to Territorial Commando 4 for further clarification. What followed was not an investigation of the conditions in the Gyrenbad camp but a summons to Dr. Heberlein to appear before Lieutenant Colonel H and Major B. They then informed him that his eulogy and his letter fell within the definition of punishable rumor-mongering and it was possible that his eulogy of Joseph Schmidt might be injurious to Switzerland's reputation in the United States!

In his written account of this conversation, Dr. Heberlein retorted: "If in fact there was anything that might damage Switzerland's reputation in the United States, it was certainly not a newspaper article but the terrible things that take place on our borders; the exclusion of refugees who seek asylum here because they believe in Switzerland and who are turned back."

Since Heberlein's "offense," however, was not so serious, he was to have been penalized with only a brief stay in prison. Finally this too was waived after a "correction" of Heberlein's article had been published.

## Fear of Competition

As early as August 8–9, 1942, *Die Basler-Nachrichten* had proposed the daring suggestion that able-bodied refugees be incorporated into the normal labor force, adding: "Most—we do not say all—of the problems of our emigrants would be resolved by such a bold step, which admittedly contravenes a guild and labor-union mentality, which indeed entails many risks, but which, viewed as a whole, at present represents a completely possible and constructive solution."

Now obviously this would have substantially increased the measure of national solidarity with the victims of persecution. In September 1943, when many refugees, especially from Italy, entered Switzerland and a large number of them was immediately taken to the canton of Berne, National Councilor Robert Grimm and State Councilor Rudolf Weber expressed their views in two parliamentary questions, inquiring of the Federal Council how it would handle the problem of their employment now that unemployment had really become a graver danger than in the past. Grimm pointed out that there must be understanding for the attitude of the working class when it saw itself faced with unemployment or the first indications of it, and that, if the need arose, consideration must be given to the methods by which the refugees would be integrated into the labor force without creating competition that might result unfavorably for the Swiss working class.

These remarks clearly expressed the understandable apprehension of a crisis like that of the 1930s, which had affected Switzerland too. This was a legitimate concern. It was self-evident that Swiss citizens should not go jobless because foreigners—even if they were refugees—had taken their places. Neither this concern nor this labor-union mentality —to the extent to which each was justified—can be invoked in criticism of officials or of private groups. Criticism was valid only when behind this concern there was unfounded enmity toward foreigners, especially "alien-thinking elements"; where obstinacy, envy, and timidity actually prevented feasible and meaningful work and, as a consequence, the solution of many psychological and material difficulties.

## Servant of the Spirit

This mentality, a peculiar mixture of justified concern for the jobs of Swiss citizens, thoroughly understandable fear of competition from foreigners, and also underlying hostility toward the Jews as such, already prevailed not only in the Police Section and the Fatherland Front, in labor unions, federations, and clubs. It was operative not only in the Federal Council. The Swiss Medical Society, by and large, took no different stand. Artists' organizations were able to express themselves most vehemently against commissions to emigrants or exhibitions of their works. Even the Swiss Writers' Union frequently and in many instances applied a strong-armed labor-union policy. This was in itself not beyond comprehension when one considered the difficult position of German-language Swiss writers, who were now virtually restricted to sales in their own small country. Germany was still open to only very few of them.

The Writers' Union stated its view in a letter of May 25, 1933, to the Federal Alien Police, on the basis of the position adopted at its general meeting eleven days earlier. It referred to the currently much-deterio-rated situation of Swiss authors to whom German newspapers were virtually barred by reason of the political changes in Germany and whose book sales there had dropped sharply as a result of the severe economic crisis in Germany. Thus the Swiss writer was forced into greater dependence than ever on the domestic sale of his literary produc-tion. Above all it was important to him that Swiss newspapers and magazines be open to him without restriction. "Hence the residence of every foreign author in Switzerland means a competitor for Swiss writ-ers. Most of the foreigners arrive penniless in Switzerland and are therefore advised to earn their livelihoods here in journalism."

Economic considerations by themselves, however, were not allowed to be determining factors in the treatment of the German refugees. These refugees included authors of truly superior stature who could not be deprived under any conditions of the right to publish freely. To any host country these literary eminences meant the enrichment of its artistic and intellectual life. Hence they ought to have not only the right to live in our country but also the opportunity to earn their livelihoods here. "They will repay our country richly in intellectual values for whatever economic gains they may take from us."

The Writers' Union believed that residence in Switzerland should be permitted too to writers who were political refugees. "Intellectual freedom is the prerequisite of our democracy. Therefore Switzerland may not close her gates against those who are persecuted because of their convictions. Since these refugees too must live, moreover, they should not be prevented from supporting themselves in Switzerland."

With the utmost vigor, however, the Writers' Union attacked "those foreign writers and journalists who want to come into Switzerland in order to exploit a situation. We stand firm against the little penny-a-liner, the irresponsible and characterless scribbler, who can be counted among neither the eminent nor the political refugees and who comes into Switzerland because he thinks he can have an easy life here." This third category of writers, then, should be denied permission to live in Switzerland.

In a letter of reply, Dr. Heinrich Rothmund stated his complete accord with these views.

Subsequently, applications for residence permits by foreign writers were submitted for approval from time to time to the Writers' Union by the Police Section, the cantonal Alien Police, and the labor offices. The results varied according to the identity of the applicant. In 1933 the Writers' Union intervened with the Federal Council on behalf of Albert Ehrenstein, who was under an order of expulsion. Dr. Wilhelm Högner, a well-known Social Democratic politician who was to be minister-president of Bavaria after the war, later applied for permission to work in Switzerland as a writer, and on February 21, 1935, the Writers' Union expressed the opinion that there could be no question of substantial competition by German writers who had fled to Switzerland. It made little difference whether the author lived here or in Germany. Out of considerations of humanity there should be no withholding of working permits from persons who fled to Switzerland for asylum. "What good does it do if they are allowed to enter the country and then left to go hungry?"

Dr. Daniel Brody, a Hungarian national who was then a director of the Rhein-Verlag, was less fortunate a year later. In a letter to the Federal Alien Police the Swiss Writers' Union asserted that, after Dr. Bermann of the Insel-Verlag had been refused permission to live and work in Switzerland, Brody's application should not be similarly denied out of hand. The Writers' Union proposed a set of rules to be followed:

1. The staff of his publishing house should be 50 per cent Swiss.

2. At least 50 per cent of its output should be sold in Switzerland.

3. Brody must give evidence of a culturally valuable publishing program of Swiss tendencies and be made to adhere to it.

4. Brody must retain a reputable and independent Swiss as a literary collaborator.

5. Brody must produce evidence that it will be possible for him to sell his books in Germany as well.

"We have no interest," the Writers' Union added, "in the establishment of a new emigrant publishing house." What that really meant, in different words, was that "the culturally valuable publishing program of Swiss tendencies" must include no books that attacked National Socialism.

Although Professor C. G. Jung had endorsed Dr. Brody with praise for him as a man of intellectual attainment and high character in whom the utmost confidence could be reposed, on 20 June 1936, Dr. Rothmund advised the Swiss Writers' Union that Brody's application for permanent residence in Switzerland had been rejected because his activity in the Rhein-Verlag would be of no particular interest to Switzerland.

## No Enrichment of Our Spiritual Life

Max Hochdorf, an author, also got a bad mark. The Swiss Writers' Union wrote to the Alien Police:

In general one has the impression that Hochdorf is one of those Jewish big-mouths who, in imitation of the prevailing trend, have been writing about anything and everything in the Berlin newspapers. According to Kürschner, Hochdorf was the dramatic critic for the Socialist *Vorwärts;* according to his own story, he wrote for the middle-class *Tageblatt.* As far as this kind of writer is concerned, it comes to the same thing.

Therefore he was to be denied a working permit. "His presence in our country means no enrichment of our spiritual life."

On February 8, 1938, the Alien Police informed Professor Franz Eichler, a German, that his application had seemed quite honest, appealing, and modest, but obviously he was neither prominent nor politically persecuted and therefore the Writers' Union felt no obligation to take a particular interest in him. The notification continued:

> Since the economic situation of Swiss authors has been growing worse month by month, every step must be taken to prevent their being deprived of their few remaining opportunities of earning money from abroad. Hence it is our opinion that permission should be refused to Professor Eichler to work here as a journalist or writer. On the other hand, we have no objection if the applicant works quietly on his book about Schiller in Switzerland.

There was much dismay in the secretariat of the Writers' Union in those days when refugee authors wrote under pseudonyms. In a letter of August 7, 1937, to the Federal Alien Police on the subject of the well-known worker-poet, Bruno Schönlank, the Union declared that emigrants should be compelled to write under their real names.

> There is something offensive about it when these gentlemen, as unfortunately occurs very often, assume the most Swiss-sounding names possible in order to deceive the public as to their origins. If emigrants are to be allowed to publish here, then they should be recognizable as foreigners. These Berliners in Swiss Alpine costumes remind us somehow of the wolf in sheep's clothing.

An application by another writer, Otto Nebel, was equally churlishly handled in a letter of May 25, 1938.

> Since we must now urgently insist that no further competition with our Swiss writers and journalists be permitted, and since we have

every reason to fight out our intellectual battles among ourselves (that is, without help from foreigners), permission should by all means be refused to Otto Nebel to work as a writer here in Switzerland. . . . The simplest way of achieving this goal would be to refuse him permission to live in our country.

In the summer and autumn of 1938, after the annexation of Austria, it would appear that intellectual honesty did not always prevail in the attitude of the secretariat of the Writers' Union toward emigrant authors. When it was learned that Victoria Wolff, at that time a widely read writer, was contributing one or two articles a month to *Die National-Zeitung* and receiving forty francs for each, the secretary of the Writers' Union expressed his discontent thus to the Alien Police:

> The aforesaid woman has therefore exploited her residence in Switzerland to engage in serious competition with Swiss writers and inject herself in undesirable fashion into our literary life. When one reflects that almost all collaboration with German and Austrian newspapers is precluded to our own writers [a fact for which the emigrants could hardly be held responsible], and when one considers the deplorable financial situation in which as a result they find themselves, it will be understood why the Writers' Union is opposed to emigrants who exploit their residence in our country to the detriment of their Swiss colleagues precisely where there is still something to be earned.

The Swiss Writers' Union therefore called on the Alien Police to take the strongest measures, which could mean only that Mrs. Wolff's residence permit should not be extended. "Literarily Switzerland will lose nothing by this." Victoria Wolff was thereupon thrown out. She found a place to live in France. Later, after temporary detention at the instigation of the Gestapo, she managed to reach the United States, where she now lives.

Even Siegfried Trebitsch's creative output was adjudged to be not so significant "that it would represent an enrichment of our country's cultural life." He too was refused permission to work, so that he could not continue his translations of Shaw in Switzerland.

The attitude of the Writers' Union created a tragedy for the married writing team of Schmidt-Ellrich. In the April 22, 1944, issue of *Das Ostschweizer Tagblatt* the editor, H. Niederer, told the story under the title, *One Fate Among Thousands*. The Schmidts, who had had to leave Germany in 1933, lived first in Dalmatia, then in Switzerland, and after that in Vienna. In 1938 they fled back to Switzerland, where they established themselves in a village in Aargau. At that time they were writing for small newspapers. One of their articles paid a specially impressive tribute to the significance of a democratic Switzerland in an epoch of upheaval. When the couple applied for an extension of their residence permit, the Federal Alien Police turned to the Swiss Writers' Union for counsel. The Union replied, among other things, that the couple wrote entertainment literature of no enduring value. "It is not inconceivable that they would be read by a public that is looking for diversion. But they do not belong among the foreign authors of significance whose works enrich our intellectual and literary life. We are therefore of the opinion that they should not receive residence permits. We have no objection if the husband remains here and writes for the foreign press." So in 1939 the couple went to southern France. When the demarcation line was overrun, both made every effort to return to Switzerland in legal fashion. The Federal Alien Police, Niederer wrote, expressed approval, and the required security bond was posted. "What put an end to the whole matter was a letter in the Schmidt-Ellrich file that had come from the Swiss Writers' Union and that urged the authorities *not* to grant an entry permit. No reason was given!"

The Schmidt-Ellrichs were deported.

## *In Re* Alfred Polgar

A letter of June 30, 1938, to the Zürich Alien Police is highly revealing of the basic attitude of the Writers' Union in that year. The letter dealt with the case of Alfred Polgar, a well known author. Since the Writers' Union has ever since attempted to cloud the issue, I reproduce the letter verbatim:

> On April 8, 1938, you submitted to us for appraisal the record in the matter of Alfred Polgar, born in 1873. Since we preferred first to observe the effects of Germany's annexation of Austria on our Swiss

literary world, we consulted the head of the Federal Alien Police and deferred our reply to your inquiry until today.

After close examination of all the evidence, we are therefore submitting to you today the *recommendation* that a working permit be refused to Alfred Polgar. At the same time the applicant is to be expressly informed that he also lacks the right to work as a journalist or writer under another name in our country.

The question whether a residence permit is to be denied to Alfred Polgar for reasons of overpopulation by foreigners does not fall within our consideration.

The foundation for our recommendation is as follows: As a result of the upheaval in Germany it has become almost totally impossible for Swiss journalists and authors to collaborate with foreign newspapers and magazines. The annexation of Austria to Germany has also excluded our writers from Austria as well. What is true of the market for newspaper articles is equally true, *mutatis mutandis*, of the sale of books. It is now possible only in exceptional instances for works published in Switzerland to have a large-scale success in Greater Germany. The Swiss writer's reading public has been reduced from more than eighty million to about three million persons. As a result our own publishers have become very hesitant to publish new works at their own risk. In many cases in which in the past they have paid good fees to authors they must now pay on a royalty basis. What that means to a country's literary culture is easy to measure. The Swiss authors were compelled to appeal for the help of the Confederation in order to continue to exist. It makes no sense that they should be subsidized by the state and at the same time competition by foreigners should be permitted.

We take this opportunity to remind you that the entrance of works in the graphic arts (without special authorization by the Department of the Interior) is in general prohibited. The writers are requesting no prohibition on the entry of foreign books, but they do wish to have at least the very small home market for journalistic production reserved to them.

The unification of Austria with Germany has resulted in a rise in the cost of both wood and paper, and as a result Swiss newspapers have had to make sharp reductions in their fees to contributors. Reputable newspapers today are paying only five, seven, or at the most twelve centimes a line. Obviously a writer can earn almost nothing more under these conditions, which rule out prolonged work on an article. It is absolutely inevitable that the intellectual level of our press should decline. Then we have the competition of the emigrants, who are often prepared to work for even less than these minimal prices, so that it is indeed impossible to see how the Swiss journalist and author can live.

There are also reasons of cultural policy that justify the denial of permission to emigrants to work in the areas of the press and literature. We are living today in a period in which opponents within Switzerland are pressing one another hard. Unquestionably it could lead only to an intellectual and probably, as a result, to a political catastrophe for our country if foreigners, no matter where they come from, inject themselves into our problems. Our history demonstrates that we have always been able to reach an understanding when we have disagreed. A common responsibility unites the left and the right, the French- and the German-speaking Swiss, the Catholics, the Protestants, and the Jews. Irreconcilability appears only in the foreign elements, which have nothing to lose.

It is known in addition that just at this time an effort is being made to extend to our territory the conflict between National Socialism and the emigration. Large sums are being invested in the struggle. We have every reason to prevent Switzerland from becoming the battlefield for this conflict. We Swiss will soon get rid of the problems in our own way. Every purely negative, foreign-directed cultural policy would be unfruitful and would bring us into political conflict with other nations.

As it now appears from the record, A. Polgar writes regularly for *Die Nation* and occasionally for other Swiss newspapers too. The editors of *Die Nation* have stated that "there is no one to replace Polgar as a literary artist." This statement must be rejected as being wholly without foundation. Naturally Polgar has his own style. There are in Switzerland, however, plenty of authors who are completely his equals in artistic and intellectual respects. Is it impossible for the management of *Die Nation* to find a replacement for Polgar among Swiss authors? At best this testifies to the paucity of their knowledge of the men in the field.

For the rest there is no necessity to say very much about Alfred

Polgar's literary merits. Undoubtedly he is a talented writer in his own way who made a certain name for himself in certain circles in the years after the First World War. Nevertheless it must be pointed out that Alfred Polgar's work is not of such significance that it would represent a real enrichment of our country's literary life. This brings us to our conclusion. Foreign authors should be granted permission to work only if they can be counted among the truly outstanding minds of our time.

It is distasteful to note, too, that in recent times, although he obviously had no working permit, Polgar has been consistently contributing articles to Swiss newspapers. This is further evidence of the indifference of these emigrants toward our laws.

Alfred Polgar's application had been endorsed by State Councilor Dr. Oskar Wettstein; Carl Seelig, journalist and author, and the Zürich Press Club. The Club, which must have felt that it too was implicated in the bill of attainder, then called on the Swiss Writers' Union to produce more specific grounds for its position on Polgar's application.

On the basis of the Union's statement, the cantonal Alien Police decided that temporary residence should be granted to Alfred Polgar on the following conditions: He was prohibited from collaborating in any way with Swiss newspapers and magazines; he was forbidden to speak or give readings in public or on the radio in Switzerland; his residence permit was limited to one year; at its expiration an inquiry would be made to determine whether Alfred Polgar had complied with the restrictions imposed on him.

## Good and Bad Marks

The Swiss Writers' Union adopted a very different position in the case of Else Lasker-Schüler. In a warm letter approving the poet's presence in Switzerland, the then secretary of the Union presented on November 2, 1938, a strong defense of the artistic personalities whose search for asylum among us was giving rise to much head-shaking here and there. In general the Swiss Writers' Union always showed more understanding toward writers or poets who concentrated on specialties in which they threatened no "competition" to their Swiss colleagues—that is, for

instance, lyricists, or travel authors. By and large the Union offered no
opposition to the publication of their books. Thus Ernst Preczang and
Erik Reger benefited by its statements to the authorities on their behalf,
while on the other hand an application on behalf of Dr. Erwin Reiche,
endorsed by Max Rychner, evoked a negative reaction.

With respect to the well-known Alexander Roda-Roda, too, whose
talents the Swiss Writers' Union explicitly recognized and of whom it
said in a letter of June 30, 1938, to the cantonal Alien Police of Zürich
that his literary level was respectable, his convictions democratic and
freedom-loving, and all his criticisms infused with a tone of human
sympathy, so that he could truly be called a humorist and not merely an
ironist or a satirist, the Union nevertheless emphasized "that the domain dealt with by Roda-Roda had very little to do with Switzerland"
and that therefore his work could hardly contribute to an enrichment of
our intellectual life. "On the basis of this appraisal," the authorities
arrived at a decision in conformance with which the Writers' Union was
able on October 26, 1938, to state that "for the term of one year the
petitioner" would be granted residence in Switzerland and authorization
to engage in literary work and publish his books, but he was forbidden
to contribute to Swiss newspapers, magazines, and broadcasts, as well as
to accept a position as editorial director, reader, or the like, or to deliver
lectures without special authorization from official sources.

But for Golo Mann, that "political artilleryman" who was to undertake the Swiss publication of *Mass und Wert*, the review directed by his
father, Thomas Mann, the Swiss Writers' Union would not open the
doors: "Inasmuch as Switzerland has now pledged herself to a comprehensive neutrality, she has no reason to allow emigrants—whether their
motives be good or bad—to wage their war against Germany from her
soil." Furthermore, "with all due respect to Thomas Mann," this family's residence in Switzerland had not proved exactly advantageous—
"one has only to recall the scandal that Erika Mann brought down on
herself with her cabaret"—and it was recommended that the permanent
visa requested by Golo Mann be refused.

Harsh terms were imposed also on the Austrian writer, Robert Musil.
He was forbidden to contribute to newspapers and magazines, speak on
the radio or in public, or accept any literary job (as reader, publisher, or
editor). If he had not had loyal friends, such as the Reverend Robert
Lejeune, Musil would certainly have starved in Switzerland. In any

event he died there embittered and alone, since our country was too stupid to appreciate the honor of his presence as our guest.

Margarete Susman, however, was given a good recommendation—according to the Union's letter of November 16, 1939—and "by way of exception" the Union agreed that she should receive permission to live in Switzerland and engage in literary work. But she could lecture only by special permission, to be granted or withheld according to the circumstances of each individual case. This recommendation was contingent on a two-year limitation on her permits and re-examination at the end of that time.

In retrospect many of these "evaluations" seem harsh and incomprehensible. One is disturbed that authors so ostentatiously dedicated to the service of the intellect and to the struggle against materialism should have maintained so stiff-necked a guild-plus-labor-union opposition and emphasized the purely material fear of competition in order to keep foreign colleagues out of "the Swiss market"—and this precisely at that period when the exiles seeking asylum among us had been stripped of everything. The case of journalists was quite different: they indeed had to depend for their livelihoods on their newspaper work, which was much more precarious than that of the writers. Then as now, far fewer than 10 per cent of them really lived—or could live—on their literary work. Ninety per cent of them worked as well in some steady occupation—as teachers, editors, government officials—and therefore were not completely dependent on their newspaper earnings. But even so, writers, too, are only men, not angels. Writers, too, here as elsewhere, then as now, are for the most part concerned first of all with their own success. "Nevertheless," Professor Zbinden asserted in his *Der Flüchtling und die Humanität* (*The Refugee and Humanity*), "the much too overemphasized economic consideration operated in so peculiar a fashion that the same refugee, as long as he remained abroad, could work unhampered for our press and collect fees from it. Once he was in the country of asylum, however, all that was at an end. He had ample time to examine what changes he might have occasioned in our labor market."

When it was a question of colleagues who were in peril, the Swiss Writers' Union espoused their cause. Thus it furthered the rescue effort begun by Hans Reinhart in Winterthur on behalf of Alfred Mombert, who pleaded for help in heart-rending letters from Gurs in the autumn of 1940. Robert Faesi, Gustav Gamper, Hermann Hesse, and others added their voices on behalf of the poet and his sister, who were in imminent danger. Late in the autumn of 1941—after an earlier refusal in March of that year—Dr. Heinrich Rothmund finally announced his approval of the Momberts' entry into Switzerland, thus snatching them out of the jaws of the National Socialist wolves at the last minute.

The Writers' Union intervened also on behalf of Paul Leons, James Joyce's secretary, who had been seized as a hostage in Paris in 1941; it acted favorably in many more such cases.

## Brain Fever

A new wind began to blow through the Swiss Writers' Union when Dr. Eduard F. Knuchel, fiction editor of *Die Basler-Nachrichten* and at that time president of the Swiss Press Club, appealed at the directors' meeting in Solothurn on October 21, 1943, for more generous behavior toward colleagues who had fled to Switzerland. Fully conceding the principle that Swiss writers' interests naturally came first, he argued that one must not prescribe an exclusively "homemade" literature or endeavor to achieve complete literary self-sufficiency; it was much more consonant with good Swiss tradition to listen to voices from other countries and allow others to hear them. Official German literary production, he said, was useless to us, and good writers still living in Germany no longer dared to risk writing for foreign newspapers that were prohibited there. Hence the Swiss newspapers had no choice but to strengthen their ties with those few long-time contributors who were now living in Switzerland as emigrants.

He had made inquiries, Knuchel added, among fifteen of his best known colleagues—Dr. Otto Kleiber (*National-Zeitung*, Basel), Dr. Eduard Korrodi (*Neue Zürcher Zeitung*), Dr. Paul Meierhans (*Volksrecht*, Zürich), Dr. Arnold H. Schwengeler (*Bund*), Dr. Max Rychner (*Tat*), Auf der Maur (*Vaterland*, Luzerne), Ernst Flükiger (*St.-Gallen Tagblatt*), Dr. Friedrich Witz (*Du*, Zürich), Eugen Felber (*Luzerner Neueste Nachrichten*), Manuel Gasser (*Weltwoche*), Dr. H. Suter (*Aargauer Tagblatt*), Dr. W. Meier (*Schweizer Illustrierte*), Max Schuler (*Thurgauer Zeitung*), Dr. E. König (*Beobachter*, Basel), and Dr. Hans Rudolf Schmid (*Schweizer Feuilleton-Dienst*, Zürich)—and had found that, with the exception of *Der Bund,* which said that it received sufficient material from domestic sources, these papers could not obtain sufficient Swiss material to meet their needs for serial fiction; moreover, they were not interested in attaining complete self-sufficiency. On the basis of this survey, Knuchel had decided to present an appeal to the Federal Alien Police on February 27, 1943, to authorize any newspaper seeking such permission to accept a maximum of four pieces a month from any qualified refugee who before his emigration to Switzerland had been a regular contributor to Swiss newspapers. He also asked for authorization for the publication of serial fiction by these writers. As a result of the strict prohibition of such literary activity, he pointed out, year-long major contracts were being made with writers living abroad, while on the other hand well known authors were being forced to live on private or public charity. There was also the danger, he added, that contributions from Germany might taint the Swiss press with un-Swiss falsifications of historical fact and attacks on democracy, often very subtly camouflaged.

In substance, however, the Alien Police had rejected his proposals. The present state of affairs was infuriating. The emigrants were developing a strong antagonism to our country, and indeed the nation's behavior thus far had not been unworthy of it.

For professional reasons alone, Knuchel insisted, it was wrong to make these fearful attempts to eliminate all competition in order to assure the support of all our talents. We should make it our business to ask: "Is it good writing?" rather than: "Who wrote it?," he declared.

Dr. Knuchel called on the Swiss Writers' Union to support his point of view in its negotiations with the authorities. He was backed up by the board of directors.

As we have pointed out, the change in the secretariat of the Swiss Writers' Union in 1943 had already brought about a significant shift to a more liberal position. On March 16, 1943, the Union wrote to Federal Councilor von Steiger urging him to rescind all restrictions on foreign writers who were living in Switzerland as refugees. They should be allowed to contribute to newspapers, the letter said, emphasizing that limitations on competition were inconsistent with the essence of intellectual endeavor.

Our picture would be incomplete if it did not also include the fact that many Swiss writers were eager and active in helping their perse-

cuted colleagues abroad and in Switzerland with contributions of
money, intervention with the authorities, and the hospitality of their
own homes. The best of them, the real artists, suffered from no dread of
competition. Nor did they forget, in these gloomy years, that the spirit
moves where it will, that it asks no questions about nationality, race,
party, or religion, and that the bearers of this spirit are brothers, a
sodality united by inner bonds. They did not turn their backs on those
who were in peril. One could list the names of many men and women
who labored in complete obscurity and did what was necessary without
ostentation. When their efforts were rewarded with success they re-
joiced with the friends whom they had saved, not forgetting that their
own safety was to be ascribed not to their merits but to the fact that
they were citizens of a country whose determination to preserve its own
dignity and whose fortunate destiny had spared it the hell of dictatorship and war. What mattered here was not the standards of the Police
Section but the power of the mind. Here the hunted had equal rights
and were taken seriously. Here as everywhere it was plain that true
humanity is not nearly so much the business of a nation or an organization—they can always make, increase, or reduce the facilities for it—as
it is the work of individuals—many individuals.

# The Turning Point

It was not until July 12, 1944, that the Police Section rescinded the orders given on December 29, 1942, and all subsequent written and oral instructions regarding specific border areas. At last the Police Section struck out the fateful sentence: "Refugees on exclusively racial grounds are not political refugees." The new instructions said: "For the present, admission shall be granted only to . . . foreigners who for political *or other* reasons are in actual peril to life and limb and who have no way of avoiding this danger other than that of flight to Switzerland."

It also followed, as the Police Section informed the Federation of Swiss Jewish Communities, that henceforth all Jewish refugees were to be admitted because they must now be deemed to be in danger in all countries bordering on Switzerland. (See Ludwig, pages 293–294.)

285

The reports now being received of mass murder of the Jews in Hungary could no longer leave even the most determined skeptic doubtful of their credibility. On June 5, *Die Tat, Die National-Zeitung, La Liberté, Die Berner Tagwacht*, and other newspapers reported that a daily average of ten thousand Jews was being deported from Hungary to Poland, particularly to the camps of Treblinka and Auschwitz. On June 28, the Juna agency distributed a detailed account of the extermination of the Jews in Hungary. Between May 15 and June 10, 355,000 Jews had been shipped out of Hungary and the areas annexed to it. The report also described the torture chambers in Auschwitz, which was called the largest of the German "death factories." Ten thousand corpses a day could be consumed in its three crematories. This report was published by a number of newspapers, although the censorship bureau protested that "this dispatch contains a deliberate collection of carefully selected quotations on the persecutions of the Jews and thus it has a propaganda character that we cannot countenance."

At the same time the Swiss were made acquainted with the narrative of Rudolf Vrba, who had escaped from Auschwitz; his report corroborated what had been related as early as 1942 by Dr. Riegner, as well as other accounts. On July 7, 1944, *Die Neue Zürcher Zeitung* declared that "no doubt is any longer possible as to the horrible thoroughness of the deportations and the inhuman cruelties practiced on the victims."

The Swiss public was profoundly shocked. The dreadful facts were made known in the press and from the pulpit, and swift help was urged. The Zürich Cantonal Council unanimously adopted a resolution of protest, saying: "According to reliable reports, one million persons of Jewish origin in Hungary are threatened with a terrible death. Thousands of men, women, and children are shipped daily to the death camps with mass-production methods. . . ."

The Evangelical Relief Agency and other organizations and prominent individuals stormed the Federal Council with demands that everything possible be done to save the threatened Jews of Hungary. Even the head of the Police Section, Dr. Heinrich Rothmund, began to call for the rescue of the Jews. In a letter of November 3, 1944, to the Swiss Legation in Berlin, he declared his willingness to take in thirteen hundred Jews—what was left of a transport from Hungary—provided that they were properly accounted for and brought to Switzerland. He also called on the Legation to "intervene against deportation and to request food and clothing for all other Jews still remaining in Germany." In furtherance of his purpose—so Professor Ludwig reported—Dr. Rothmund attempted to bring pressure to bear on a particular official in the Foreign Ministry so that he would appeal to Himmler.

> This is a question of hundreds of thousands of human lives, and so, if necessary to give one man somewhat indecorously the courage that perhaps he lacks. . . . That we are very much in earnest about saving the Jews who are still alive can be seen from the fact that, when our Legation in Budapest notified us that the Hungarian and German governments had agreed to allow eight thousand Hungarian Jews to travel to Switzerland, we answered by telegraph two days ago saying that in principle we were ready to admit them . . . If we are now committing ourselves to such positive measures of assistance, surely we have a right to take a stand against further deportations.

In Berne, too, the turning point had been reached. The outcome of the war was now clear and its end was in sight. Tens of thousands of children from the war-torn countries could now come to Switzerland to regain their health. The Federal Council announced its readiness to accept fourteen thousand Jews from Hungary, and preparations were set in motion. Former Federal Councilor Jean-Marie Musy negotiated with leading. figures of the Third Reich and succeeded in obtaining the liberation of a large number of Jews. Bargaining began, and it was not always altogether above-board and indeed not always altogether honorable, despite the fact that this time it was in the hands not of the "smugglers" denounced by the Federal Council but of upstanding Swiss. The Germans demanded merchandise or money for the Jews whom they let go. Even in the final stages of their disintegration, the Aryan men of honor showed their true faces. The money was transferred by way of Swiss banks. It was a traffic in human beings. But the stake was human lives—and so one did things that were or seemed disreputable.

It was an irony of history that we Swiss were now taking in those whom we had kept out earlier, and that others with whom we had made deals against the Jews were now being turned away from our borders.

High-level policy often takes strange paths.

## *Bonjour, Monsieur le Bureau!*

And yet the cantonal and Federal Alien Police would not allow even the end of the war to alter the operations of the machinery that they had designed for the repulse and re-emigration of the refugees. Even if worlds are falling to pieces, rules are still rules. On September 14, 1945, the Federal Police Section issued a circular letter that declared: "Although refugees are once more reminded that Switzerland can be regarded only as a transit country for them, we still note that individual refugees continue to believe that they can remain in our country permanently."

On December 25, 1945, *Der Nebelspalter* published an article entitled *Bonjour, Monsieur le Bureau* (*Good Morning, Mr. Office*)! It said in part:

> Switzerland has long prided herself on being the shield of freedom and democracy and, as such, offering asylum to all the persecuted. Between 1933 and 1945 the borders of Switzerland were stormed by thousands of persons persecuted, plundered, and hunted by Hitlerism. Many were in fact admitted and came to know the proverbial hospitality of our country and its free, democratic customs in their camp barracks surrounded by barbed wire. Most of the refugees and emigrants, however, had already learned about this kind of living from German concentration camps, and so—and this we must certainly put to their credit—they bear no rancor against Switzerland; after all, she saved them from the worst. It was quite the opposite for the other thousands who were driven away from our borders into suffering and, often, certain death. This was described by that New German-Swiss word, *exclusion.* Meanwhile, thousands of military and civilian internees have left our country again, though other thousands are still here because for the moment they have absolutely no idea where they can turn; for the makers of world peace in San Francisco include no recognizable Pestalozzis. In Europe, however, suffering, hunger, and need are dominant, and it is now winter. This situation is regarded by those gentlemen in Berne who very suddenly perceived that the war of weapons had ended as the best suited to the special-delivery dispatch of question-

naires and summonses to the twenty or twenty-five thousand refugees and emigrants who are still here, so that they can be tormented and driven into a corner. These frightened, helpless people
are reminded that at such and such a time a transport will be
leaving Switzerland for the west or the north or the east, and they
are threatened with internment in camps if they do not make up
their minds to leave Switzerland; preparations are made to evacuate
all of them to the frontier. . . .

The Nazis, the half-Nazis, the quarter-Nazis, the one-tenth-Nazis
are left unmolested now, while the victims hunted down by their
system are driven out into the winter cold and starvation.

Regards, but unkind!

So men, women, children, and old people had lived out miserable
existences among us for years, fled their homes and countries, lost
families, relatives, friends to the gas chambers or the execution squads
of the SS and the Gestapo, been spiritually and physically enfeebled,
uprooted in the deepest sense of the word; they did not know where
they could turn, and more than anything they needed rest—yet they
were reminded again and again that they were strangers, tolerated but
unwanted. Perhaps this was not malice, but it was that cold bureaucracy
that at times can be no less inhuman.

The thought that as "stateless persons" on the grounds of race we
have become the victims of a shipwreck who can nowhere find a
haven and who are nowhere welcome is a heartbreaking thought.
The loss of money and property does not grieve us so much as life
without a country and without any rights whatsoever; the impossi-
bility of working has been a grievous wound to my beloved husband. . . . Where shall we settle, where shall we turn, where shall
we go? We do not want to be driven forever. Germany? Reverend,
I am afraid we cannot. . . . Yes, it is a country that we once loved
more than anything else . . . because so many fine people gave us
joy there by their mere presence. They have all gone away—or they
are no longer what they were. . . . It makes me shudder. Is there
never to be an end to this homelessness? . . . This eternal wander-
ing, being tolerated, having to hear the same thing: "You are
foreigners, you must leave the country as soon as possible. We did

not send for you! You came here of your own accord!" But surely
you can understand that one makes the effort to save oneself.
Before our flight—our second—we thought differently of Switzerland! We did not want to fight any longer—only finally to rest! We
got up our courage again, we came here—and they wanted to send
us back! Then my husband, who could no longer control himself,
reached for the border guard's pistol—he pulled it from the wall
and wanted to make an end of everything. We stopped him. Then
he went into convulsions, and after that he was unconscious for
three days. So we paid the bitter, heavy price of health for our
residence here. . . .

This letter was written by the wife of a man who had once been a
responsible executive on the staff of one of the most important newspapers in Germany.


## Dust-Covered Folders

Dust has gathered now on the innumerable folders in which the refugee-relief organizations filed the documents of similar life stories. The
papers are yellow between the lines of shaky script in which frightened
men and women made their appeals for help at a time when they were
again beginning to feel like human beings and to look forward to peace
and to a simple, quiet old age. The folders also hold the letters to
authorities in which the refugee workers begged for understanding and
insight and a little human sympathy.

They testify to the uncounted hours spent by officials paid by the
state—and so by us, its citizens—in further tormenting already tormented men and women. They attest to the strength and the exertions
of clergymen, lawyers, welfare workers, politicians, and unknown individuals attempting to avert tragic conclusions in the worst cases. They
bear witness to the stubborn battle between narrow-minded legalism
and compassionate human feeling.

Yes, now these papers are covered with dust. Perhaps they will be
destroyed one day in order to make room for others. But perhaps, too,
one day someone will come and look through them and note with
amazement how important these records are, how admirably suited they

are to the completion of the historical picture of those disordered years. Then—perhaps with a certain degree of shame—he will observe what resolute bargaining and haggling over every centimeter of human kindness was required even then, until finally a settlement was evolved in 1947 that made it possible for at least a restricted number of the persecuted to take up permanent residence in Switzerland. He will encounter the names of men and women who labored together in nonpartisan committees to obtain the nation's "Yes" vote.

Dr. Urs Dietschi, National Councilor and Privy Councilor of Solothurn, was particularly energetic in his efforts on behalf of permanent asylum through his work in the National Council. When the decision was made, Dr. Nettie Sutro wrote:

If one reflects that this permanent asylum also involved emigrants who since 1933, perhaps, had had repeatedly to return at intervals of three or at most six months to apply for extensions of their residence permits—so that in the course of the years they had appeared as petitioners perhaps fifty or sixty times before a functionary of the cantonal Alien Police—it must have seemed like a miracle at last to hear: "You may stay among us as long as you work; you may work as long as you are able, and, when you are no longer able, we—the Confederation, the canton, and your relief agency—will take care of you."

# The Helpers

It would be impossible to present an accurate picture of the relations between Switzerland and the persecuted victims of National Socialism who sought her protection if one omitted the statistics revealing the country's willingness to help and the assistance that it actually rendered.

During the war years—1939–1945—a total of 295,381 fugitives found asylum in Switzerland for varying periods. When the war in Europe ended in May 1945, more than 115,000 refugees were still in the country. More than 103,000 of the almost 300,000 who had entered had been interned (escaped prisoners of war, deserters, and hospital patients); more than 55,000 were civilian refugees in the strictest sense; about 10,000 were emigrants—in other words, refugees—who had sought and found shelter with us before August 1, 1942; 251 were political refugees; 60,000 children either had come to us as fugitives or had been brought in organized groups for health cures of several months' duration; more than 66,000 persons were so-called border refugees, who for the most part had sought only short-term refuge in Switzerland. About thirty thousand of the refugees and emigrants were Jewish by belief or by ancestry. The most heavily represented nationalities were Italian, French, Polish, German, Austrian, Russian, Dutch, Yugoslav, Hungarian, Czech, Rumanian, Belgian, Greek, Spanish, and Lithuanian. The number of nationals of forty-four other countries totaled fewer than two hundred.

The Confederation's financial outlay for the refugees amounted to 178,000 francs before the war; from 1939 to 1945 it totaled 82,836,849.60 francs; by 1950 the net outlay had risen to 127,830,703.72 francs.

The total of private expenditures should probably be reckoned even higher. Ludwig's report put it at 87 million francs, although this figure did not include individuals' expenses, often over periods of years, in providing refugees with housing, food, clothing, and linens, as well as with household furniture and equipment. These expenditures obviously cannot be calculated. They must have amounted to many millions of francs.

(Between 1940 and 1950 the Confederation made more than 350 million francs available for aid to refugees abroad through the Swiss Red Cross, the International Red Cross Committee, and Swiss charities, while more than 630 million francs were contributed to the various relief agencies from private sources.)

These figures offer impressive evidence of the Swiss nation's readiness to help.

We do not wish to forget, however, that these sacrifices amounted to infinitely less than the damage inflicted by the war. In the report that it published on the refugee policy of 1933–1950, the Federal Justice and Police Department observed: "The accidental bombing of Schaffhausen by American planes caused damage amounting to more than thirty million francs. In a few minutes property worth a huge amount at that time was destroyed. One day of war brought almost unimaginable consequences in damage."

Nor can we Swiss simply preen ourselves on large numbers. Francs expended do not reflect unlimited human kindness. They can serve as a cheap way of simultaneously avoiding actual help and easing the conscience. What counts for much more is actual effort, being available, willingness to act. What counted was the fact that there were police commissioners like Privy Councilors Briner in Zürich and Brechbühl in Basel who remained human beings and ignored the orders from Berne whenever possible.

What was important then was the fact that not all border officials docilely obeyed Dr. Rothmund's orders, that there were border guards who, when they saw refugees approaching, looked the other way until the fugitives had disappeared into the sanctuary of Switzerland's midnight darkness. What was important was the fact that at every level there were police officials who carried out not only the duties laid on them by their superiors but also the obligations imposed on them by their consciences, and to whom the commands of human decency outranked the orders of an often unjust national policy.

There were such men, just as there were the cruel and the heartless. I am thinking of the police captain in an eastern canton who refused to obey the inhuman orders issued from Berne and who had to pay for his humanity with his discharge—on a very shoddy pretext. I am thinking of officials in the Police Section in Berne who did not lose their compassion even when the orders of their chief made life difficult for them. They are forever obscure. They do not wish any recognition. The refugee-relief workers know them. Justice demands that they too be thanked.

What counted was the fact that there were men who had the courage to admit the innocent "illegals" and, when necessary, to conceal them from arrest and expulsion over the border. What counted was the fact that there were families that invited the refugees to their meager repasts and shared what little they had with them. Whoever, knowing the emergency, stood aside in those days has more than forfeited the right to cast a stone today.

What was important was the fact that there were men and women—physicians, clergymen, politicians, lawyers, writers, housewives, laborers—who made it their business not to allow the voice of humanity to be silenced among us or the nation to be seduced by the arguments of an insensate, unfounded phobia of inundation by foreigners.

What counted was the fact that there were men and women who had the courage to say what had to be said.

No, the refugee policy was not the creation of the Justice and Police

Department, the Police Section, and the cantonal police commissioners alone. It was also shaped and executed by the men and women in our country whose consciences gave them the strength to recognize what the time required of them as Swiss and as human beings. Humanitarian Switzerland was not asleep. It was an incalculable community that was not dedicated to *"sacro egoismo"* but rather fulfilled its duty of humanity with a clear mind and a warm heart.

There was the motherly Gertrud Kurz-Hohl, the Appenzell-born wife of Dr. Albert Kurz of Berne, scientist, vice chancellor of a university, and colonel in the Swiss army, in whose house at Sandrain released prisoners and wanderers had found a friendly welcome for years; in 1938 she assumed the new and great task of refugee assistance without a second thought. How many lives did she save by her appeals to the authorities, going up even to the Federal Council? She herself does not know the number. How often she herself made bold decisions on the spur of the moment and only later arranged formalities with the authorities—for example, on that day of prayer in 1942 when a border trooper telephoned her from an inn and asked her whether refugees should really be allowed to enter, since he was so far away and was not precisely informed. Mrs. Kurz did not even stop to think. "Yes," she said, "let the people in, the frontier is open." Two families entered. Later Mrs. Kurz went to the Police Section and explained the matter. The refugees were allowed to remain. What kind of influence emanated from her that she could make Dr. Rothmund, Dr. Jezler, Federal Councilor von Steiger, and other magistrates and officials give way, that she could move them to make concessions to so many persons in danger of death? And what gave the woman herself her absolutely unbelievable stamina to travel virtually day and night from one official to another, from one needy refugee group to another, explaining their position to them, distributing money, collecting clothes, finding quarters, delivering lectures in order to enlist understanding, writing letters, telephoning? Certainly she had loyal, helpful, influential friends: Professor Karl Barth, National Councilor Albert Oeri, and others. But that alone was not enough. It was also, as she always said, the strength of her unshakable belief in man's God-given duty, it was the matter-of-fact manner in which she did what she regarded as her own duty, and it was her comprehension of other people's situations—not only that of the refugee but also that of the official. Not least it was the magnificent sense of humor, born of a great heart, with which she eased many a tense crisis. What her fellow-citizen, Federal Councilor Dr. Johannes Baumann, lacked in courage and human warmth was outweighed by her virtues.

And there was Regina Kägi-Fuchsmann, the founder of the Swiss Worker Relief Agency, a convinced Socialist and a warm-hearted, astute, incessantly active woman. She was a helper from the earliest moment. When she heard of the emergencies in the French camps, she organized *Les colis suisses* (Swiss Packages), a food-parcel service that enabled many persons to survive the horror camps. Earlier than many others, earlier too than many of her political friends, she recognized what was going on and what National Socialism would mean for Switzerland. With such friends as Dr. Hans Oprecht, Dr. Werner Stocker (later a federal judge), Franz Schmid, an editor in St. Gallen, National Councilors Huber and Walther Bringolf, and many others, she did whatever was to be done. She knew that political refugees, most of them Jews, were crossing the border; she knew that Dr. Stocker and others were helping them. Not only did she know it; she approved of it and she furthered it. Above the nation's law she ranked the duty of rescuing human beings. Hundreds, perhaps thousands, knew and know what they owe to this woman. If ever the history of this period is written, her name will stand among those that we shall read with pride.

There was also Sasha Morgenthaler, an artist, housewife, mother, and teacher, whose husband, Ernst, was a painter. She turned her home into a residence for the persecuted; when the trains full of suffering children arrived, she went to the frontier to meet them, driven by their need to do her utmost for them.

And there was the Reverend Dr. Paul Vogt, who had long regarded his clerical vocation as a social obligation to his neighbor. "A church that offers no haven to the suffering can never be a church of Jesus Christ," he declared in the 1930s, and he had joined the battle against the sufferings of the victims there where he served in an official capacity. "In a time of any kind of emergency," he said, "the church may never stand aloof and wring its hands"; he threw himself into the exhausting task of refugee assistance when the emergency was at its worst. For him preachment and practice were inseparable. In his sermons he called for practical service, and in his actions he preached more convincingly than any word could do.

His words and his actions were guided not by so-called reasons of state but by the obligation that he felt in his heart. He was first of all a servant of God, and only secondarily an official of his country. When his God bade him speak, he spoke, even if the state—and sometimes, too, the church—called for caution, circumspection, and silence. From his pulpit he preached no prudently phrased platitudes; he spoke from an overflowing heart, anguished by the agony of the persecuted, convinced of and dominated by the mission that had now been laid upon him.

*Armor Has No Fear* was the title that he gave to the little periodical sent to contributors to the refugee fund that he had established in cooperation with the Reverends Gottfried Ludwig of Biel and Alfred Hübscher of Zürich. There could be no thought of fear when the defense of human kindness was at stake. He had no fear. He wrote strong outspoken letters to the authorities, he spoke up unafraid in their offices and explained to the officials exactly what was at issue. He made malevolent, hard-hearted camp commanders aware of what was reprehensible in their actions. Not because his was a rebellious character or because it gave him pleasure to make the officials' work harder, but because he had recognized and accepted the duty of being the voice of the silent, the emissary of the hunted.

And too there was Emil Oprecht, the Zürich publisher, to whom principle was more important than profit and who, when the need required him to do so, converted his publishing house into a branch office of human decency. He and his indefatigable wife, Emmy, collected money, underclothing, outer garments for the use of the sufferers in the French camps. Every day he received letters that were cries for help. And he listened to them all. To those who were intellectually starved he sent books and magazines. He wrote letters to powerful friends and acquaintances, to partnerships and corporations, to universities and officials. He renewed the courage of the despairing. He went to Berne whenever it was necessary. He put to work all his connections in England, the United States, and Sweden for the rescue of human beings, above all the imperiled writers and artists and intellectuals. He sent such people money by legal and by illegal means. And every so often his letters would be sent back with the prosaic rubber stamp: "Return to sender." The addressee had disappeared, had been deported, or had committed suicide.

His many files contained hundreds of letters recounting appalling

fates, unlimited helpfulness and powerlessness, generosity and stubbornness, successes and wasted efforts. These files are filled with famous
names: Franz Werfel, Heinrich and Thomas Mann, Maria Fein and
Leonhard Frank, Ferdinand Hardekopf and Konrad Heiden, Lion
Feuchtwanger and Friedrich Wolf, Theodor Wolff and Hermann Kes-
ten, Frans Masereel, and many more.

There was also Nurse Anny Pflüger, a quiet, overworked Zürich
woman who was surely never cut out for heroism. In her confession of
faith she wrote: "He who knows God in his inmost heart must also
accept his creatures. He who loves God must also love God's creatures.
He who seeks to serve God must also serve men. To him who really
loves God there can be no valuation based on nationality, race, class, or
sex." And, because she meant what she had written, to her the persecuted Jews were no "alien-minded element" on whom doors must be
closed. When they knocked, shivering with fear, bearing no papers, no
residence permits, "illegals" guilty of unauthorized entry into the land
of asylum, Anny Pflüger opened the door, welcomed them into her
father's house, and gave them food and beds. Frequently every room
was filled with refugees. If all the beds were filled, they slept on the
floors. But at least they felt safe. For Anny Pflüger never did anything
that "proper" citizens were supposed to do. She never went to the Alien
Police and said: "There are three Jewish boys in my house who came in
illegally. You can take them away." She did not inform on some Jewish
family from Austria so that they would have to be thrown out the next
day. She set everything in motion to prevent people's expulsions. She let
her work slide, going off to Berne to deal with one functionary after
another. She interceded with the cantonal Privy Councilor of Zürich.
And then, when all her efforts came to nothing, she concealed her
fugitives in some mountain village. The local burgomaster and notables
were her "accomplices." She violated articles and sections and committed the crime of saving lives. She also saved the honor of Switzerland, if
necessary against the laws made by the authorities. We owe her thanks.
"He who loves God must also love God's creatures." To Anny Pflüger
this was a categorical imperative that could not be evaded.

There was also Professor Hans Zbinden in Berne. He was the publisher of Iris Reproductions, magnificent prints of European and other
art works. His interest was the history of culture; politics did not interest
him. But when it came to a question of men's and women's lives, he
knew that culture without kindness was a farce. In the fateful month of

August 1942 he lifted his voice on the side of those who wanted to preserve Switzerland as the "shield of freedom and humanity." He went into the camps to visit the exiled intellectuals, writers, artists, got them to their feet, proved his solidarity with them, exerted himself to ease their situation, and poured out articles and speeches calling for compassion for them.

There was another helper: the editor Hermann Böschenstein of Berne, a pugnacious democrat whose principles were beyond reproach. And there was Max Rychner, poet, essayist, and editor of *Die Tat* in Zürich. He knew that he was forbidden to publish work by emigrant writers. His mind was not easy about breaking the law. But he knew how vitally important it is to poets to transmute their experiences and their reactions into works of art. And he knew, too, how important it was that a hearing should be given to precisely these voices that came to us from out of the dark night of suffering. So he did what many of his colleagues also did, and what redounded to his and to their honor.

There was Robert Faesi, the Zürich professor of literature in whose hospitable home so many of the uprooted found shelter in which to resume the battle for life in freedom. Carl Seelig, untiringly helpful, similarly assisted many literary colleagues intellectually and financially through the difficult years. Robert Musil, Jakob Wassermann, Fritz Wotruba, the sculptor, and others found a real friend in the Reverend Robert Lejeune. Erwin Jaeckle interceded with the authorities on behalf of poets driven out by the Nazis, and opened his house to the fugitives. There were also Abbé (now Cardinal) Journet and Dr. Otto Karrer, who in word and act symbolized human kindness and compassion for the persecuted. On the same side stood Albert Maag-Socin and Max Wolff, and those fighting, ever-helpful editors, Oskar Hürsch and Adolf Galliker. Fritz Schwarz and Werner Schmid, the economists, constantly raised their voices. Young Oskar Reck, imbued with the ideals of liberal humanism, hid refugees threatened with "exclusion" until their safety was assured. Clara Nef, then president of the Federation of Swiss Women's Clubs, put into practice what she had written in a letter in 1940: "Either one acknowledges one's obligations, which then extend to all men, or one does not acknowledge them, and then one is equally selfish when it comes to the needy in one's own country. May Switzerland prove her right to exist by recognizing her duty today and performing it." History will not forget her courageous, inexhaustible efforts on behalf of the threatened Jews of Hungary—her interventions of July 13, 1944, with Paula von Horthy and Federal Councilor von Steiger, which paralleled those of Dr. Vogt though neither knew of the other's action.

Elsbeth Kasser was a helper of rare quality. Wherever there were wounds to be healed and needs to be met, she was there. With Rodolfo Olgiati and Karl Ketterer she had gone to Spain to aid the innocent victims of the Civil War. Then she went to the camps in France, lived there with the refugees, nursed them, organized the procurement of medicines, food, and clothing. And, when the refugees came to Switzerland, she devoted all her energies to them, often to the point of exhaustion. She was called "the angel of the helpless," and she deserved the title.

There were also Erwin Haymann and Armand Brunschvig, Abraham Silberschein and G. M. Riegner, Georges Bloch, Otto Heim, Veit Wyler, Benjamin Sagalowitz, the unforgettable Sylvain S. Guggenheim, Sally Mayer, Carl Silberstein, Jean Nordmann and his future wife, Georges Brunschvig, Nathan Schwalb, and A. Syngalowski, who organized the ORT's work in the camps. These few names of important and wholly dedicated helpers inside and outside the Jewish organizations must serve also as symbols for those many others like them, all of whom were at once victims, rescued, and rescuers.

There were Fritz Wartenweiler and Dr. h.c. Adolf Maurer, whose Christianity was one of deeds. There were Nettie Sutro and Georgine Gerhard, women of the utmost dedication and helpfulness. There were the Reverend Adolf Freudenberg in Geneva and Monsignor Crivelli in Lucerne—one the representative of the Protestants, the other the director of the Catholic *Caritas*, but both united in their determination to save lives. There were the eminent liberal, Paul Lachenal, in Geneva; the diplomat, Charles Lutz, in Budapest; the Reverend Thurneysen and Professor Wilhelm Vischer in Basel.

All these, as well as the many unidentified, unknown helpers, were the representatives of humanity, the defenders and restorers of a tradition that belongs to the innermost essence of Switzerland.

## At the Strangers' Table

> My husband gave me money for Christmas so that I could buy something for myself. He knew what I had been wanting for a long time. We went into town together to shop, and I was almost

carried away by temptation. Then I remembered what you had said. We went back home, and now I am sending the money to you for the children you are helping, the refugees. My gift is small in terms of their need, but at the moment it is all that I can do for the poorest of the poor.

This was the letter that a woman wrote to Dr. Vogt.

Another family decided to do without its "expensive Christmas tree" and cut down on its celebration so that with the money thus saved "we can give a little joy to our persecuted brothers and sisters." The God's Help Children's Home in Says renounced meat for a month "so that we can do at least a little to help ease the sufferings of these poor people." The director of the institution added in her letter: "It gave me so much happiness to see how quickly and gladly the children made this small sacrifice."

The pastor of a rural community wrote: "I have two winter overcoats —one for Sundays and so forth and the other more for ordinary use. I can always get along without this one. If I could help a refugee with it, I shall be glad to do so, remembering the counsel: 'He that hath two cloaks . . .' "

The chairman of a church welfare organization wrote on behalf of a woman who had taken in refugees: "She received her reward for her hospitality and helpfulness at once, for as a result of taking in these refugees she has been cured of her nervous depressions." A Swiss woman wrote that "there was a time when my husband and I were not free of prejudices. And now we cannot thank Jesus Christ enough . . . that he has sent these people to us."

There was a working-class family with seven children. The income was small and had to be stretched, with considerable scrimping. Nevertheless this family took in a refugee child with its mother and grandmother. In another instance a church welfare group even placed flowers in the house that it had rented and furnished for a refugee family. This was far more than a question of money. It was the expression of the response to the commandment: "Thou shalt love the stranger."

A child who had earned five francs selling Zwingli calendars turned over the money to a refugee fund. An old couple often had frequently-repaired shoes repaired again so that the shoe-ration cards could be given to refugees.

A woman who worked for the clerical refugee agency had this story:

On Thursday, August 5, I took a young refugee woman and her eighteen-month-old son to the home of a very simple, hard-working farm family in Bündnerland. The refugee was expecting her second child in October. When we reached the railway station nearest to the farm, the family's twelve-year-old son was waiting there with a little hand-drawn wagon. We loaded the eighteen-month-old baby and all the luggage into the wagon. After an hour's walk in the noon heat we reached the family's village. There the farmer's wife was waiting for us in front of the old Bündner farmhouse that goes back to 1597, with her darling eleven-month-old baby in her arms. It was her sixth child. But in September she was expecting the seventh. Immediately she asked when her homeless guest was expecting her own confinement. It was impossible to resist the surge of emotion that rose at the sight of the blissful joy of the two pregnant women, who virtually threw themselves into each other's arms in happiness: now there would be even more merry young lives in the house!

Where healthy attitudes prevailed, the refugees could not be a burden.

Things are going very well with us [said a woman who had offered hospitality to a refugee woman]; we have a delightful companionship. When people in the shops ask me stupid questions sometimes —"What do the Jews do? Aren't they nervy? Are you still not sorry that you took these people in?"—I have to answer every time from a heart full of gratitude: "No, we enjoy being together." Now Christmas is just over. The smart-alecks asked: "Are you going to have a Christmas tree just the same?" Yes, of course! Our guest herself decorated the house with fir branches, and every evening during the whole Advent she opened another window of the little Advent house for her baby; then finally she also trimmed the Christmas tree and we celebrated.

"Our refugee has truly become a cherished guest," another woman wrote. "As much as we wish that this dreadful war would end, it makes us unhappy to think that then we shall have to give her up. I must admire the integrity of these people."

"Those were simply marvelous times that we had while our refugees were here," another letter said, "and every time they went away it left a great void. They have no reason to thank us; it is we who have every reason . . . to thank them from the bottom of our hearts."

Encounters with Jews were significant spiritual experiences for many persons. "The Jewish question and the refugee question had formerly disturbed us deeply," one letter said, "and then God so arranged things that we could no longer evade the issue or make excuses: we *had to* say 'yes' when we were asked whether we could take in Jewish refugees. It would take too long to tell you everything that followed—but all of it was only good, truly only good!"

Here again these few excerpts must speak for the thousands of letters that bore witness to practical good will. The Federal Council's doubts were exposed as lies, the malice and hostility of the Fatherland Front backfired against it from the people. The weak grew strong by giving. The call issued by Dr. Vogt on his day of prayer in 1942 aroused action by sixty-four thousand persons. At the end of the war sixty thousand were making monthly contributions for refugees to the Evangelical Relief Agency alone. This was the Switzerland that was the subject of a letter sent from a concentration camp on October 12, 1942, by a father who had sacrificed his own flight to our country:

> In a measure that in today's times is incalculable and generous, Switzerland has granted the right of asylum to those who have fled there—a gesture, an act that will never be forgot and that has saved the lives of thousands of persons and their children. I too spent some time weighing the question whether I should not go there with my two friends, but after much deliberation I decided not to do so. . . . I feel that I have no right thus perhaps to deprive someone else of what means his salvation. [From Dr. Vogt's archives.]

Can we help blushing at this?

## Voices of the Rescued

A letter from the *Società israelitica di Soccorso* (Jewish Relief Agency) of Lugano told of the harrowing adventures of two groups of refugees from Italy who finally found safety on Swiss territory after the exhaustion and suffering of a hazardous escape and whose expulsion it was at last possible to prevent with immense effort. The letter continued:

> What cannot be praised enough was the heartfelt help of many people in the little mountain village, who were constantly bringing warm drinks for the poor fugitives to refresh them and give them strength, as well as the humane compassion of the border guards and the commune officials. [From Dr. Vogt's archives.]

One refugee described his reception in Switzerland:

> Police station. A stairway, gray walls, a green wooden door. Two policemen took charge of us. They made us walk ahead of them. This is one of the many rules: Keep a watchful eye on prisoners. They did not know that for us there could be nowhere to run. In the office there were several police officials in civilian clothes. The lieutenant was in uniform. We watched his every movement, the expression in his eyes, his gestures, we listened breathlessly when he spoke. Was he a good-hearted or a hard man? Would he send us back? Did he have the power to decide what would become of us? Something choked up in my throat. I began to weep. But soon I wiped away all my tears: "Are you tired?" he asked. In the midst of his writing down the name of my friend's husband he had given me a look. He broke off his questioning and ordered that we be taken to the kitchen of the police station, where we were welcomed by a fat giant of a cook. The regular lunch hour had passed. He gave us coffee and bread and a dish of cheese—a month's rations in France —and ladled applesauce out of a huge jar and kept urging and urging us to eat.
>     When the hearing was resumed we were asked where we had come from, which mountains we had climbed, who had guided us. We gave truthful answers. I handed over my "assets"—three thousand French francs. A young official asked me· "Where were you born?" "In Vienna." "Where is your child?" "In North America." Suddenly a question forced itself out of me: "Tell me, please: are you going to send us back?" "Certainly not," the official said. But I still had not gained confidence. I asked this question many more

times. The official always answered patiently. Then we were told
that for a few days we would be kept in a hospital, the women and
children too. The men were segregated and given straw mattresses.
My friend had to say goodbye to her husband. "Why can't Daddy
go with us?" little Andrée asked. "Will he come home again
tonight?" How could we explain what was so hard for us to
understand ourselves? Come home? A child's innocence that could
not yet understand that for us there was no more "home."

The nurses were wonderful to us. We were allowed to take hot
baths. That gave us a marvelous feeling. The dirt and dust of our
flight were washed away. We ate and went to sleep. The beds were
ranged close together. The room was almost full. Everyone was a
refugee. Children too. Some were already asleep. Two children near
me were whispering. "I'm so afraid of the police," one of them said,
but the other reassured her: "Here you don't have to be afraid.
We're in Switzerland." The light was turned off. The first night of
peace sank over our weary eyes, our palpitating hearts.

One morning we were taken to the office of the border police.
We could hear the telephone conversations—orders and counter-or-
ders. The official himself hardly knew where he stood. A telegram
arrived. A friend of my family had interceded. We had to go to the
nearest large town, and report to the police there. An official
certificate that we had registered would keep us out of trouble. It
was a beautiful late-summer day. The sun was hot and we could
breathe the rooty smell of mountain air. But it was not yet time to
relax. We were still under military supervision. And now a gendarme came up. We were full of fear and distrust. Perhaps we
would now be thrown out of here. But he was very friendly. He
invited us into his house, which was in that street. His wife made
breakfast for us. Her motherly eyes turned to my friend's child.
"Did the little one come over the border too?" She warmed some
milk, put bread on the table, and offered us all the good things in
the house.

With the gendarme we boarded a train. We told him how on
the other side of the border children's papers were taken away and
the children themselves were separated from their parents. "Terrible, terrible," he said, full of real sympathy.

The other passengers were very interested in us. Their glances

were full of good will. But for us it was as if we were on display, as
if the word *refugees* were written on our clothes in large letters. A
lady put a package of candy into little Andrée's hand. Sharing.
Compassion.

To a refugee such a natural act, so long forgotten, was a deeply
moving experience.

Another described how a poplar on the border served as a guidepost
on the road to Switzerland:

Switzerland. The moon shone on the poplar. It gave us the sign. It
was a signal. It heightened our confidence. We laughed among
ourselves. Let's go! We ran to the poplar. Over the barbed wire!
Everyone helped everyone else. We were in Switzerland! Thank
you, wonderful poplar tree! Thank you, wonderful Switzerland!

We went to the border post. We were interrogated. We told
about the poplar. A lieutenant said: "Everyone tells us that about
the poplar." I said: "*Ach*, lieutenant, if you knew what that poplar
meant to us!" He answered—and I will never forget how terribly
serious a man can be and yet laugh: "I understand you very well."

He was an officer on duty. He could not offer an embrace of
welcome when a refugee climbed over the barbed wire into the
country that he was guarding. But he had said—and it was plain
that he meant it: "I understand you very well." Thank you, dear
Swiss officer, for this word of welcome, thank you!

"Please accept the deepest thanks," another letter said, "from a
stranger whom you have snatched out of the hell and the martyrdom of
the Third Reich. I find words too trivial for your divine goodness."

Another letter:

When I came to you I was embittered, and the only emotion of
which I was capable was deep-rooted hate. I hated everything,
including myself. And then, though you did not know me, though
to you I was a frantic foreigner, who for all you knew could have
been an impostor, you did everything for me as perhaps only my
mother could have done. . . . To us you are the physician who
heals our deepest wounds. You make everything so clear, and you

do not wait for us to tell you of our gratitude in any way. You help
us . . . for the sake of helping . . ."

"We are constantly encountering the miracle of love for one's neighbor," still another letter said.

Slowly we are learning to feel no longer harried and persecuted.
Slowly we are learning that it is not necessary to feel the fear of
death at the sight of a man in uniform. Slowly we are beginning to
understand that it is not necessary to tremble when one approaches
an official; we know it in our minds, but our legs do not learn it so
quickly, and they still tremble when they must climb the stairs; it is
with amazement that we recognize that behind the all-powerful
desk sits not a functionary but a human being, a human being who
is kind to us.

Suddenly we recognize that there is a country that does not want
to exterminate us, that wants to help us *to live,* to live and be
healed.

This letter came from Toggenburg:

I cannot find words for everything that has made so strong and
deep an impression on us here. . . . Everything is so wonderfully
beautiful and indescribably good: the air and the mountains, the
view, the sounds, the care—and *the people!* And all this in wonderful Switzerland—in freedom! Often it seems to me that I am only
dreaming. Most particularly I should like to thank our dear hostess.

Or:

When I arrived today, Thursday, at my new home with bag and
baggage, there was the scent of colorful, gay flowers in beautiful,
tasteful vases. A floor lamp with a delightful shade, carpets, bed-
spreads, a washstand—and a fully equipped writing desk with
writing things, ashtray, paper everywhere for my literary work and
my letters, envelopes, pencils of every color, blotters, ink, pens, a
penholder, notepads that are so useful and necessary for writing
down memoranda, and a pencil on the night table too, a package of

cigarettes, a couple of small cigars as well, just in case, matches,
more writing equipment and blotting paper, a calendar, pillows.
Very efficiently the pastor and the community workers and the
men from the church relief agency had come the day before and
seen to all these things. . . . At last I was at home. Really at home.
And it was Christmas Eve in midsummer. All that was lacking was
a Christmas tree with lighted candles.

When a refugee wrote an article for *Die Nation* in February 1944,
describing his experiences in Switzerland, and said that even under
changed conditions it would never be possible for him in the future to
visit this country, which to him was the country of disillusionment, a
woman refugee answered him in the same publication:

How well I understand his letter—not only I but certainly all my
fellow-victims—because I too am a refugee and for me too these
eighteen months that I have spent in your country were full of
pain and disappointment and the bitterest suffering.

Yet, in spite of everything that I have experienced and had to
endure, in spite of all the indescribably miserable days and nights,
weeks and months, that my fellow-victims and I could easily have
been spared, in spite of everything the time that I have spent here
was also good—not only good but impressive. And I will always
remember the good things that I was allowed to enjoy in your
country; these memories will remain alive longer than the offenses
to our human dignity that all of us have undergone here.

Because there is also another Switzerland, and it is this Switzerland and her people that I want to talk about here. The simple,
ordinary people, who themselves have a difficult time staying alive
and yet regard us refugees not as unwanted, alien visitors but as
human beings whom they must help and inspire with new courage
to go on and with the feeling of human solidarity through their
love and understanding.

It is these simple, ordinary people . . . who represent Switzerland to me, . . . and whom I shall remember in the future with a
warm heart and a surge of gratitude. . . .

A workman's wife in Winterthur—she did not know me, she had
got my address by chance—wrote to me: "My husband gave me

twenty francs for Christmas; I know how hard it is for you refugees, I feel for you, and I want you to know it. Take this little bit of help, which will show you that we Swiss too feel friendship for you."

An Appenzell housewife who was in a hospital wrote to me when I was in a camp: "You have suffered so much and after all these agonies you have come to our country and now you are in a camp. This upsets me, and I can't rest. Please take these two little francs as a small token of my sympathy. . . ."

An eighty-year-old teacher in a home for the aged in Zürich sent me a Christmas parcel—a little vial of toilet water, a cake of good soap, a bar of chocolate. And a note: "I know the little pleasures of life are often harder to do without than the big ones." On December 24 I found at my door another package with coffee, chocolate, and other delicacies, and a letter: "You do not know me—who and what I am are of no interest. But I do want you to know that you are not alone here, that we Swiss feel with you and pray that your life will again be beautiful and easy in the future."

For months now I have not lived in the camp—a Swiss woman has taken me in and made room for me in her small house. She and her sister look after me with unremitting, touching self-sacrifice. In a foreign country I have found not only a home but also human beings who stand by me and to whom I belong, with whom I am bound even if destiny separates me from them again.

This is the Switzerland that we love. This world and these ordinary people are what symbolize the country of the white cross and the Red Cross.

I could tell of many former refugees and emigrants who still live among us, perhaps have even become citizens, follow their vocations, speak our language; we have learned to love them. Assuredly the tragedy and the agony that they have known and survived will never be wholly erased from their memories. But they have learned that the Alien Police of the 1930s and 1940s is not the whole of Switzerland. They have seen that there is also the other Switzerland, the Switzerland of decent men and women of good will.

I have spoken with Henryk Kreski, who was born in Lodz in 1926. In 1942 he was separated from his parents and sister. In 1944 he was sent to Buchenwald. His martyrdom lasted six months. He was beaten and tortured. His fingers have no nails. In April 1945 the Americans liberated the camp. Nurse Elsbeth Kasser brought him and others to Switzerland. He became acquainted with a few Swiss camps. And he was glad when at last his camp days were at an end. Then he went to Winterthur. When he talks about Winterthur his face glows. There were friendly people there, human people. They took him in and were true friends to him. He was able to complete a technical course. In 1953 he received permanent residence authorization; six years later he was naturalized in Zürich. He is now a department director in a firm in Berne. "I was lucky enough," he said, "to come into contact almost exclusively with friendly people in Switzerland."

It would be too much to say that Henryk Kreski's sufferings have left no mark on him. One cannot lose one's parents and sister in concentration camps and oneself go through the horrors of this hell without being affected by it for the rest of one's life. But, as far as that is possible, he has found a country among us. He has married. He has a daughter. He has a home. He belongs to us.

One could also tell of Richard Maurice Wagner, who was saved in 1942 thanks to Mrs. Gertrud Kurz. He had hardly reached Switzerland when he began to help other refugees in turn. Today he owns a business and, with his family, enjoys Swiss nationality. A warm-hearted, sympathetic, upstanding Swiss.

Rachel M was a Polish medical student of Jewish ancestry. She did not have an easy time. She went through all the procedures of the Alien Police for years. All her closest relatives were murdered by the Germans. But she still speaks of the simple Swiss mother who took her in and who was prepared to defend and conceal her if the Nazis had come here. Today Rachel is the wife of a Swiss scientist and the mother of three children.

Martin Freudenberg, also a refugee, put his thanks into a poem:

Thanks to Switzerland
You hurt us often, we tell you plain;
With best intentions, yes—you cut
Families apart, and freedom's reign
Turned out to be police again.
But now that's all long since forgot.

You took us in when life seemed lost:
This we always remember most!

Outlawed, hunted, we had gained
The right to stay in France's land,
Then the Gestapo was unchained,
And everywhere the travel-stained
Survivors found that they were banned.
You and you only were our host,
This we always remember most!

Now back we go again to France,
The barriers have fallen all away.
Another life, another chance,
And future hopes will steel our stance.
We know whom we must thank today.
In every heart this is our boast:
This we always remember most!

In 1943 Louis Heilbronner, a writer, devoted a letter to the people
who had befriended him during the year that he spent in Switzerland:

I can still see that border-command captain who took into his
home a political refugee half out of his mind after a trip through
the "forbidden zone" that he made three days after he had been
turned back by the Swiss border patrols at St.-Gingolphe and
handed over to the French (Vichy) constabulary for deportation.
Even more clearly I see the captain's wife laying out bread and
cheese and coffee with cream and sugar for that refugee.

I see a nurse who herself was often ill, for whom her arduous
profession was a true vocation, who assumed even the heaviest tasks
and forever examined in her own conscience whether what she was
doing for her patients was enough, especially when she thought
that she could save a receptive mind; she was only one of many
equally warm-hearted nurses.

I see an elderly physician with a severe heart ailment, who
regarded his calling as the highest that he could imagine, who had
sacrificed his own health for forty years and devoted the last years

of his life to good works and serenity. He is one of the most selfless persons imaginable.

I see that camp commander who with his family was moved by human decency to make the sacrifice of living among the refugees and to govern them *without* military force and power but only with good will and deep understanding, with better results than many a soldier can obtain even in your country.

I see my friend, the old teacher, with his warm-hearted wife, both of whom went to great efforts to help the refugees by serving as correspondence agents and by giving hospitality.

I see a printer who for years sent his Swiss newspapers to an internee in France whom he did not even know in order to provide intellectual nutriment and solace, and who, when at last I briefly met him (in St. Gallen), crowned his earlier efforts and expenditures with the warmest hospitality.

I see clergymen who in inexhaustible love for their fellows dedicated themselves exclusively and selflessly to arranging quarters and placating national and local officials—and who at the same time unendingly looked into their consciences for the answer to the question whether they and all their predecessors in the past nineteen hundred years had really worked sufficiently in the spirit of the Gospels—for example, with regard to the stiff-necked race of Israel.

I see Professor Staehelin of Basel, that good man who died too soon, a sacrifice to humanitarian science, telephoning to every research laboratory in Switzerland until he finally found the typhus serum that saved me from death.

I see the enormous effectiveness of the Red Cross, the "association of twenty-five members" and fifteen million card holders, in addition to the thousands of volunteer helpers, men and women, the organizations of the FHD, the refugee-relief agencies, the agencies for the relief of prisoners of war, the foster parents of children from Belgium, France, Greece, Italy, etc. . . . and I see the Swiss children who went from door to door to collect funds for them.

And I am firmly convinced that sooner or later all these actions will bring their own blessings and rewards to the people of the Confederation, contributing to the day when *every* government of force and terror and police mentality will long since have fallen into the abyss of oblivion! Just as today we can hardly imagine any longer that there should ever have been so *barbaric* a period, in which two quite different words—*hospes* and *hostis*—were translated as if they meant the same thing—*stranger, enemy;* just so, in that day, *hostis,* the stranger, will become *hospes,* the guest.

# For We Know What We Do

This, then, is the story of Switzerland's refugee policy during the era of the Third Reich—as far as it can be told on the basis of a rather general survey of the evidence available to us today. It is a complex story, and a tragic one. Not all the records have yet been opened, nor do we yet know in full detail who interceded with the federal authorities or by what means. The refugee policy was conceived by human beings, and so it was neither all bad nor all good. It is easy to make accusations, but it can be immeasurably difficult to do what is right in the hour of need. Many who seemed to be strong were weak, and others in whom there had been no previous sign of heroism suddenly became models of courage and integrity. When Europe collapsed like a sand castle under the onslaught of the National Socialist armies in the unforgettable year of 1940, even firm believers in democracy and opponents of National

314

Socialism were haunted by the question whether perhaps after all, they
had not erred in their appraisals of the new Germany. This bewilderment extended in those days even into government circles. The statements of the Federal Council in June 1940 offer the evidence of that.
They were in no way heroic—they were merely human. Let him who is
without sin cast the first stone. Let those of succeeding generations who
are absolutely certain that they have always acted justly set themselves
up as judges.

As far as her refugee policy is concerned, Switzerland behaved no
worse than the other nations. Her situation was in many ways far more
difficult than that of the United States or even Sweden. Such problems
as unemployment, food supplies, the military defense of the country,
and also foreign policy in the heart of a Europe dominated by the
National Socialists were incomparably complicated. The capacities for
the admission of refugees and emigrants were indeed not unlimited. No
government—even with the best will—can renounce its primary responsibility to its own citizens. Any government in a democratic state—and
this is inevitable by the nature of democracy—is the government not
only of the generous of heart and the noble of mind but also of the
apprehensive and the self-centered.

These basic facts are not the issue. At issue is the question of what
was possible. And on this question, of course, opinions vary.

The Federal Council asserted in its report on the refugee policy of the
war years:

> In retrospect it is perhaps possible to recognize that at a given point
> in time we could have taken in more of one or another category of
> refugees. But who at that point in time could have given the
> persons then responsible the assurance that a short time later it
> might not have been necessary to turn back other refugees who
> perhaps were even closer to us? The limited accommodations avail-
> able in our country should not have been completely taken up first
> by refugees who were less closely related to us so that then it would
> no longer have been possible to help the endangered and the
> persecuted in our immediate vicinity. [See page 55.]

This is the voice of the dread of inundation by foreigners. It overlooks
the fact that "at a given point in time" those most immediately imperiled were also those closest to us geographically.

It was this dread of inundation by foreigners, this "stockpiling of inhumanity," that more than anything else motivated and inspired the official refugee policy. All other arguments were of secondary importance, and also proved—on closer examination—to be of less validity, at least in that fearful summer of 1942 when the death trains began to roll eastward out of western Europe. Not once could the argument of pressure of foreign policy have been legitimately raised. The Federal Council's report continued: "No pressure of any kind was ever exerted in this connection. Nor were any 'courteous wishes' or requests made of the Swiss authorities. They would have been equally courteously but definitively rebuffed by the Federal Council."

We were cruel of our own free choice—so cruel that the German government never found any necessity to intervene with Berne.

In normal times it might be understandable that I should refuse to open my house to a man whom I found uncongenial, and that I might refuse his appeal that I share with him whatever I had. It would be somewhat less acceptable if I were to extend my antipathy to his whole family sight unseen. But it is inhuman if I bar the door at the very moment when this man and his family are fleeing to my house in terror of death, pursued by armed criminals—and I do so purely out of fear lest I never be able to get rid of these people.

That is what we did.

We thought that our hands were clean if we caused the murderers not to hunt their victims in our direction, so that we should not have to turn them back. But it is not easy to acknowledge this.

"Even today," Mrs. Gertrud Kurz wrote, "I ask myself why at that time I did not make a demonstration of protest by refusing to leave the Federal Council's premises night or day." What Mrs. Kurz meant was that even those who helped could weary.

"For everything," Dr. Paul Vogt declared, "was allowed to happen only because we turned our backs on one another. When the synagogues of Germany went up in flames, and the Jews were driven out and tortured, the priests and the Levites saw what was happening and they stepped aside. When injustice extended its rule ever more widely, the church people saw it and stepped aside. When the refugees fled for their lives and begged for admittance at our borders, we Swiss saw their peril and we stepped aside. Not just some of us: All of us stepped aside."

When the war was over, Federal Councilor Eduard von Steiger

declared, in connection with a lecture by Mrs. Kurz: "You have done a magnificent work for our country. We owe you our thanks." Unfortunately the recognition came too late.

When the war was over, Dr. Heinrich Rothmund went from one cantonal government to another to advocate that the refugee children be given Swiss citizenship. This should not be overlooked. But it did not undo what had been done before.

The limit of capacity was never even approached. The lifeboat was never full. We could have taken in many tens of thousands more without harm. In 1942, the Germans had established a security belt six miles deep on our western border. They wanted to prevent any more Jews from entering Switzerland. We cannot know how many Jews fell into their claws before ever reaching the Swiss border. We cannot know how many did not even make the attempt because they had been forewarned that we would send them back. Whoever did get through could call it a miracle. According to reports reaching the Police Section, some twenty-six hundred persons were turned back between August 1942 and July 1943. We could have taken them in. We turned our backs.

It is proper to ask today what all of us—our people and our government—have learned from those years. The Federal Council and the Police Section have learned from experience what is involved in the control of a possible new flood of refugees. On February 1, 1957, the Federal Council issued its *Basic Principles for the Administration of the Right of Asylum in Times of Increased International Tension or War,* in which a new spirit is manifest:

> The Swiss "right of asylum" is not mere tradition but a maxim of national policy; it is an expression of the Swiss concept of freedom and independence. . . .
>
> The experiences of the refugees' presence during the Second World War have led to the conclusion that Switzerland should admit foreign refugees—in other words, individuals who may seek safety in our country because of grave danger to their persons or their lives—to the extent of her capacities, and that as a matter of principle the authorities should establish no numerical restrictions. . . .
>
> It has been recognized that the granting of asylum must be

318                                    The Lifeboat Is Full

treated not only from the point of view of the Alien Police but also as a humanitarian and political problem of extraordinary importance. . . .

In conformance with the duty of maintaining a policy of asylum in keeping with Swiss tradition, the free, generous admission of refugees is to be envisaged.

This is the foundation that makes possible a more generous procedure. In terms of organization, we have been told, we are now prepared for any future influx of refugees. The acceptance of the ten thousand Hungarian refugees of 1956–1957—unquestionably under far more favorable conditions—proceeded almost without friction. All the refugee-relief workers confirmed unanimously that "working with the Alien Police today is a pure pleasure." Does this mean that everything is as it should be? I think not. Organizational measures and good laws are not in themselves a policy. What is important is the spirit and the inner attitude of the men who set and carry out this policy: in short, the spirit and inner attitude of every citizen, since no one can evade the responsibility that has been laid on him.

I have tried to show what can happen even in a democratic country when arrogant officials set themselves up in defiance of the desire for human kindness expressed by people and Parliament; when higher authorities who are under no responsibility to answer to Parliament for their actions flout the wishes of the sovereign.

I should like to show that what happened yesterday can happen again today or tomorrow if too many people relinquish the responsibility imposed on them by democracy. We know what totalitarian ideologies of every stripe can make of men. The pogroms in the Third Reich and in Mao Tse-tung's China are harrowing examples. The end is always an Auschwitz. We know, too, that soulless bureaucracy begets that coldness of heart that made us sharers in the guilt for the massacre of the Jews through our brutal exclusions and surrenders of helpless refugees—a behavior that was the fruit of indifference, selfishness, envy, and prejudice.

These things, however, are not dead. Anti-Semitism and intolerance are not dead; among us too they are not dead. They still glow beneath the ashes. Sometimes this demon suddenly flares up, as harsh and anti-human as it ever was. It can happen in the ordinary conversation of friends and acquaintances, when one man suddenly says: "Is he a Jew?"

and the other's silence is itself the answer: "Certainly!" It flares up in a naturalization hearing, when citizenship is refused to an artist who has lived for years in Switzerland. The real reasons are only too easy to identify. Or when some overzealous functionary, exhibiting his cleverness and his intimate knowledge of every subsection of the law, finds that a refugee who has been at home in Switzerland for twenty-five years —and who is also one of the most important poets of the Jewish people —cannot be granted citizenship because for a few years, in pursuance of his profession, he worked abroad and, because of his ignorance of all the requirements for naturalization, did not strictly comply. Of course, this is completely correct according to the statute book. According to the statute book the expulsions were completely correct also.

The spirit of anti-Semitism and arrogance leers out of a pamphlet on the right of suffrage for women in the canton of Zürich. The pamphlet makes the "revelation" that the president of the Swiss League for Women's Rights first became a Swiss citizen through marriage at the age of thirty-six; perhaps she had been compelled for deplorable reasons to leave her native country. Quite apart from the vicious intent of the statement, it was untrue. Mrs. R., the woman in question, who held a doctorate in law, had emigrated to Switzerland from South Africa before the First World War, studied in Zürich schools and the University of Zürich, and acquired Swiss nationality on her own initiative a year before her marriage.

Extremists are not fastidious about truth. In their envy, their hatred, and their irrationality they sow other hatred and race superstitions. If we keep silence about such things, they can flower into new Auschwitzes and Maidaneks.

It is in our hands to contribute to the realization of human kindness, tolerance, respect for others and for other ways of thinking. The roads to that realization are not new. They were pointed out to us in the Sermon on the Mount and the Declaration of Human Rights of the United Nations. They mean communication and mutual understanding in defiance of all barriers of race and class, religion and sect, politics and geography. The exemplars are there, even today: Fritjof Nansen, Mahatma Gandhi, Albert Einstein, Albert Schweitzer, Carl von Ossietzki, Martin Buber, Abbé Pierre, Dag Hammarskjöld, Father Pire, Gertrud Kurz, Tullio Vinay, Danilo Dolci, Paul Vogt. These "idealists" are the authentic realists.

Human kindness is not a talent that one has or lacks. Nor can it be

created by decree. It can, however, be desired and practiced. It begins
with you and me, in the family, the school, the job, politics, art, the
economy, science. This recognition and the conclusions that we draw
from it will determine whether any sort of totalitarianism—it need not
be political alone—will ever be allowed to emerge again, or whether it
must retreat. We must make it as difficult as possible to approve it in
our consciences. Scapegoats can be only progressively less effective in
unburdening us. What we have or have not done we cannot unload on
Heinrich Rothmund.

In October 1934 the secretary general of the European Central
Organization of Church Relief Agencies wrote to the Federal Alien
Police in opposition to unlimited admissions of refugees. These, he said
during a conference with Dr. Heinrich Rothmund, would create a
burden on the general welfare; and in addition the refugees often
included "menacing elements." (See Ludwig report.)

In reply Dr. Eduard Behrens wrote in *Die Nation* on August 27,
1942: "The day of the great reckoning will come. The day will come
when Switzerland too will have to prove her moral right to exist. Nation
of the oldest democratic tradition, old land of refuge for all who are
persecuted, have you been worthy of your renown, have you been true to
your heritage?"

This question cannot be evaded. Whoever tries to evade it does his
country a disservice.

In a prayer written by Pope John XXIII that he was to have spoken
shortly before his death he said:

> Today we recognize that for many, many hundreds of years our
> eyes were so blind that we were no longer capable of recognizing
> the splendor of Thy chosen people nor to descry in their faces the
> lineaments of our privileged brothers. We know now that the mark
> of Cain is branded on our foreheads. For hundreds of years our
> brother, Abel, lay in blood and tears for our errors, because we had
> forgotten Thy love. Forgive us the curse that we unjustly put upon
> their Jewish name. Forgive us that we have crucified Thee a second
> time in them, in their flesh: for we knew not what we did.

Today we know.

# Chronology

## 1933

*January 30:* President von Hindenburg of Germany names Adolf Hitler Chancellor. Thus the National Socialists take over the government. This is the beginning of the most menacing threats and persecutions for Jews, Communist and Social Democratic party members, union leaders, pacifists, active opponents of National Socialism in all sectors, certain religious sects, democratic writers, intellectuals, and artists. Laws excluding Jews from government service and professional associations follow in rapid succession.

*March 31:* The Federal Justice and Police Department of Switzerland— headed by Federal Councilor Dr. H. Häberlin—issues regulations, approved by the Federal Council, under which in general the borders are to be kept open but refugees are to be granted only temporary residence. Economic activity is forbidden to them (because of unemployment in Switzerland). We must defend ourselves with all the means at our command against the establishment of "alien-thinking elements" in our country, various groups declare.

*April 7:* Federal Council's decree on the treatment of political refugees: They must register within forty-eight hours of their arrival; they must be under police supervision; the Alien Police must approve their assumption of any work; they are subject to expulsion for violation of any of the regulations; they are under the tutelage of the federal government.

*April 20:* Circular letter from the Federal Justice and Police Department concerning the refusal of persons found unqualified for asylum; undesirable persons—specifically Communists without papers—must leave the country quickly; others are required to reside in specific places and to report periodically to the authorities.

*July 20:* Concordat between the Vatican and the Third Reich.

## 1934

Circular letter of instructions from the Federal Justice and Police Department to the cantons: Stateless Germans shall be granted tolerated residence, but

321

they are strictly forbidden to engage in any work, including even voluntary unpaid cooperation with relief agencies or household service.

## 1935

*September 15:* The Nürnberg racial laws are approved by the German Reichstag. The deprivation of Jews' rights grows constantly harsher.

## 1936

*June 17:* The Swiss Central Office for Refugee Assistance is founded; all the principal relief agencies are represented in it. One thousand thirty-five refugee children from France are authorized to spend three- to six-month vacations in Switzerland.

## 1937

*August 18:* Circular letter from the Federal Justice and Police Department to the cantons: Because of the inundation of foreigners, it states, Switzerland can serve only as a transit country for refugees. Residence for a few months shall be granted to those found qualified. Lack of papers shall not be a valid ground for the refusal of residence. Certificates of toleration shall be issued without charge to refugees lacking means and employment. No security bonds shall be posted. Refugees shall be returned to Germany only in exceptional cases. Moderation is urged toward illegal entrants.

## 1938

*March 12:* German troops invade Austria and complete her annexation to Hitler's Germany. Field Marshal Hermann Goering predicts: "In five years Vienna will be Jew-free."

*March 28:* The Federal Council orders the reinstitution of visa requirements for holders of Austrian passports.

*April 8:* The Federal Justice and Police Department calls on the cantons to exercise the greatest caution in the admission of refugees.

*July 6–15:* Evian conference is held for the discussion of the refugee question. Thirty-two nations take part. Results: zero.

*August 10:* Switzerland increases her border controls. Holders of Austrian passports who have no visas are to be turned back and handed over to the German border guards. The Federal Alien Police informs the Federal Justice and Police Department that thus far one thousand persons have entered illegally. If illegal entries cannot be halted, the report adds, they will lead to a situation beyond Switzerland's control.

*August 17:* Cantonal Police Commissioners' conference demands the closing of the borders.

*August 18–19:* The Federal Council orders the borders sealed. Refugees who have no visas are to be turned back without exception. Tragic scenes on our eastern frontier arouse protests by the population.

*September 7:* The Police Section instructs the border forces: "Emigrants holding German passports are to be turned back. Whether the persons are emigrants is to be determined as much as possible by the officials of the border police." Holders of German passports who are or most probably appear to be Jews are to be sent back. It must also be determined whether holders of Czech and Hungarian passports are emigrants: "Almost all . . . emigrants . . . are Jews." In such case, they are to be turned back and the fact is to be noted in their passports.

*April–October:* Negotiations among the Police Section, the Swiss Legation in Berlin, and the German Foreign Ministry. Switzerland insists categorically that Jews' passports be distinctively marked, otherwise she threatens to require visas for all Germans. These negotiations lead in the end to the "J" stamp.

*September 29:* The Munich Agreement. Czechoslovakia is abandoned by the western powers.

*October 4:* The Federal Council approves the accords with Germany, informs its legations and consulates, and issues specific orders to the border forces. The negotiations are not only concealed from the relevant committees in Parliament but omitted from the Council's annual report.

The first fund solicitation by the Central Office for Refugee Assistance brings in 360,000 francs.

*November 9–10:* Kristallnacht in Germany. Pogroms and ever harsher restrictions against Jews. The accords of October 4 between Switzerland and the Third Reich are officially confirmed.

*December 7:* As the result of a question in Parliament by National Councilor Dr. Guido Müller of Biel, the refugee question is debated.

## 1939

*January 20:* The Federal Council orders that visas be required for all foreign emigrants.

*February 20:* Dr. Rothmund, head of the police section, announces that at present Switzerland is harboring ten to twelve thousand refugees, three thousand being penniless Jews for whom the Swiss Jewish community has to contribute approximately 250,000 francs monthly.

*February 22:* The cantonal police commissioners' conference emphasizes once more that Switzerland can be only a transit country for refugees; it demands that entry permits be issued only when there is a guaranty of reemigration.

*March 15:* Czechoslovakia disappears as an independent nation. The Protectorate of Bohemia and Moravia is proclaimed.

The Federal Council requires visas for holders of Czech passports.

*June 19–20:* At a meeting of the Intergovernmental Committee for Refugee Relief in London it is announced that there are fifty-two thousand Jewish refugees from Germany in England, thirty thousand in France, twenty-five thousand in Poland, twelve thousand in Belgium, ten thousand in Switzerland, and five thousand in the Scandinavian countries.

*September 1:* The German armies invade Poland.

*September 3:* England and France declare war on Germany.

*September 5:* The Federal Council imposes a universal visa requirement for all foreigners, both for entry and for transit. Border security is tightened. As the war begins, there are still seven to eight thousand refugees in Switzerland.

*September 19:* National Councilors Maag-Socin of Zürich and Rittmeyer of St. Gallen propose Parliamentary questions and statements sharply criticizing the actions of the Alien Police against illegal immigrants. Further criticism is voiced by the press and in the cantonal legislatures. National Councilor Stöckli, on the other hand, demands that emigrants be prohibited from residing in larger cities and border areas. Refugees requiring support will be employed in labor camps.

*October 17:* The Federal Council orders that foreigners who enter Switzerland illegally shall be immediately expelled to the countries from which they came, with the exception of deserters and persons recognized as political fugitives. It reiterates its earlier prohibitions dealing with economic activity. Henceforth a distinction will be made between emigrants and refugees. Emigrants are foreigners who have entered Switzerland since 1929, have lost their nationalities, or can no longer return to their home countries. In order to be allowed to reside in Switzerland they require cantonal certificates of toleration. Their travel papers will be marked with the perforated stamp, *Emigrant.* Refugees, in general, are considered to be those who have fled into Switzerland since the outbreak of the war. They are the direct responsibility of the Confederation. Regulations concerning police obligations, permissible residence areas, etc., for both categories are issued.

*December 8:* Federal Councilor Baumann, head of the Justice and Police Department, replies to the attacks of Maag-Socin, Rittmeyer, and Stöckli in the National Council.


**1940**

*March 12:* The Federal Council orders the construction of labor camps. Their management is entrusted to the Central Office for Volunteer Labor Service. But all instructions are issued through the Police Section.

*April 9:* The Germans invade Denmark and Norway. Norway declares war on Germany.

*May 3:* The Federal Justice and Police Department orders a census of refugees living in Switzerland.

*May 10:* The Germans invade The Netherlands, Belgium, and Luxemburg. Many Swiss move to the fortified interior.

*May 14:* The Netherlands lays down her arms.

*May 17:* The Federal Council reinforces its decree of October 17, 1939. Henceforth foreigners entering illegally can be expelled at any time without any opportunity to appeal. The earlier order restricting the term of internment to two years is abrogated. Refugees with means can be compelled to pay the costs of their internment.

*May 28:* King Leopold of Belgium capitulates.

*June 10:* Italy enters the war.

*June 14:* Paris falls.

*June 16:* The commander-in-chief informs the Federal Council that it is impossible for Switzerland to admit the French civilian population driven out by the advancing German troops.

*June 18:* Circular letter from the Federal Justice and Police Department instructs the cantonal police departments that military personnel are to be disarmed and interned by the army; civilian fugitives—with the exception of women, children up to the age of sixteen, men over the age of sixty, and invalids—are to be turned back.

*June 19:* The commander-in-chief issues an order under which members of labor detachments are also to be treated as civilian refugees and hence are to be turned back when they cross the border unless they are in danger of being fired on by pursuing troops.

*June 19–20:* The French XLV Army Corps, including a Polish division—a total of twenty-eight thousand men—crosses our frontier and is disarmed. Within a few days we admit more than forty thousand military personnel. Approximately seventy-five hundred French civilians are admitted; a few months later they are returned to France.

*June 25:* Armistice between France and Germany. Federal Councilors Pilet-Golaz, Etter, and Celio broadcast their highly controversial statements on the radio.

*July 12:* The Federal Justice and Police Department issues orders for the complete surveillance of all refugees and emigrants in Switzerland.

*July 25:* The commander-in-chief, in a report, calls the nation to resistance and denounces defeatist tendencies.

*October 28:* Italy attacks Greece.

*November 15:* Dr. F. T. Wahlen discloses his land-cultivation plan in Zürich and it is immediately hailed and understood by the entire nation as an act of resistance to threats from abroad.

*December 13:* The Federal Council orders the frontiers partly closed. Entrance into and departure from Switzerland in evasion of the border forces, as well as preparations for and collaboration in such action, are made subject to punishment.

## 1941

*January:* War in Africa.

*February–March:* The Germans invade Bulgaria and Rumania.

*March 1:* Bulgaria adheres to the Axis Powers.

*March 18:* The Federal Council decrees that refugees with assets abroad shall be subjected to a solidarity contribution to their penniless fellow-victims.

*April 6:* The Germans invade Yugoslavia.

*June 22:* Germany attacks the Soviet Union.

*November 30:* The Russian counter-offensive begins.

*December 7:* Japan attacks Pearl Harbor.

*December 8:* The United States and England declare war on Japan.

*December 11:* Germany and Italy declare war on the United States.


## 1942

Conditions grow steadily worse for the Jews in German-occupied territories. Arrests and murders of hostages are the order of the day. Deportations to the east begin in the spring. Dr. Rudolf Bucher of Zürich, a member of a medical mission to the eastern front, describes his observations in a number of lectures; his major revelation deals with the extermination of the Jews. Reports on the deportations appear more and more often in the Swiss newspapers. The pressure of refugees for entrance to Switzerland mounts. One hundred are admitted between April 8 and 30, 132 in May, 183 in June, 248 in July.

*July 29:* Dr. R. Jezler, Dr. Rothmund's deputy, gives the Federal Council a detailed report on the increase in the number of refugees living in Switzerland. He discusses the Police Section's admission procedures in the light of the grisly conditions in the Jewish areas in the east, and says that in such circumstances the refusal of entry to refugees can hardly be permitted to continue. At the same time, however, he urges an even more severe policy of exclusion because the influx of refugees has assumed huge proportions.

*August 4:* Adopting the recommendations in Jezler's report, the Federal Council orders them put into practice "even if the foreigners thereby affected may incur the gravest perils (danger to life and limb)."

*August 13:* In the absence of Federal Councilor von Steiger, Dr. Heinrich Rothmund issues orders that all civilian refugees be turned back at the border. These orders are enforced to the letter. They soon become public knowledge and encounter the fiercest opposition by the people and the press.

*August 20:* The Central Committee of the Federation of Swiss Jewish Communities meets and hears Dr. Rothmund. Sharp protests against the Police Section. Reports on the horrible events in the east.

*August 23:* Gertrud Kurz and Paul Dreyfus-de Günzburg visit Federal Councilor von Steiger in his vacation hotel on Mount Pélerin and urge him to reopen the border to refugees.

*August 24:* The Swiss Central Office for Refugee Assistance meets in Zürich under the chairmanship of Privy Councilor Dr. Robert Briner. Dr. Rothmund is bitterly attacked. By telephone Federal Councilor von Steiger orders a relaxation of the instructions of August 13.

*August 25:* The Police Section issues appropriate orders to the border forces.

*August 28:* The Police Commissioners' conference in Lausanne approves the new instructions and urges further caution in the admission of refugees.

*August 30:* In Zürich-Oerlikon, the Youth Church holds its national congress, attended by eight thousand persons. The refugee policy is severely criticized. In his address Federal Councilor von Steiger invokes the metaphor of the "overcrowded little lifeboat."

*September 11–12:* The cantonal Police Commissioners confer again in Altdorf. Questions addressed to the Federal Justice and Police Department concerning the maintenance of refugees and requesting financial assistance are answered predominantly in the negative.

*September 22–23:* Long debate in the National Council on the refugee question. The principal political parties back the Federal Council. Six of eleven speakers make severe criticisms.

*September 26:* New instructions telephoned to the border forces by the Police Section. Admissibility is still further restricted. "Under current practice, refugees on the ground of race alone are not political refugees" and "French Jews are to be turned back without exception, since they are in no danger in their own country."

*September 30:* In a speech to the Swiss Reformed Pastors' Association, General Henri Guisan, discussing the refugee question, asserts that he "fully understands the impulses of the heart that move us but in the solution of this question, too, concern for the security of our country must take the first place."

*October 3:* Federal Councilor von Steiger requests that the commander-in-chief initiate preparations to reinforce the closure of the border.

*October 9:* The army reinforces the border patrol in the west. Barbed-wire emplacements are erected. While thirty-eight hundred refugees were admitted in September, the total falls by 50 per cent in October. An agreement is reached between the Police Section and the clerical authorities providing that periodically the church will submit the names of prominent persons whom the Police Section should not turn away if they cross the border.

*November:* The Fatherland Front publishes a *Declaration on the Refugee Question* that reveals a strongly anti-Semitic character; it also organizes a campaign of newspaper articles opposing any further admission of refugees. Reports of the ghastly circumstances of the deportations and the extermination of the Jews in the east appear increasingly often even in the Swiss press, despite frequent objections by the censors. A fund solicitation by the Central Office for Refugee Assistance produces more than 1.5 million francs

*December 17:* In the British Parliament, the American Congress, and in Moscow, identical declarations are read concerning the mass murders of the Jews by the National Socialists. Anglican Bishops appeal to the Allied and neutral governments to help the Jews and admit them into their countries.

*December 29:* The Police Section issues new, more severe orders to the border forces. Among other things, it prescribes that "in every case care must be taken to see that refugees who must be turned back receive no opportunity to communicate directly or indirectly (specifically, by telephone) with . . . anyone."

## 1943

*January 26:* Casablanca Conference.

*February 2:* The German troops at Stalingrad collapse. The retreat from Russia begins.

*March 12:* The Federal Council issues new regulations covering refugees who have entered Switzerland since August 1, 1942.

*May 9:* The Synod of the Evangelical-Reformed Churches of the City of Basel adopts a resolution condemning the current exclusion of refugees and urges the church authorities to make representations on the matter to the Federal Council.

*June:* The Federal Council's refugee policy is criticized again in the National Council's summer session.

*July 10:* The Allies land in Sicily.

*July 25:* Italy's Fascist government falls.

*July 26:* The Police Section issues supplementary orders to those of December 29, 1942, with certain relaxations. The maximum age for admissible girls is raised from sixteen to eighteen.

*July 27:* New orders from the Police Section for the southern border.

*September 8:* Italy surrenders. The German army occupies the country.

*September 14–15:* New orders from the Police Section.

*September 17:* More new orders from the Police Section. "All male refugees above the age of sixteen are to be sent back."

*September 29:* National Councilor Robert Grimm and State Councilor Rudolf Weber challenge the Federal Council because of their fear of new unemployment and the competition between Swiss workers and the many foreign refugees.

*October 13:* Italy declares war on Germany. The Swiss commander-in-chief intervenes by telegraph in the refugee question. Persecutions of Jews in German-occupied Italy increase. At first this rise is followed by exclusions of refugees on our southern border, but then Jewish refugees are no longer turned back if they raise any objection or their return cannot be expected. Between September and the end of the year more than twenty thousand military personnel and seventy-eight hundred civilian refugees enter Switzerland from Italy.

*December 9:* National Councilor Jacques Schmid of Solothurn demands that a federal commission independent of the government be created to counsel and supervise the refugees and hear their complaints.

### 1944

*February 23:* Federal Councilor von Steiger invites leading citizens to Berne to discuss Schmid's proposal.

*March 6:* A fact-finding committee for refugee questions is created with forty-seven (later sixty-three) members, all prominent Swiss. Even earlier, refugees had been consulted on the question of their leaves. In 1944 they were consulted as well on matters of re-emigration.

*March 19:* German troops enter Budapest. Persecution of the Jews in Hungary, Rumania, and Yugoslavia assumes increasingly brutal forms. From Hungary alone more than a hundred thousand Jews are deported to Auschwitz during the year. The Federal Council announces its readiness to admit fourteen thousand Jews from Hungary and begins its preparations for them. In actuality it proves possible to bring only a small proportion of this number to Switzerland.

The refugee pressure on our borders continues. The orders of December 29, 1942, are still in force, but are executed "leniently." The maintenance of the refugees entails mounting difficulties. Of almost 35,000 emigrants and refugees, 22,500 are in the labor force on May 1. There are occasional conflicts between the population and the refugees: for instance, on December 5, 1943, in Visp, on March 11, 1944, near Siders, on April 17 in the Murimoos camp, and during that month in Lausanne and Lugano. In a Parliamentary question on June 7 National Councilor Dr. Eugen Bircher vigorously attacks the refugees. On September 21 Federal Councilor von Steiger dismisses Bircher's extravagant distortions as fantasy. Maag-Socin also sharply denounces Bircher's calumnies.

*June 24:* The commander-in-chief inquires what the Federal Council plans to do about the refugee question in the future. He points out that everyone must be allowed to enter or else everyone must be turned back. He recommends steps to prevent the crossing of the frontier by persons lacking valid passports and visas. The Federal Council recommends that the border forces practice the utmost discretion in admitting refugees.

*June 6:* The Allies land in Normandy.

*July 4:* The Allies enter Rome.

*July 12:* The Police Section issues new orders superseding those of December 29, 1942. The statement that "refugees on the ground of race alone are not political refugees" is eliminated; instead the instructions now state that "for the present admission is to be granted only to . . . foreigners whose lives and persons are actually in danger for political or other reasons and who have no alternative but flight into Switzerland in order to escape this danger."

*July 20:* The attempt to assassinate Hitler fails. An increased number of French refugees enters Switzerland; most leave again after a short interval.

*August 21:* Three hundred eighteen Jews from Hungary cross the Swiss border.

*August 25:* Paris is liberated.

*September 1:* Budapest is liberated.

*September 2:* American troops reach the Rhine.

*September 3:* Brussels and Antwerp are liberated.

*September 7:* The army issues new regulations for the admission of military personnel. No asylum will be granted to those unqualified.

*September 15:* Russian troops enter Sofia. From September to October fourteen thousand children and two thousand mothers enter Switzerland from France. A thousand children, most of them accompanied by their mothers, are admitted from the Val d'Ossola.

*October 20:* Russian troops capture Belgrade. Soviet armies enter Germany.

*November 3:* Dr. Rothmund orders the Swiss Legation in Berlin to protest to the German authorities against the deportations and announces that Switzerland is prepared to accept more Jews. Clothing and food are offered. Former Federal Councilor Musy negotiates with the Germans for the rescue of Jews. In response to a question by National Councilor Kägi of Zürich, the Federal Council gives assurances that no asylum will be granted to war criminals.

*December 1:* More than a hundred thousand refugees are now in Switzerland.

*December 7:* After long, exhausting negotiations, 1552 more Jewish refugees enter Switzerland.

### 1945

*January:* Russian troops in Budapest, Warsaw, and Memel. Numerous military and civilian fugitives seek sanctuary in Switzerland. The refugee total on February 1 is 104,673. Germans subject to draft for the *Volkssturm* (militia) are in general turned back at the border.

*February 6:* The Federal Council intercedes with the German government against the mass slaughter of the Jews.

*March 7:* The Allies cross the Rhine.

*March 29:* The Police Section issues new instructions to the border forces that are intended to prevent a mass influx of refugees from Germany. Nazis are to be turned back.

*April 13:* The Federal Council orders the closing of part of the border, especially in the north, the east, and the south. Nevertheless, thousands of refugees cross the border every day, particularly foreign workers and escaped prisoners of war.

*April 15:* Russian troops in Vienna.

*April 21:* Russian troops in Berlin.

*April 29:* The Germans in northern Italy surrender.

*May 1:* Switzerland is housing 106,470 refugees and internees, including 46,470 military fugitives. Just before the armistice the total rises to 115,000, including ten thousand Russians.

*May 8:* All German troops surrender. The war in Europe ends.

# Appendix

## Statistics Dealing With the Refugee Policy

When the war started in September 1939, there were about seventy-one hundred refugees in Switzerland. By July 31, 1942, this figure had been increased by twelve hundred more refugees. By December 31 the number of civilian refugees stood at approximately eighteen thousand. Between January and July of 1943, Switzerland admitted 4733 refugees, between August and December, 8719 civilian refugees. The number of military fugitives was very high. At the end of 1943 there were 39,713 internees— escaped prisoners of war, military refugees from Italy (more than twenty thousand after the collapse of Fascism), hospitalized Frenchmen and Finns—and 34,232 civilian refugees: a total of 73,944. In the first half of 1944 Switzerland admitted 5763 civilian refugees. On December 1, the total of military and civilian refugees reached 103,162. When the war ended on May 8, Switzerland was sheltering more than 115,000 refugees.

## Exclusions at the Border

How many refugees who tried during the war to find a haven in our country and were sent back over the borders cannot be established precisely, since a complete census of the influx was impossible at certain periods. Much greater even than the number of those turned back was the number of those who did not even attempt to reach our country because of the measures already adopted by Switzerland. When a figure of many thousands is mentioned in this domain it is surely no exaggeration. [From Professor Ludwig's book.]

On the basis of reports made to the Police Section, however, we have the following figures for exclusions at the border:

| | | |
|---|---|---|
| August–December 1942 | | 1056 |
| 1943 | | 3344 |
| 1944 | | 3986 |
| 1945 | | 1365 |
| | Total | 9751 |

## Who They Were

Of the total of 295,381 refugees who found a sanctuary in Switzerland for shorter or longer periods during the war, 103,869 were internees, escaped prisoners of war, deserters, and hospital cases; 55,018 were civilian refugees in the strict sense; 9909 were emigrants; 251 were political refugees; 59,785 were foreign children cared for by the Swiss Relief Agency for Emigrant Children and the Swiss Red Cross (Children's Agency), who either were brought in via organized transports for rehabilitation periods of several months or came to us in flight; 66,549 were border refugees, most of whom sought haven in Switzerland for only a brief time.

Jews accounted for 6654 of the 9909 emigrants and 21,858 of the 55,018 civilian refugees. Of the 64,927 emigrants and refugees, 14,599 were Italians, 11,524 were Frenchmen, 10,109 were Poles, 9119 were Germans, 3655 were Austrians, 3104 were Russians, 2401 were Dutchmen, 2013 were Yugoslavs, 1814 were Hungarians, 1718 were Czechs, 928 were Rumanians, 920 were Belgians, 687 were Greeks, 599 were Spaniards, 347 were Lithuanians, 220 were stateless. The total of nationals of 44 other countries came to fewer than 200 (of whom 189 were Britons and 64 were North Americans).

## Prominent Emigrants and Refugees

These well-known individuals who found temporary or permanent refuge from National Socialism in Switzerland between 1933 and 1945 included:

| | | |
|---|---|---|
| Fritz Adler | Kurt Hirschfeld | Max Ophüls |
| Hermann Adler | Wilhelm Högner | Rudolf Pannewitz |
| Albert Bassermann | Kurt Horwitz | Karl Paryla |
| Maria Becker | Gertrud Isolani | Wolfgang Pauli |
| Ernst Bloch | Georg Kaiser | Hermann Rauschning |
| Otto Braun | Alfred Kerr | Erich Maria Remarque |
| Bertholt Brecht | E. L. Kirchner | Wilhelm Röpke |
| Alfred Döblin | Arthur Koestler | Hermann Scherchen |
| Käthe Dorsch | Oskar Kokoschka | Joseph Schmidt |
| Walter Fabian | Wolfgang Langhoff | Ignazio Silone |
| Paul Geheeb | Herbert Lewandowski | Margarete Susman |
| Therese Giehse | Wilhelm Lichtenberg | Kurt Tucholski |
| Ernst Ginsberg | Emil Ludwig | Bruno Walter |
| Jakob Haringer | Thomas Mann | Jakob Wassermann |
| Stefan Hermlin | Hans Mayer | Erich Weinert |
| Wilhelm Herzog | Alexander Moissi | Carl Zuckmayer |
| Rudolf Hilferding | Alfred Mombert | |
| Paul Hindemith | Robert Musil | |

This list was supplied by the Police Section of the Federal Justice and Police Department.

## The Camps

The various types of camps for the refugees included:

*Collection camps*—For newly arriving refugees. Here the decision was made as to exclusion or admission, and civilian refugees were separated from military refugees. Camp residence might last a few hours or three days. Contact with the outside world was restricted to the minimum.

*Quarantine camps*—For medical examinations by the army's health service. Police investigation of each case. No contact with the civilian population. Camp residence three weeks.

*Reception camps*—For refugees whose cases could not be sufficiently clarified during their stays in the collection and quarantine camps. Residence in the reception camp could often continue for a very long period. In general these camps were inadequately equipped.

*Labor camps*—For able-bodied refugees between the ages of twenty and sixty. The men were employed in road-building, civic improvements, or farming. The women were assigned to mending, laundry work, etc.

*Training camps*—For young refugees between the ages of seventeen and nineteen.

A compilation made by the Police Section on January 17, 1944, provides the following over-all picture of the distribution of refugees:

| | |
|---|---:|
| In labor camps | 3681 |
| In internment institutions | 4028 |
| In special camps | 262 |
| In punishment camps | 24 |
| Working individually on farms (men) | 1057 |
| Working individually on farms and in homes (women) | 222 |
| In various cantons with permits for special occupations | 81 |
| In university towns with study permits | 471 |
| In private homes | 754 |
| Children placed with families and institutions | 1950 |
| Placed with relatives or in hotels and boarding houses by the Police Section | 2505 |
| In military quarantine and reception camps | 5612 |
| Restricted to special residence under military control and limitations on freedom of movement | 1809 |

## After the War

By the end of 1950, Switzerland had admitted 65,037 emigrants and refugees, of whom 52,064 had subsequently left the country.

On March 7, 1947, the Federal Council decided that permanent asylum should be granted to a limited number of refugees and emigrants. Several thousand emigrants and refugees were given permission to settle in the country. Of the approximately ten thousand refugees and emigrants still in Switzerland in 1950, about half were working.

# Illustrations

"Halt! Swiss territory. Crossing of the border forbidden. Violations of this order will be put down by armed force." This notice, legally correct and required by national policy, had a tragic import for thousands of refugees for whom asylum in our country was prohibited during the Second World War.

Spokesmen for the defensively-oriented refugee policy included Federal Councilor Eduard von Steiger; Dr. Heinrich Rothmund, head of the Police Section; National Councilor Dr. Heinrich Walther, and Dr. Eugen Bircher, physician (*all shown below*). The infamous "J" stamp in the passports of German Jews in no way contravened the desires of Switzerland (*opposite page*).

Dr. Eduard von Steiger

Dr. Heinrich Rothmund

Dr. Heinrich Walther

Dr. Eugen Bircher

Leading figures in the church had very early recognized the special responsibility of Christians in the face of the horrible persecutions of the Jews undertaken by the Third Reich, and they had raised their voices in furtherance of this responsibility. Not infrequently this brought them into conflict with the authorities.

Professor Dr. Karl Barth

Dr. Arthur Frey

The Reverend Dr. h. c. Paul Vogt

Professor Dr. Leonhard Ragaz

The Reverend Walter Lüthi

Superior Judge Dr. Max Wolff

In the National Council's major debate on the Federal Council's refugee policy in September 1942 the tradition of the Swiss right of asylum had prominent and resolute defenders. They came from all parties, left and right.

Dr. Albert Maag-Socin

Dr. Ludwig Rittmeyer

Pierre Graber

Dr. Albert Oeri

Professor Dr. Walter Muschg

Dr. Paul Meierhans

The refusal of entry and residence permits to Renate Stein, Jewish step-daughter of Jochen Klepper, the Evangelical poet, had tragic consequences. *Below:* the official form letter denying the application. *Bottom:* An urgent appeal for help by Jochen Klepper on January 8, 1942. *Opposite page:* The face of the Front's press.

## Verweigerung der Einreise- und Aufenthaltsbewilligung

Je

Eidg. F.P.Nr. 12389 EL/St          Kanton-Nr. 216031          Kant. Antrag oder Entscheid vom 19.4.40.     1. Mai 1940. Bern

Die eidgenössische Fremdenpolizei, nach Prüfung des Gesuches

S t e i n  Renate, geb. 5. März 1922, ledig, deutsche Reichsangehörige wohnhaft in Berlin-Nikolassee,

teilt folgendes mit:

Das Gesuch um Erteilung der Aufenthaltsbewilligung in Zürich ist von der kantonalen Fremdenpolizei Zürich

**abgewiesen.**

Die Einreise in die Schweiz —

ohne ausdrückliche Bewilligung der eidgenössischen Fremdenpolizei in Bern ist untersagt.

*Begründung:* Der Kanton Zürich verweigert den nachgesuchten Aufenthalt.- Ueberfremdung.- Belastung des Arbeitsmarktes.- Die Wiederausreise ist nicht gesichert.-

Geht an:
Gesuchsteller    Frl. R.Stein, Berlin-Nikolassee  Eidgenössische Fremdenpolizei
                 Teutonenstr. 23

zuzustellen durch  Schweiz.Gesandtschaft Berlin (Lo250)    sig. Steiner
Arbeitgeber  Hrn.Tappolet, Steinwiesstr. 54

JOCHEN KLEPPER                    BERLIN-NIKOLASSEE, den 8.I.1942
                                 TEUTONENSTRASSE 23

Zürich, Freitag, 2. Februar 1934. Nr. 10 (2. Jahrgang).

# Die Front

## Zentrales Kampfblatt der Nationalen Front

Redaktion, Verlag und Inseraten-Verwaltung: Zürich 2, Talstraße 67. — Telephon: Redaktion 87.917. Inseratenverwaltung 70.200. — Verlag und Abministration 32.200. — Postscheck-Konto: „Die Front" Zürich VIII 5180. — Druck: Buchdruckerei H. Roth, Zürich 2, Talstraße 67, Telephon: 32.200.

Abonnementspreise: Inland: Jährlich Fr. 11.—, halbjährlich Fr. 6.50, vierteljährlich Fr. 3.50. Ausland: Jährlich Fr. 15.—, halbjährlich Fr. 8.50, vierteljährlich Fr. 6.—. Inseratenpreis: Die einspaltige Millimeterzeile oder deren Raum 15 Rp., für das Ausland 20 Rp. Reklamezeile 60 Rp., Ausland 90 Rp.

# Im Kampf gegen die Judenpresse

## Der Jungfrontist

### Brutalität als politisches System.

# Der Jude als „Arbeiterfreund"

## Die planwirtschaftlich verkrachte Arbeiterbank.

*Wie der sozialistisch - jüdische Vorsteher des Basler Konkursamtes dem Arbeiter hilft*

### Totalrevision der Bundesverfassung.

### Ein jüdischer Beitrag zur Erklärung des Antisemitismus.

### „Sozialer Faschismus und Nationale Front"

# Gegen die Wühlerei der Emigranten

## Gewaltige Kundgebung in der Stadthalle — Ueber 2300 Volksgenossen demonstrieren gegen die Emigrantenplage — Hunderte können keinen Einlass erhalten

### Robert Tobler

# Neues von Jud Rosenbaum.

### Die Angst als Ordnungswächter.

### Jud Rosenbaum als Kolonisator.

### Neubestellung der Landesleitung.

---

Einzelpreis 25 Rp. • Erscheint jeden Freitag — Zürich, den 16. November 1934 — 2. Jahrgang • Nr. 4

# der Reichsdeutsche

## Das deutsche Wochenblatt in der Schweiz.

### Parteiamtliches Organ der Landesgruppe Schweiz der NSDAP.

**Aus dem Inhalt**

# Emigranten machen in Kultur

Thousands of children from the war-ravaged countries of Europe found hospitality in Switzerland for longer or shorter periods (*immediately below*). *Bottom:* In the autumn of 1944, 1352 rescued Hungarian Jews came to Switzerland, where they were immediately placed in quarantine camps. *Opposite page:* More Swiss Fascist newspapers.

Extrablatt

# Schweizervolk
### FÜHRENDES WOCHENBLATT FÜR SCHWEIZERISCHE POLITIK

Herausgeber u. politische Leitung Ernst Hofmann

## Für

**Wir**

### Eidgenosse!
kann nur sein, wer Volksg
unseres Blutes ist

Wir soziale Nationalisten wissen
nur Sein Sinn und Geist des bi
gegründeten ewigen Bundes der E
schaft ist. Er ist das Wesen der
echten Eidgenossenschaft überhau

«Kein Fremdling soll uns
sein oder über uns her

Heute, nach 640 Jahren, haben w
kommen: jüdische Richter,
Bonzen, jüdische Offiziere,
Gerichtsherren, jüdische Ärzte,
Advokaten, Juden, Juden, J
Herren über uns Freie Eidgenosse

Wie war das möglich?

Die französische Revolution u
partikel, der Liberalismus, hat d
der Eidgenossenschaft auf häufig
ten uns vieren anderen die

### Emanzipation der Ju

Die Gleichstellung der Juden mi
nanten auf allen Gebieten. Der ei
ordnete Gastjude konnte nun s
werden! Der jüdische Pseud
«rechtsunzäsiger» Besitzer una
Ahnenblatt geheiligten

### eidgenössischen
### Grund und Bo

Acker an Acker, Land un La
Jüdling zusammen, nicht um na
sondern um es zu verschachern,
lieren, — zu

### verwuchern.

Der freie Eidgenosse und Bauen
Einsknecht. Wie mancher Baue
Frau und Kindern vom Haus un
ben, vom Juden ausgeplündert,
weil er den Wucherzins und di
lang dem jüdischen Makler und
nicht pünktlich bezahlen konnte

Tausende von Eidgenossen wa
kis den Hannsise im jüdischen J
besiehen. Ueber 70 Prozent der §
Wohnungsmarktes in der Schweiz
von in- oder ausländischen Juden
Der freie Eidgenosse ist dah
eigenen Heimat geworden, unter f
Doch zu leben!

### Die Volksverräte

Grösser als der materielle Schaden
uns der verschmende, geschä†zende,
nude Jüdling zuf†gt, ist der Schad
und Volkstum!

Die jüdisch-bolschewistische Vere
serer Volksgemeinschaft, unserer K
Kultur, unserer Politik, ja sogar un
gion (geschäftenne Sekten, oder si
mit dem Himmel) ist ein ungeheuer
Schaden,

**sie ist die Wurzel allen**

Jüdische oder verjudete Schrift
teilpolitiker, System-Redakteure un
haben — mit einem Wort die beg
nannte geistige Grösse — verspulle
lich in Wort und Schrift die «Läch
der Behauptung der A
Volkstums zu «beweisen». Sie «vers

ZÜRICH, Donnerstag 8. November 1934 — 2. Jahrgang  Preis 20 Cts.  Deutschschweizerische Ausgabe. — No. 2

# Schweizer Fascist
### Kampfblatt des Schweizerfascismus

Verlangen Sie: "Le Fasciste Suisse"

Bestellen Sie heute noch den "Schweizerdegen", das ein-
zige "Schweizerisch-Nationalsozialistische Kampfblatt"!  Sie müssen unsere Obmann sprechen
Zürich, den 1. Oktober 1938  Einzelnummer 25 Rp.  Erscheint vierzehntäglich am Samstag – Nr. 5

# Schweizerdegen
### Schweizerisch-Nationalsozialistisches Kampfblatt
Gegen Hochfinanz, Judentum, Freimaurerei und Marxismus. – Für eine wahrhaft freie Eidgenossenschaft

Verantwortlicher Herausgeber: Alfred Zander

Genève, le 12 Mars 1937  No 245 (14me ANNÉE)  Prix : 20 centimes

# LE PILORI
### Organe de libre critique paraissant tous les 15 jours - Directeur: Georges Oltramare

ABONNEMENTS : UNE ANNÉE, Fr. 6.— SIX MOIS, Fr. 3.— ÉTRANGER, Fr. 9.—  CHÈQUES POSTAUX

Zürich, April 1934, Nr. 1 – Einzelnummer 20 Rp.

# Freiheit
## IN DER GEMEINSCHAFT
### NATIONALE FRONT ORTSGRUPPE AUSSERSIHL

Sion  20 Centimes  No 1

# LE
# PILON
### FRONT VALAISAN

As the war came closer to Swiss borders, thousands of refugees streamed out of adjoining territories into Switzerland (*immediately below*). *Bottom:* Many refugee camps were under military leadership. Military discipline alone, however, was not enough for the delicate task. *Opposite page:* More Swiss Fascist newspapers.

# Haarus

**Zentral-Kampfblatt**

des

### Nationalsozialistischen Eidgenössischen Kampfbundes
und Nationalsozialistische Eidgenössische Volks- und Wirtschafts-Partei (N.S.E.B.W.P.)

Einzelpreis ... 20 Rp.
Jährlicher Bezugspreis ... Fr. 4.—
Erscheint je 1. und 15. jeden Monats

Anzeigenpreis: Die Petitzeile 15 Rp.
Bei Wiederholung Rabatt
Anzeigenverwaltung: N.S.E.B.

Druck: ... Zürich
Geschäftsstelle: ...
Nationalsozialistischer Eidgenössischer Kampfbund Zürich
N.S.E.B.

Redaktion: G. Weber

ZÜRICH, den 15. September 1933 — Erscheint am 1. u. 15. des Monats - 1. Jahrgang - No. 2 — Einzelpreis 20 Rp.

# Schweizer NATIONAL SOZIALIST

**Für Heimat, Kultur** — KAMPFBLATT DER S.N.S.V.P. — Religion, arische Rasse

Abonnementspreise:
1 Monat Fr. 1.20 - 4 Monate Fr. 2.20
12 Monate Fr. 4.50

Herausgeber:
Schweizerische National-Sozialistische Volks-Partei
Verwalt. Redaktion: R.G.SKG, Postfach 16200 Zürich-Wiedikon

Insertionspreis:
Für den Raum einer einspaltigen Millimeter-Zeile 10 Kappen, Reklamezeile 40 Rappen.
Wiederholungen Rabatt.

## Was wir woll...

**Wir wollen:** Eine verantwortli...
Ein aufrechtes Bü...
Eine Arbeitersch...
Deckmantel der F...
Verklärung entge...
Uns frei machen...
Schachergeist.

### Politischer Kri...

Unser Vaterland befindet sich in einem K...
zustand, in einem Kampfe gegen die nigrendtigs...
...wirtschaft des Grosskapitals, gegen das hin...
...gen Treiben des Judentums, gegen die Volks...
und Aufwiegler zum Klassenkampf und gegen die...
...orer.

Es ist ein Krieg der Niedertracht unter...
Missachtung der Moral, ein Hordentreiben. Unser...
wird angeworben wie Söldner. Die Pflichterwe...
zur Vaterlandsliebe und Treue ist ver...
...hen besteht nur darin, einem Fronv...
Macht zu verhalten.

Das Volk — dahinter die Krall...
wittung, diejenige den Juden steckt —...
die Wortführer mit Blindheit schlägt...
Söldnerheer einzelnen.

Im Grundzwischg weiss es sig...
für was zu kämpft, es kämpft nur e...
Dunkeln.

Eidgenossen, habt ihr die Bew...
men, Unterdrückten und Wehrlosen...
rassenherrschaft vergessen? — Ich...
...licherweise konstatieren, ja! —...

Schweizer, Volksgenoss, wir...
...ten, für den richtigen Kampfweg zu E...
wine, für was Ihr kämpft, schliesst I...
...zusammen. Wir bilden eine Schutzru...
Helvetia, eine Kampflegion, die Leg...
National-Sozialisten.

Unser Kampf, derjenige der...
offensiv gegen das Grosskapital, Ju...

## Der Eiserne Besen

Zürich, 3. März 1933 — 2. Jahrgang, Nr. ...

**KAMPFBLATT FÜR NATIONALE UND SOZIALE POLITIK**

Abonnementspreis bei täglichem Erscheinen
durch die Post bezogen
6 Monate Fr. 4.80 — 12 Monate Fr. 8.80
Einzelnummer 20 Rp.

Herausgeber: Zollwein Front, Schweiz, politische Vereinigung Zürich
— Erscheint jeden Freitag —

Inseratenpreis:
Für die einspaltige Millimeterzeile
oder deren Raum 10 Rp., Ausland 15
Reklame 40 Rp.

Zürich, 15. Juni 1933 — Erscheint monatlich zweimal — Nr. 12 Dritter Jahrgang

## Der Eidgenosse

### Kampfblatt der Nationalsozialistischen Eidgenossen

Herausgeber Theodor Fischer

Verwaltung und Anzeigenannahme:
Postfach Prenzberger 447, Zürich
Postcheckkonto VIII 988

Sprechstunden von 10—11
Uhr, ausgenommen Sonntags
Buchhandlungen an den Verlag
Erhältlich an allen Kiosken

Verlag und Schriftleitung:
Bund Nationalsozialistischer Eidgenossen
Zürich 1, Kirchgasse 21, 1. Stockwerk, Postfach 23.408

Bezugspreise:
Inland: Ausland:
Vierteljährlich Fr. 1.30 Fr. 1.50
" " 2.50 3.—
Einzelnummer:
Eidgenossisches 10 Rappen
Deutsches Reich 15 Pfennig
Oesterreich 20 Groschen
Frankreich 70 Centimes

Zürich, den 15. Juli 1933 — Chronique de la Suisse Romande, p. 1 — Achter Jahrgang — Nr. 14

# Schweizerbanner

### Unabhängige nationale Zeitung

Organ der „Schweizer Heimatwehr"

Jährlicher Bezugspreis:
Schweiz Fr. 9.—
Einzelnummer 20 Cts. Erscheint zweimal monatlich

Schweizer Heimatwehr:
Landessekretariat, Postfach Rathausgasse 14, Zürich 7
Postcheckkonto VIII 12991

Redaktion und Administration:
Postfach Rathausgasse 14
Zürich 7

# in der Schweiz.

Noch selten sah der politische Himmel der
Schweiz verworrener aus als jetzt. Neue Bewe-
gungen schiessen in regendammerlicher...
Pilze aus dem Boden. Die politische P...
in Andrän. Der bieten Schweizer Erl...
Weg führt? Keiner zufriedenstellend...
ihm zuteil. Begreiflich: Wer nicht...
lassen stellt, der könnte sich hinterness...
gegen Einblick in die politischen D...
hat, der ist restlos im Bilde; der ist st...
wenn die Welt heute in den Fugen k...

Die gehteinen „Wegdagdeur",...
fühlten, sind von der erwählenden...
auf den Sportplätzen und bei den Kinos...
ten, jäh überrascht worden. Jahrelang...
Jugend vom parteipolitischen Pasch...
kümmen, für ein Titel vor der Politik...
sich genügte nach von der Südelhaft...
Kanchen laut ist, brachen...
dessen Seite Abrechnung wartag, das...
Sesselkleber wird diesen streitig gut...
...tem" ist entdeckt und soll fallen, ent...
schaft sich die Notzuskleber auf Kocht...
ganzen eingerichtet und in Frondien...
Die Jugend will ihren Platz an d...
hait vor allem und mit dem „System"...

Dieser Zug sei Freiheit hat für die...
in Verwaltuung gebracht...

Ueber die Schweizer Heimatwehr, für das „System" unbedingt die massgebende Freiheits...
... Lützen gekommen sind, haben die Freimaurer...

Zürich, 1. März 1934 — 2. Jahrgang —

# Eidgenössische Zeitung
### für Volk und Heimat

171 2 Herr Paul Schmidt,
Buchhandlung und Zeitungsfiliale, Basel 2

Erscheint jeden Donnerstag
Einzelnummer 20 Rp.
Vierteljährlich Fr. 2.20 — jährlich Fr. 10.—

Verlag: Keutmann & Co., Buchdruckerei, Nebengasse 20, Zürich 8
Postcheckkonto VIII 22846
Redaktion: Zürich, Postfach Hauptbahnhof 1740, Telephon 51.774

Inseratenpreise:
Einspaltige Millimeter-Zeile
Reklamezeile...

Gegen falsche Gerüchte

The terrible truth was treated for much too long as mere atrocity propaganda. When Dr. Paul Vogt obtained and displayed two photographs taken in concentration camps (*immediately below, left and right*) and another taken in the Warsaw ghetto in 1943 (*bottom*), he came face to face with unbelievable horror. *Opposite page:* It began with "*Juda verrecke* (Croak the Jews)!" and ended with the extermination camps. The Swiss Nazis shouted as loudly as the rest.

# Volksbund

## Kampfgemeinschaft für Schweizerische Nationale und Soziale Erneuerung.

## Die Nationalsozialistische Bewegung der Schweiz

## Gehört Zürich der israelitischen Gemeinde?

Die „Neue Zürcher Zeitung" hat sich wieder einmal herrlich als Sprachrohr des Judentums bewährt.

Prangt da am 20. November 1934 in großen Lettern ein Aufruf des schweizerischen israelitischen Gemeindebundes, Lokalkomitee Zürich", worin er der Hoffnung Ausdruck verleiht, daß die Zürcher Bevölkerung unentwegt festhält an der Gleichberechtigung aller Bürger, welcher Konfession oder Rasse sie auch immer angehören mögen.

**Was war der Grund zu diesem Angstschrei?**

Die skandalösen, jedes Sauberkeitsempfinden verletzenden Cabaretaufführungen der „Pfeffermühle", in denen nicht nur der Nationalsozialismus und unsere deutschen Nachbarn, sondern auch Oberstkorpskommandant Wille in gemeinster Weise besudelt wurden, steigerten den Unwillen der neutral und eidgenössisch denkenden Zürcher dermaßen, daß sie ihren Abscheu gegen diese Juden- und Emigrantenschmiere in dem Ausdruck:

# Juda verrecke!

Luft machten.

Nicht nur beim deutschen Michel, sondern auch bei den urchigen Eidgenossen wird das Maß einmal voll! Und wenn es zu voll ist, läuft es notgedrungen über. —

Der israelitische Gemeindebund sagt in seinem Aufruf folgende wahrlich entwaffnend unschuldige: „Wir lehnen es ab, den Kampf gegen diese Provokatoren, gewissenlosen Aufwiegler und Feinde der Demokratie zu führen!"

## Wer müßte nicht neidlos bekennen, daß das Judentum im Verleumden und Aufwiegeln seit Menschengedenken den von keiner anderen Rasse je erreichbaren Rekord geschlagen hat!

Was nun die „Feinde der Demokratie" anbetrifft, so scheint dies für das Judentum gleichbedeutend sein mit: Feinde der Zersetzung, der Schweinerei, der lügnerischen Hetze und der Schamlosigkeit. Denn nur Feinde all dem vom Judentum uns tagtäglich vorgesetzten Dinge ließen aus übervollem Ekel über Erika Mann und ihre „Pfeffermühle" den Kampfruf:

# Juda verrecke!

tönen.

Das Schönste an dem Aufruf des Israelitischen Gemeindebundes sind die Worte: „Wir legen Verwahrung ein gegen den aus dem Dritten Reiche seitens der sogenannten Erneuerer übernommenen Kampfruf

# Juda verrecke!

der in schändlichster Weise mitten in unserer Stadt dieser Tage erneut erhoben wurde."

Hat wohl der israelitische Gemeindebund die Stadt Zürich tatsächlich gepachtet? — oder gar gekauft? — oder gedenkt man vielleicht im Einverständnis mit dem roten Stadtrat, der ja weder an der „Pfeffermühle" noch an allen anderen jüdischen Propagandastücken etwas auszusetzen hat, ein regelrechtes Versuchungsinstitut zu gründen, in dem man sein arisches Vieh durch Juden und Emigranten solange „abhärten" lassen kann, bis die ganze ........

---

## Die Systempresse macht für uns Reklame!

Die „Zional-Zeitung Basel" und die „Fasler-Nachrichten" übertreffen sich wieder einmal gegenseitig in Verächtlichmachungen, falschen Mutmaßungen und haltlosen Verleumdungen über den Volksbund.

Daß sich so große führende Intelligenzblätter überhaupt noch mit dem „erbärmlichen", ach so „lächerlichen Volksbündelein" befassen, ist doch wirklich rührend.

Die „Zionale" schreibt:

### „6 Mann suchen ein Lokal"

Müssen das aber fabelhafte Kerle sein, die nicht nur die ganze israelitische Gemeinde, sondern sogar die „hochbedeutsame" Freimaurer- und Judenpresse in Angst und Aufruhr bringen! — Ein kläglicheres Zeugnis als das, sich vor 6 Männlein und deren so „lächerlichem" Führer zu fürchten, könnten sich wohl diese Presseluisen nicht geben. Diese armen Teufel klammern sich heute an jeden Strohhalm, um das völkische Erwachen in der Schweiz heimzuleugnen! Sie wissen so gut wie wir, daß sich immer breitere Massen für die Ideen des Volksbund interessieren.

Echt jüdisch sind die Märchen der „Fasler-Nachrichten", die von einer Versöhnung unseres Führers mit Dr. Zander zu erzählen wissen. Nein ihr armseligen Judenknechte, im Volksbund handelt man nicht nach dem Grundsatz: „Pack schlägt sich, Pack verträgt sich." Wen Major Leonhardt einmal heimgeleuchtet hat, den holt er nicht wieder; das dürft ihr euch merken!

Das Verächtlichmachen unseres Kampfes und das Lächerlichmachen unseres Führers ist der beste und größte Dienst, den ihr uns erweisen könnt; denn erstens gereicht es jedem gesunden und sauberen Menschen zur Ehre, von Zeitungen eurer Sorte beschimpft zu werden, und zweitens gewinnen wir durch nichts leichter die Aufmerksamkeit des Volkes und die Anhänglichkeit unserer Gesinnungsgenossen, als wenn die „Zionale", die „Fasler-Nachrichten" und die „Züritante" uns lächerlich machen.

Die Geschehnisse der letzten Woche waren nicht zuletzt dank der betreffenden Zeitungsangriffe für uns sehr erfolgreich.

### Wir danken der Systempresse herzlich.

Ebenso fehlgeschlagen haben die Mutmaßungen betreffs Redaktion unserer Zeitung. Wir verstehen ja die Neugier! — Aber bei aller Hochachtung vor der weiblichen Intelligenz sehen wir doch die Aufgabe der Frau im Nationalsozialismus auf anderen Gebieten als im Zeitungschreiben. Außerdem sind wir mit hiefür geeigneten Kameraden so reichlich versehen, daß die „Zionale" wie alle anderen Käsblätter mit Recht neidisch sein können. Wir haben Ringlein und Kreuzlein, samt Kobern und Salandern, nur keine abstinenten Freimaurer! Die verschämten wir ihrer ganz besonderen Verlogenheit wegen!

---

## Nationalrätliche Neutralität.

### Stimmt es, daß der Verleger Dr. Hans Oprecht Nationalrat ist? und daß er Jude also jüdisch Schweizer ist?

Wie vereinbart es sich dann mit dem Amt eines Nationalrates, als Verleger die Auslieferung der gemeinsten Lügen- und Hetzliteratur gegen das nationalsozialistische Deutschland zu betreiben? — — —

Sind schweizerische Regierungspersonen ihrem Amt nicht die Verpflichtung schuldig, sich als Vertreter eines neutralen Staates zum mindesten der Wahrheit zu befleißen? Oder ist es im Sinne unseres gesamten Nationalrats Adolf Hitler als Mörder, seine Politik als niedrigste Barbarei, den Nationalsozialismus als Kulturschande zu bezeichnen? — — —

Die durch Dr. Oprecht im ganzen Schweiz als „wertvolle" Literatur empfohlenen Bücher sind eine fortgesetzte Beschimpfung und Verleumdung des nationalsozialistischen Deutschland und seiner Regierung. Außerdem sind sie eine niederträchtige Irreführung unseres Volkes.

Wo bleibt die Neutralität, wo bleibt die Gerechtigkeit, wo bleibt das Verantwortungsgefühl unserer Regierung? — — —     Rober.

In spite of much opposition from the authorities and the censorship, the truth about National Socialism's mass murders had to be brought to public knowledge. Unfrightened men helped the Swiss press to perform its task in an admirable fashion.

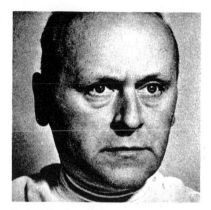
Rudolf Bucher, M.D.

Johann Baptist Rusch

Dr. Fritz Heberlein

Dr. Benjamin Sagalowitz

Professor Dr. Hans Zbinden

Hermann Böschenstein

When helpers were required to meet the refugees' needs, they were at hand. Men and women from every sector of the population heeded the call and fulfilled their simple human duty as a matter of course and without stint.

Dr. h. c. Gertrud Kurz

Dr. h. c. Regina Kägi-Fuchsmann

Sister Anna Pflüger

Georgine Gerhard

Dr. Werner Stocker

Dr. Emil Oprecht

Not only did the refugees obtain food and shelter; in addition they labored in agriculture, on highway construction, in land reclamation, drainage, etc. In October 1942, *Die Neue Zürcher Zeitung* declared: "So we and the refugees are givers and getters at the same time, and both sides have reason to be thankful."

# Index